1986

DIMENSIONS OF TELEVISION VIOLENCE

Dimensions of Television Violence

BARRIE GUNTER

St. Martin's Press   New York

All rights reserved. For information, write:
St. Martin's Press, Inc., 175 Fifth Avenue, New York, NY 10010
Printed in Great Britain
Published in the United Kingdom by Gower Publishing Company Ltd.
First published in the United States of America in 1985

ISBN 0 312 21077 9

Library of Congress Cataloguing in Publication Data

Gunter, Barrie
 Dimensions of television violence

 Includes index.
 1. Violence in television
 I. Title
 PN1992.6.G86   1984   302.2'345   83−40145

ISBN 0 312 21077 9

Contents

301.162
G977

119,412

Preface

At the beginning of 1980 the Independent Broadcasting Authority appointed the writer as Research Fellow to undertake a feasibility study to develop if possible a system to assess television programme content, with particular reference to the portrayal of violence. This research project, which covered a period of two years, examined certain methods of classifying and weighting the seriousness of violence portrayed in fictional TV drama programmes.

An experimental approach was adopted that involved investigation of the ways in which ordinary viewers perceptually differentiate and evaluate a wide range of different forms of violence extracted from current TV drama output. Violent episodes were taken from British-made crime–detective shows, American-made shows of the same genre, westerns, science-fiction series and cartoon shows. Effects on viewers' perceptions of TV violence of the types of characters involved, the types of weapons or instruments of aggression that were used, the physical setting and the consequences of violent incidents were systematically explored to indicate that ordinary viewers can and do use many different attributes or features of aggressive TV portrayals when judging how seriously violent they are. Whilst this research cannot claim to have covered *all* aspects of programme content that are likely to mediate viewers' perceptions of violent TV episodes, it does demonstrate unequivocally the complexity and variety of violent forms on television, and more importantly, of viewers' appraisals of them.

Acknowledgements

It would not have been possible to complete this research had it not been for the invaluable help and assistance of a number of people. Among those I would particularly like to single out for thanks are Dr Ian R. Haldane, then Head of Research at the IBA, for giving me the opportunity to carry out this research and for providing financial support and a base to operate from; Colin Tyler and Mike Brown of the IBA's engineering section at Brompton Road for their tireless efforts during countless, long and often monotonous editing sessions needed to set up the TV materials used in this research; Douglas Kerr and Geoff Reardon of the IBA's Research Department for advice and help with computing and data analysis; Dr Adrian Furnham for his help in setting up and running the sessions; and to Mallory Wober for comments and advice on my early ideas and scribbles. I would also like to thank Stanford University Press for their permission to reproduce Table 2.1 from the text W. Schramm, J. Lyle and E.B. Parker *Television in the Lives of Our Children*, to Professor George Gerbner of the Annenberg School of Communications, University of Pennsylvania for permission to reproduce Figures 2.1 to 2.4 from Gerbner, G., Gross, L., Signorielli, N., Morgan, M. and Jackson-Beeck, M. The demonstration of power: Violence profile No. 10 *Journal of Communication* 1979, Vol. 29, pp.177–196, to the American Psychological Association for permission to reproduce the sub-scales from the Buss-Durkee Hostility Inventory, Buss, A.A., and Durkee, A. An inventory for assessing different kinds of hostility, *Journal of*

Consulting Psychology, 1957, Vol. 21, pp.343—349 in Table 5.4, and to Professor H.J. Eysenck for permission to repeat the items from the Eysenck Personality Questionnaire in Table 5.5.

1 The analysis of violence

The evidence for the possible harmful side-effects of exposure to TV
violence and the widespread public concern accompanying it have led
to calls for strict controls on the depiction of violence in programmes.
These calls in turn necessitate some consideration of how to classify
and measure the violent content in TV programmes in order to
monitor and limit the extent and form of its occurrence. But whilst
there are many sources, in academia, viewers' associations and
popular journalism which are ready to condemn the depiction of
violence in TV programmes as a potentially dangerous and antisocial
act on the part of those who make and transmit programmes, there
has been little attempt to formulate explicit statements about what it
is exactly that should be controlled. This observation is encapsulated
perfectly in a quote from a BBC Working Party document on the
portrayal of violence in TV programmes:

> Our reading of some of the academic work and
> newspaper reports has suggested that 'violence on
> television' is in danger of becoming a portmanteau
> phrase, convenient for journalists, but in fact
> capable of the widest variety of meanings and
> applications. (BBC, 1979, p.5)

It is with the problem of specifying what is meant by 'violence' in the
broad context of drama programming that the research in this book
is mainly concerned. Thus, rather than placing emphasis on the possible

effects of watching TV violence on viewers' subsequent behavioural tendencies, the focus of the experiments discussed in this book is on the development of a system of TV programme content assessment, whose reference point is the portrayal of violence in programmes. The eventual aim of this work is to make specific statements, based on the objective empirical analysis of fictional TV drama materials, about the nature and extent of violence in these programmes. The first step along this road is to decide how the concept is to be defined, classified and measured. We shall begin by considering the inherent complexity of the concept, and then discuss briefly the relative merits of two methods of assessing violence on television.

Defining violence

Violence is a topic which has interested philosophers, social scientists and laymen for many years both within and outside the field of mass communications. However, despite all that has been written about violence, there remain several unresolved issues concerning its definition. The terms 'violence' or 'aggression' receive almost indiscriminate use, not simply by journalists with reference to TV portrayals, but also by ordinary people in everyday life. These terms are used to refer to a host of different actions or behaviours, and a major difficulty facing writers on violence and its causes has been to reach common agreement on what actually constitutes a violent act.

The problem of defining violence in itself reveals something fundamental about the nature of the concept. The fact that many different psychological and sociological definitions of violence and explanations of its occurrence have been formulated reflects not simply the complexity of the definitional problem, but perhaps more essentially that violence does not represent a unitary process or a single set of events or happenings with common antecedents or consequences. This observation has led some writers to suggest that a better understanding of the nature of violence might be attained via a multi-faceted analysis of its causes and characteristics (e.g. Fraczek, 1979). In most discussions of the definition of violence, however, emphasis is usually placed on some aspects of violence only. Two broad definitional perspectives can be identified: one that focuses on the behaviour of the perpetrator of violence; and another that examines the consequences of violence from the victim's point of view.

Violence is often defined in terms of the intensity or seriousness of the harm-doer's behaviour. The concept of violence in this respect refers to behaviour that is considered excessive or unrestrained, and accompanied not uncommonly by an appraisal of the justifications for

2

the harm-doer's actions. Violent behaviour tends often to be that which is judged by people to be aimed at antisocial ends or which is unjustified. Much of the controversy surrounding the definition of an act as violent or not relates to the problem of justifications. In society today, many pain- or injury-inflicting acts serve socially acceptable or useful functions, and hence may not be classified by many people, strictly speaking, as 'violent'.

Destructive and injurious behaviours such as murder for financial gain, school vandalism, juvenile gang assaults and football hooliganism, are generally disapproved in the strongest terms by most of society. Other pain-inducing behaviours though may be approved under particular circumstances or when used within certain degrees only, e.g. fighting and even killing in self-defence, physical violence in a prize-fight ring, a parent spanking a child for misbehaviour, or police using physical force to capture dangerous criminals or to control a riot. However, if the force used by an individual in self-defence against an attacker or by the police to control a public disturbance oversteps the mark and reaches a degree of severity not merited by the provocation, it becomes less tolerable. Thus, various kinds of injurious or 'aggressive' behaviours differ in their severity, not simply in terms of the amount of pain and suffering they cause, but also in terms of what they are intended to achieve and in their legal and moral justification. As we shall see in a later section of this chapter, the legal or moral context of coercive or injury-inflicting behaviour is an important mediator of public perceptions and definitions of violence.

Further distinction can be made between instrumental and expressive violence and between intentional and unintentional violence. *Instrumental violence* is designed to achieve some end or goal, while *expressive violence* occurs spontaneously in a state of anger or rage. Thus the latter is often a goal in itself, while the former is a means to another goal. As an illustration of instrumental violence, an armed bank robber may not set out to shoot a cashier, and does so only when the latter fails to co-operate with his demands. The threat or actual use of violence in this case is not employed in the service of some intrinsic gratification derived from performing the action itself, but as a necessary means of getting money out of the bank. As a purely hostile and expressive violent act, a sadistic killer may attack, rape and even murder a female victim, simply for the pleasure of doing so.

Intentional violence covers those acts in which injury or the expectation of injury to a victim is an essential functional component of the perpetrator's behaviour. Thus the perpetrator acts deliberately to harm another person. *Unintentional violence*, on the other hand, involves incidents where the harm-doer does not know that his behaviour has caused harm or injury to another person. The harm done may have been accidental, as in a situation where the harm-doer acted without knowing that his behaviour would have any consequences. Alternatively, the harm-doer may have attempted to benefit the victim of his unintentionally painful actions. Thus a dentist may cause his patient some agony during an extraction, but his actions are intended to prevent further discomfort from the decayed tooth.

The concept of unintentional violence permits another distinction between the terms 'violence' and 'aggression', the latter of which places an emphasis on a perpetrator's intentions to do harm. Unintentional violence allows one to categorise as violent those harmful acts caused by non-human agents, such as animals or natural disasters. Fires, floods, earthquakes, volcanic eruptions and hurricanes can be considered as violent incidents, since they result in harm to those in their path. The concept of unintentional violence draws attention to the need to consider not only the perpetrator's actions but also the consequences of those actions for the victim.

Another perspective in defining violence is to consider killing, injuring and inflicting pain as 'violence' and to classify violent events in terms of the seriousness of their outcomes for victims. From this angle, determination of the intensity of a violent incident would thus be achieved independently of any appraisal of the magnitude of the perpetrator's behaviours or intentions underlying them. The importance of the consequences of violent actions for victims in violence was recognised by the Surgeon General's Scientific Advisory Committee on Television and Social Behaviour (1972) which wrote:

> In order to define violence as realistically, as ethically and with as much psychological accuracy as possible, the definition should be broadened to include the experience of its victims ... when a society legislates and institutionalizes the definition of violence in terms of victims, then all violent experience becomes a matter of concern. When the definition reflects only accountable destructive behaviour, much, if not most, violent experience may not even be acknowledged (p.9).

Measuring TV violence

Turning to the question of measuring TV violence, what kinds of criteria might be used in identifying and profiling this content? A number of different methods have been used by researchers to provide both quantitative and qualitative analyses of the nature and extent of televised violence. In the current discussion two broad perspectives will be distinguished.

First, a programme-based approach concerned with the structure and content of media output and in relation to the topic of TV violence focuses on a quantitative analysis of the prevalence of violence on television. Second, an audience-based approach which emphasises audience reactions to TV content and focuses on a qualitative analysis of violence in terms of ordinary viewers' evaluations and perceptions of programme materials.

Each of these perspectives has its own advantages and shortcomings as effective methods for comprehensive and ecologically valid analysis and measurement of TV violence, and will be discussed briefly in the following sections.

Quantitative assessment of TV violence

The programme-based or content-analytic perspective places emphasis on the specification of profiles and structures of programme content. With regard to measurement of TV violence, this technique of assessment involves counting up those aggressive incidents occurring in programmes which match a single, normative definition of violence. The most detailed quantitative content analysis has been carried out on network TV programming in the United States by George Gerbner and his colleagues at the University of Pennsylvania, and it is their research that will be the focus of detailed critical discussion in Chapter Two.

Gerbner and his co-workers used a definition of violence which emphasised incidents resulting in the infliction of injury or suffering, but which largely ignored the context in which incidents occurred. Thus, any events likely to cause or actually causing injury to a character were catalogued and given equivalent weightings of intensity or seriousness whether they occurred in action-adventure programmes or comedy or cartoon shows. Although narrow, Gerbner believed that his definition of violence served well enough as a heuristic device. Yet it has already been noted that psychology theorists found it necessary to look beyond the simplistic notion of violence as behaviour that causes injury to a victim for explanatory and heuristic purposes. Furthermore, viewers' responses to violent portrayals can vary widely for different forms of violence and according to the contexts or settings in which violence is depicted. Whilst there is little doubt that the technique of counting up incidents in this relatively simplistic way can yield reliable data (i.e. the same violence scores for a programme may be produced by two teams of coders working independently), all forms of violence are not equivalent, either in their meaning or their impact on viewers, and many of the incidents in TV programmes catalogued as violent under this definitional scheme would not be perceived as such by the public at large. Gerbner has argued, in defence of his content-coding procedure, that audience assessments of programme sequences do not logically belong to his system of content analysis. But this argument is not consistent with inferences he and his colleagues have made about relationships between public attitudes and beliefs, and rates of exposure to certain patterns of TV portrayals, as revealed by their counts of violent incidents in programmes.

A fundamental contention of these writers is that portrayals of violence in fictional TV drama programmes provide symbolic demonstrations of the power structure of society, and through the differential involvement in violence and victimisation of various character-types, these programmes teach viewers about the risks and dangers of the real world. Heavy viewers of TV are hypothesised to be strongly influenced by these content profiles and to exhibit distorted conceptions of the prevalence of violence in society and exaggerated fears of personal risk and victimisation. Yet nowhere have Gerbner and his colleagues provided unequivocal evidence for the actual assimilation by ordinary viewers of the symbolism of the messages identified in programmes by content analysis. Much of this theorising about the impact of TV-drama content on viewers' conceptions of social reality is based on the assumption that because violence is prevalent in TV fiction, it must also be a highly salient aspect of programme content for the audience, conveying much of the meaning of the programme. However, highly trained, professional content analysts probably view TV content at a different level than ordinary viewers, and see in programmes many themes of which the audience is largely unaware (Gans, 1980). Indeed, research on viewers' perceptions of TV programmes has indicated that viewers evaluate or classify programmes in terms of many features and that violence is not necessarily the most salient or important of these (BBC, 1972; Howitt and Cumberbatch, 1974).

Recently, a number of writers have called for an interactionist perspective in which coding schemes are developed whose dimensions and categories of media content are isomorphic with those employed by the audience (Gans, 1980; Gunter, 1981; McLeod and Reeves, 1980). We need to be sure that the messages identified by content analysts are recognised by and received into the consciousness of members of the audience. In this vein, Gans (1980) suggested '... that if we are to understand the relationship between content and audience, *professional* content analyses must be complemented by audience content analyses. Viewers must be asked to content analyse the television fare they watch so that we can learn not only what they see in the content but also with what concepts and categories they approach it' (p.57). This book will report a series of experimental studies in which panels of ordinary viewers were invited to make personal judgements about extracts from TV programmes that depicted various kinds of violent incidents. This work represents an initial effort to develop an audience-based system of classification and coding of TV violence. In the next section, the discussion will turn to examples of experiments on public perceptions of violence which indicate the variability of individuals' assessments of coercive incidents and the need to take into account the judgement of ordinary people in the development of a comprehensive taxonomy of violence. The section following the next will introduce the research paradigm for an audience-based analysis of TV violence that was adopted in the original experiments reported in later chapters. Finally, the main findings from these experiments will be summarised.

Qualitative assessment of TV violence

Assessments of televised violence based on single, normative definitions are inadequate essentially because they fail to represent the variety and complexity of violent forms. These coding schemes may be capable of providing replicable counts of a narrow range of incidents, but they indicate little about the kinds of distinctions that can be made and which ordinary people often do make between different types of violence, whether as experienced in everyday life or as seen on fictional TV programmes.

Research on public perceptions of violence has indicated that people evaluate and differentiate between violent incidents in a multi-faceted way, and not necessarily in terms of their perceived degree of harmfulness (Forgas, Brown and Menyhart, 1980). Evidence on variations in the strength and quality of viewers' behavioural or emotional reactions to violent film portrayals according to the context or setting in which they occur (e.g. Berkowitz and Alioto, 1973; Feshbach, 1972; Lagerspetz, Wahlroos and Wendelin, 1978; Noble, 1975) indicates the necessity to give careful consideration to public definitions, labels or conceptions when classifying or assessing violence in TV programmes.

Intuitive definitional frameworks such as those used in previous content analyses of TV violence have tended to emphasise a conception of violence as injury-inflicting behaviour. But whether or not the use of force or the infliction of injury is *perceived* as violent depends on a number of factors relating to the circumstances under which this behaviour occurs. It is important to recognise the difference between the behaviour of an actor and its labelling by observers, who often rely on their understanding of the social conditions under which an action is performed in making judgements about it. This distinction was clearly noted by Bandura and Walters (1963) who wrote:

> Strictly speaking, of course, it is not aggressive responses that are learned, but only classes of responses that are labelled as aggression on the basis of social judgements that themselves must be learned. An adequate learning approach to the problem of aggression must consider both how responses usually labelled as aggressive are acquired and maintained and how a child learns to make the social judgements that enable him to discriminate an aggressive from a non-aggressive response (p.114).

Here these authors were talking about how children learn to make distinctions between different kinds of aggressive and non-aggressive behaviour, but the implications of what they are saying for the analysis of TV violence are clear enough. Violent incidents in programmes cannot be taken at a common face value. The determinants of how violent portrayals are perceived include social norms and personal values as well as the physical form of the violence itself. It is an important point that social factors are rarely taken into account in studies of violence and, in particular, in laboratory experiments investigating the effect of TV or film violence on viewers' propensities towards aggression. Indeed, research by James Tedeschi and his colleagues on the 'social psychology' of social psychology experiments has indicated that most naive observers (i.e. laymen) would not label behaviour studied in most laboratory experiments as violent at all because respondents are usually provoked into taking defensive or retaliatory action, and defensive actors are not generally perceived as violent (Brown and Tedeschi, 1976; Kane, Joseph and Tedeschi, 1976). The following example serves to illustrate this point.

In one study, Tedeschi and his co-workers presented groups of people with descriptions of four versions of a typical social-psychological experiment on aggression which they were asked to evaluate. In the experiment described, person A rated an essay expressing personal views on a topic written by person B by giving the latter either one electric shock (for a good essay) or seven shocks (for a poor essay). Person B was then given a chance to rate an essay by A and to return either two or six electric shocks to the latter. In this scenario, person A was perceived by most respondents as more violent when he delivered seven shocks initially to B than when he gave only one, but B was not perceived as violent when delivering six shocks rather than two as he had already received seven shocks from A. B was perceived as violent, however, if he returned six shocks having received only one to begin with. Disproportionate retaliation led observers of this scenario to label person *B* as violent; proportionate retaliation, on the other hand, did not.

Usually, in experiments of this sort, *B* is considered by the researcher to be more violent the more shocks he delivers to *A* regardless of how many he received in the first place. As this scenario typifies the kind of procedure used in many laboratory experiments on the effects of TV violence on the subsequent aggressiveness of viewers, the above findings throw certain doubts on the way experimental evidence on the impact of TV violence has been interpreted. Usually in laboratory studies of the impact of TV violence, person *A* is shown either a violent or non-violent TV scene after being electrically shocked (and hence 'annoyed' or 'made angry') by *B*, and immediately before being given an opportunity to return shocks to *B*. If a person shown a violent scene returns more shocks than one who saw a non-violent scene, this is taken as evidence of the capacity of violent TV portrayals to enhance levels of aggression in viewers. Experimenters have tended to focus on the magnitude or number of injury-inflicting acts (i.e. delivery of electric shocks) displayed by the retaliator whilst ignoring the totality of the context in which this behaviour was performed. Naive observers, by contrast, who evaluated the events in this laboratory scenario in terms of normal social rules of conduct evaluated them in quite a different fashion.

Parallel social judgements of violent scenarios from real life have also been recorded. For example, Lincoln and Levinger (1972) found differences in how the actions of a white police officer were evaluated depending on the context of his altercation with a black man. Respondents were shown a photograph of the police officer grabbing the shirt of a young black man. When the scene was described as taken from a peaceful civil rights demonstration, the officer's action was rated unfavourably; but when no such information was presented to justify the victim's conduct it was presumed by most respondents that the officer's action was legitimate and therefore non-violent.

Finally, in an experimental investigation of naive observers' reactions to a staged violent incident performed by live actors, Brown and Tedeschi (1976) found that whilst the *offensive* use of coercion is generally labelled as violent, the *defensive* use of force is not. In a live dramatisation of a bar-room scene, one man started an argument over a seat that was being saved by another man for his girlfriend. The first man either simply threatened the one who was saving the seat or else made a threat and attempted to use force by taking a swing (which missed) at the latter. In two other versions, the defensive man either made a counter-threat or used counter-force by striking his intimidator hard in the stomach.

Ratings by observers indicated that the man who started the

argument was perceived as violent in all versions of the scenario. However, the defensive use of force, where the only real damage occurred, was not seen as violent. When the defensive actor used force he was already under attack, and since it is usually difficult to use rational argument and persuasion while someone is attacking you, he was perceived to have little choice but to use counter-force against his intimidator. The fact that the most damaging action in this scenario was rated as least violent is testament to the importance of the context of an incident when judging whether or not it constitutes a violent act.

Research has shown that individuals often do not spontaneously mention the violence in a programme, even though it may, according to a programme-based content analysis, be classified as violent (i.e. in terms of the number of actual injurious or violent incidents it contains) (BBC, 1972). This suggests that many of the incidents counted as violent by a normative definitional scheme of content analysis are not labelled as such by ordinary viewers, perhaps because of their form or the contexts or settings in which they occur. Another reason for the lack of spontaneous awareness or recognition of violence amongst viewers may be that other features of programmes may be more prominent, such as the realism or humour of the content, or preoccupation with characters and their personal relationships with each other. Content analyses have indicated extensive involvement in violence of leading characters in fictional TV programmes. Yet research with the audience has shown that violence does not feature as a prominent attribute in viewers' judgements of characters (Reeves and Greenberg, 1977; Reeves and Lometti, 1978). Viewers make complex judgements about the characters and settings depicted in programmes and these judgements are reflected in their degree of awareness of violence in programmes and perceptions of the seriousness of any such violence.

Perceptual analysis of TV violence

From the discussion so far it is clear that violence is a complex concept which cannot be comprehensively construed as a single entity. Studies of public perceptions of real-life violent scenarios have indicated that ordinary people often make highly refined, multi-faceted judgements about violence. This fact has important implications for the analysis of televised violence because most people will experience a far greater variety of violent forms via TV than they are ever likely to come into contact with in normal, everyday life. One might therefore expect them to show a range of judgements about violent episodes on TV at least as complex as those made for violence in actuality.

To recap, violent scenes in fictional drama programmes, in

particular, may differ in terms of many attributes or features and it is already known from previous research that viewers often show markedly different reactions to violent episodes of different forms, or which occur in different contexts or settings. Analyses of audience response to TV materials, whether at behavioural, emotional or perceptual levels, have indicated many subtle distinctions that viewers make between violent portrayals. Whilst 'effects' research as such has identified a number of important dimensions along which TV portrayals (and the impact they have on the audience) may vary, as yet no really comprehensive taxonomy of TV violence has emerged.

Content analysis has produced much more elaborate breakdowns or categorisations of the types of violent episodes occuring on television. This perspective, however, has focused on monitoring frequencies of distribution of different kinds of violence rather than assessing in any direct fashion the impact (potential or actual) of these 'violence profiles' on the audience. There is a need, therefore, for an investigative empirical framework which provides an objective and comprehensive analysis of televised violence and which has some form of correspondence not only with the content that is actually shown on television but also with the way the public perceives it.

In this book new experimental research is reported which was designed to explore a method of assessing TV violence in terms of how ordinary viewers perceive and evaluate different kinds of violent portrayals from fictional programming. This analysis began with selecting programme extracts whose characteristics exemplified certain attributes either which had been previously identified by content analysts and included in the latters' coding schemes, or which had been manipulated to a limited extent by 'effects' researchers and shown to affect audience reactions to content. An important question was whether or not the categories of TV content considered as important by content analysts would be perceived similarly by ordinary viewers. Are violent incidents from different types of programmes, occurring in different settings, involving different characters and taking on different physical forms, and which would be given equal weightings of intensity or seriousness by content analytic coding schemes, judged in the same way by the audience? In the effects research literature, it has become clear from behavioural, emotional, and perceptual measures of viewers' reactions to media content, that the audience can be highly discriminating about violent portrayals and that unitary definitions of violence are relatively meaningless.

2 The volume of violence on television

Early quantitative assessments

The first efforts to document the quantity of violence on TV drama occurred in the early 1950s in the United States just as television was becoming established in American homes. Smythe (1954) reported evidence from several studies sponsored in 1952 and 1953 by the National Association of Educational Broadcasters. In one week of content analysis of prime-time output on seven New York City channels, any acts or threats of violence that occurred in all programmes except news, current affairs and sports shows were recorded.

Altogether 3,421 acts and threats were observed, averaging 6.2 violent incidents per hour. Serious drama shows accounted for 87 per cent of all violent portrayals, an average of about 10 incidents per hour. Crime-drama contributed 28 per cent of all violent incidents and western drama a further 23 per cent. Turning his attention next to violence in children's programmes, Smythe found a much higher incidence of aggressive acts than in adult programming, although perhaps more important than the actual volume of violent episodes here is the way they were distributed throughout different categories of programmes. Children's fictional entertainment programmes had three times the frequency of violent acts or threats recorded in adult programmes, but this was largely a reflection of the very high incidence of violence in children's comedy and cartoon programmes, which averaged nearly 37 incidents per hour. In fact, about one-quarter of all violence observed in adult and children's programmes monitored by Smythe occurred in a humorous context.

Further evidence showing that violence was a frequently occurring feature of TV drama programming during the early days of TV in America was obtained as part of a larger study on the impact of TV on children by Schramm, Lyle and Parker (1961). They coded the number of violent incidents occurring in 100 hours of weekday programming broadcast between 4 p.m. and 9 p.m. during one week in October 1960 on four TV channels in the San Francisco area. Schramm and his colleagues observed that violence was a prevalent feature of children's programming put out by these TV stations, with shootings and fist-fights occurring frequently. Once again though, much of this violence was found in comedy programmes. Unlike many content analysts, Schramm *et al* made a clear distinction between incidents occurring in humorous and serious contexts and based their measures of the volume of TV violence exclusively on the content of non-humorous programmes.

Table 2.1 shows the seriously violent incidents listed by Schramm *et al* from the non-humorous entertainment fraction of their programme sample. These figures indicate that whilst aggressive portrayals are quite numerous, exclusion of incidents occurring in comic contexts resulted in a substantial reduction in both the volume and rate of violent portrayals compared with previous studies in which context was not used as a defining variable of violence (e.g. Head, 1954; Smythe, 1954).

Most early studies of TV content were one-off affairs and provided only a brief cross-sectional glimpse of the nature and extent of violence on television. It is difficult to produce a cohesive analysis of trends in violent content across the years from these studies because different investigators chose different definitions of violence or used different indices of the rate or quantity of violence in TV programmes. Thus, some researchers counted the number of violent acts, and others coded the number of hours of violence. Some recorded the proportion of programmes containing any violent incidents at all out of all programmes monitored, whilst others categorised only those incidents occurring in a serious dramatic context as 'violent'. Given the inferences that have been made (some substantiated by research evidence) that the impact of TV violence over a long-term may be more significant than the short-term effects measured in many social-scientific experiments, it is important to have some measure of any changes in the levels of violence on television which occur over the years.

Table 2.1

Violent incidents coded from one week's prime time
non-humorous entertainment programming on four TV
channels in the San Francisco area, 1961

12	murders
16	major gunfights
21	persons shot (apparently not fatally)
21	other violent incidents with guns
37	hand-to-hand fights
1	stabbing in the back with a butcher knife
4	attempted suicides, three successful
4	people falling or pushed over cliffs
2	cars running over cliffs
2	attempts made in automobiles to run over persons on the sidewalk
1	psychotic loose and raving in a flying airliner
2	mob scenes, in one of which the mob hangs the wrong man
1	horse grounding a man under its hooves

A great deal of miscellaneous violence, including a plane
fight, a hired killer stalking his prey, two robberies, a
pickpocket working, a woman killed by falling from a
train, a tidal wave, an earthquake and a guillotining.

Source: Schramm, Lyle and Parker, 1961

The cultural indicators project

Perhaps the most comprehensive analysis of TV violence so far has
been conducted by George Gerbner and his colleagues at the Annenberg School of Communications, University of Pennsylvania. Using a
technique called message system analysis, these investigators have
monitored samples of prime-time and week-end daytime TV for all
major American networks every year since 1967, and during this time
this analysis has come to be regarded by many commentators as the
definitive indicator of the nature and extent of violence on TV.
Certainly the internal consistency of the analytical technique in the
features coded provide a reliability of measurement from year to year.

But whether or not this procedure produces a meaningful indicator of the changing trends or levels of violence on TV across the years depends not only on internal consistency or *reliability* of measurement but also on *validity* of measurement. Does message system analysis provide a valid indication of the amount of violence on TV? In the following discussion, in-depth examination of the methods used by the Annenberg group will reveal a number of fundamental flaws with message system analysis which throw considerable doubt on the validity of purely programme-based assessment techniques as measures of the seriousness or degree of violence on TV.

The Violence Profile

Gerbner and his team limit their analysis of TV violence to dramatic entertainment programming which means that news, documentaries, variety and quiz shows and sports programmes are excluded during coding. Typical hours for weekday and Saturday evenings are 7:30 p.m. to 11:10 p.m.; and for Saturday and Sunday mornings, 8:00 a.m. to 2:30 p.m. A single normative definition of violence is employed: 'the overt expression of physical force (with or without a weapon) against self or other, compelling action against one's will on pain of being hurt or killed, or actually hurting or killing' (Gerbner, 1972, p.31). Further specifications were made that the incidents must be plausible and credible; but that no idle threats should be included. However, violent accidents or natural catastrophes, whose inclusion in dramatic plots was reasoned by Gerbner to be technically non-accidental were included (see Gerbner and Gross, 1976).

Using the above scheme to guide them, a team of trained coders are employed to record such features as the frequency and nature of violent acts, the perpetrators and victims of violence, and the temporal and spatial settings in which the acts occurred. From certain combinations of these measures is derived the 'Violence Profile', which purports to represent an objective and meaningful indicator of the amount of violence portrayed in TV drama.

The Violence Profile itself consists of two sets of indicators: the Violence Index and the Risk Ratios. The amount of violence occurring on TV is represented directly by the Violence Index. Essentially this index represents the percentage of programmes containing any violence at all, the frequency and rate of violence episodes per programme and per hour, and the number of leading characters involved in violence either as aggressors or as victims. The Risk Ratios signify a character's chances of involvement in violence in TV drama programming and, once involved, the likelihood of positive or negative consequences for him or her. The Risk Ratios too, are a composite of more than one measure: the violence-victim ratio, for example, denotes chances of being an aggressor or a victim, while the killer-killed ratio denotes the risk of killing or being killed. Both ratios are calculated within each dramatic and demographic category for a wide spectrum of character types. A close inspection of the findings generated by each of these indices reveals an overall picture of the world of TV drama as a particularly violent one.

The Violence Index. This index is comprised of three types of direct observational data called *prevalence*, *rate* and *role*. They show the extent to which violence occurred at all in the programmes monitored and are combined according to the formula shown in Table 2.2.

Table 2.2

Computation of Gerbner Violence Index

Violence Index = %p + 2 (R/P) + 2 (R/H) + %V + %k

Where,

%p	=	percentage of programmes studied in which there is violence
R/P	=	number (or rate) of violent episodes per programme
R/H	=	number (or rate) of violent episodes per hour
%V	=	percentage of leading characters involved in violence — either as violent or victim
%k	=	percentage of leading characters involved in killing — either as killer or killed

Source: G. Gerbner, 1972. Violence in television drama: Trends and symbolic functions. In G.A. Comstock and E.A. Rubinstein (Eds.). *Television and Social Behaviour, Vol. 1, Media Content and Control*. Washington, D.C.: U.S. Government Printing Office.

Prevalence represents the per cent of programmes containing any violence, according to the definitional system employed, in a particular programme sample. Rate expresses frequency of these acts in units of programming and in units of time and each of these frequencies is entered into the Index. Role is defined as the portrayal of characters as perpetrators of violence, or *violents*, and as those who are submitted to violence or *victims*. This category yields several measures: per cent of violents out of all characters in a sample, per cent of victims out of all characters in a sample; per cent of all characters who feature as violents or as victims (%V); per cent of killers out of all characters in a sample; per cent of killed out of all characters in a sample; and per cent of all those involved in killing, either as killers or killed (%k). Only %V and %k measures are entered into the Index. What has the Violence Index shown about the nature and extent of violence in American TV drama programming since its inception?

Levels and trends of TV violence. Violent incidents are very prevalent in prime-time entertainment TV drama in the United States. Gerbner and his colleagues (1979) reported that since monitoring began in the 1967–68 TV season, an average of 80 per cent of programmes contained violence and 60 per cent of major characters were involved in violence. The average rate of violent episodes was seven and a half per hour, and in weekend, daytime children's programmes, violent episodes averaged almost 18 per hour. Indeed, programmes directed at children typically scored high on most measures of violence except for killing; cartoons in particular consistently exceeded all other categories of programmes, including adult action-adventure and crime-detective shows.

As Figure 2.1 shows, however, few definite trends in the extent of violence on TV drama programming are evident from the Violence Index measure. In terms of violence, there has been considerable stability in the violence content of American entertainment programming across the years. The rate of violent incidents per hour, however, declined between 1969–70 and 1974–75 for cartoon, comedy and children's programmes, and then rose again in the late 1970s. This is illustrated in Figure 2.2 by the inverted U-shaped curve for the rate of violent episodes in weekend, daytime programmes. Among action-type programmes aimed mainly at the adult audience the violence rate rose gently over the 1970s, although the proportion of this genre of programmes with some violence remained about the same.

Certain trends were noticeable in the involvement of leading characters in violence and in killing particularly. Figure 2.3 shows that there was a marked decline in the percentage of leading characters involved in violence between 1967 and 1973, before character involvement rose again during the mid to late 1970s. From the data displayed in Figure 2.3, however, it is evident that this trend was more pronounced for prime-time (adult) programming than for weekend,

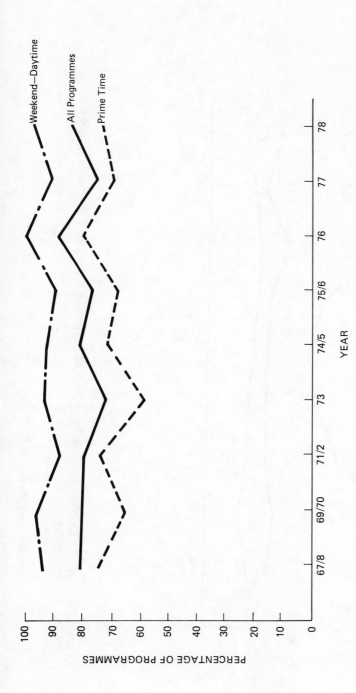

Figure 2.1 Percentage of programmes with violence on American TV - 1967–78

1. These figures are based on two samples — one autumn and one spring.

Source: Gerbner, G., Gross, L., Signorielli, N., Morgan, M. and Jackson-Beeck, M. (1979).

19

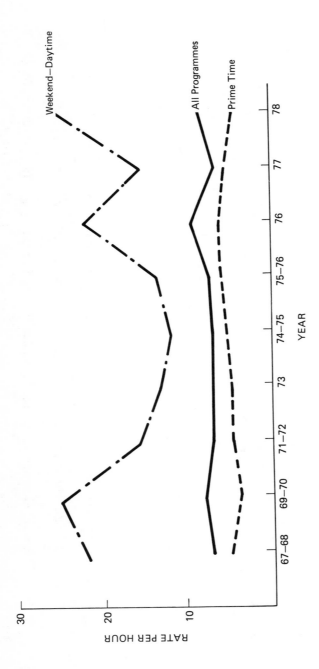

Figure 2.2 Rate of violent incidents per hour of peak-time American TV - drama programming 1967–78

Source: Gerbner *et al* (1979).

20

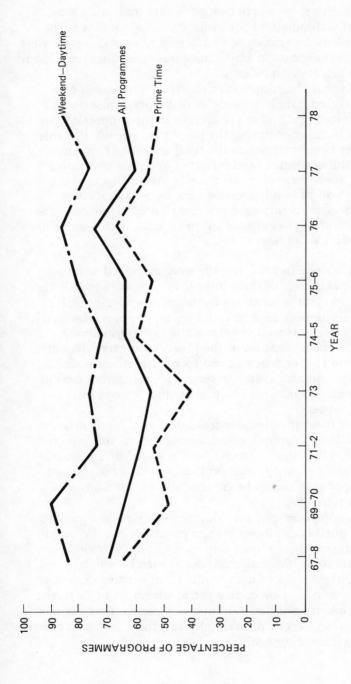

Figure 2.3   Percentages of characters involved in violence on American TV - drama programmes 1967–78

Source: Gerbner *et al* (1979).

daytime (and mainly children's) programming. In the latter category, the proportion of characters involved in violence remained at a fairly constant, high level. Not shown here though is data indicating that killing was practically eliminated from children's programmes at the weekend, whose violent content consisted largely of episodes occurring in comedy or cartoon contexts in which injurious consequences seldom appeared to follow aggressive incidents.

Figure 2.4 shows that the adoption in the 1975—76 season of a more carefully protected 'family viewing' time before a nine o'clock watershed in the United States saw a reduction in the proportion of characters involved in violence during the pre 9 p.m. period. But this reduction was offset by an increase in the total amount of violence, as measured by the Violence Index (and reflected in character involvement), after 9 p.m. for several years afterwards. According to some writers, the termination of family viewing time by a federal court decision a few years after its introduction contributed significantly to increases in the amount of violence on TV to unprecedented levels in American prime-time TV drama.

Risk Ratios. The Violence Index is not the only or indeed necessarily the most significant part of the Violence Profile. Although coded as unitary entities, on certain occasions Gerbner has conceived of violent TV portrayals in more sophisticated terms, as complex social scenarios involving victims as well as perpetrators of aggression. As such, it is a dramatic demonstration of the power of certain characters to inflict violence and the tendency of less fortunate others to fall victim to it. This scenario may cultivate several lessons for viewers in general, and also perhaps a number of quite distinct lessons for different groups of viewers.

For some viewers these may include lessons of victimisation and ways to avoid as well as to commit violence. For others, the depiction of violent interactions between characters in the world of TV drama with whom they closely identify, represents a calculus of one's own risks as well as of opportunities to be gained from personal involvement in violence in actuality.

The Risk Ratios component of the Violence Profile is designed to analyse patterns of portrayals among certain groups of the TV population and thus to represent in an objectively quantifiable way the intrinsic power structure of the violent fictional society which is brought by TV into the homes of many millions of viewers each day. This particular analysis begins by coding the involvement of different character-types in violent episodes. An 'involved' character is defined as one who takes part in a scene of overt physical force and who either commits or suffers violence, or both.

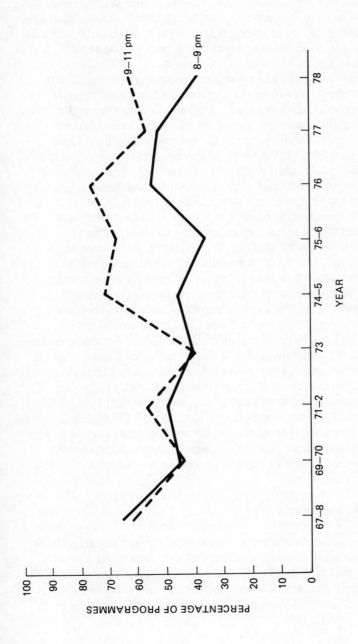

Figure 2.4 Percentages of characters involved in violence on American TV - drama during early and late evening programmes 1967–78

Source: Gerbner *et al* (1979).

23

The Risk Ratios index is derived from the 'involvement' data and consists of a composite of two measures which are calculated separately for each of a broad spectrum of character-types: (1) the *violence–victim* ratio, which denotes a character's chances for being a *violent* (perpetrator of violence) or a *victim*; and (2) the *killer–killed* ratio which signifies the risk of a character-type being involved in killing or actually being killed. For those characters involved in violence, each of the ratios is derived by dividing the more numerous of the two critical roles (i.e. violent or victim, killer or killed) by the less numerous. According to Gerbner and his colleagues the portrayal of violence on TV drama programming demonstrates a pattern of unequal relative risks among characters of different sex, age, socio-economic and ethnic groups, in which certain character-types are victimised consistently more often than others. Victimisation risk data reported for prime-time TV samples between 1969 and 1978 have indicated that victims are generally more prevalent than perpetrators of aggression but that the ratio of attackers to victims is greater for some character-types than others. Whilst men were much more likely than women overall to become involved in violence of some kind, once involved they were much less likely than their female counterparts to be victimised.

Risks of victimisation were high among children and adolescents and unmarried women, and were especially high for elderly women who were more than three times as likely to be victims as aggressors when involved in violence. Further analyses indicated that 'good' characters were more likely than the latter to be killed. 'Good' male characters who frequently feature as heroes in action-drama series were much more likely to be killers than to be killed. 'Good' female characters, on the other hand, were much more likely to be fatally victimised than 'bad' female characters, even though they were less often involved in violent episodes. Irrespective of character-type involved in violence though, all such episodes are given equal weightings of seriousness in this programme-based content-analytic perspective of TV violence measurement. In later chapters, however, we will see that scenes depicting violence perpetrated or suffered by different types of characters are not always judged as equally serious by ordinary viewers.

Violence on British television

Two studies of programme content were carried out in the early 1970s which provided quantitative measurements of the volume of violence on TV in the United Kingdom. James Halloran and Paul Croll of the Mass Communication Research Centre, Leicester, analysed broadcast material of BBC1 and one ITV region (Midlands) during one week of

April, 1971, and coded violent incidents occurring in fictional drama programmes and news, current affairs and documentary programmes (Halloran and Croll, 1972). The coding instruments for violence were based on those used by Gerbner and programmes were coded for the amount and type of violence they contained, the kinds of characters involved in violence and certain themes or contexts in which violent events happened.

At around the same time the BBC's Audience Research Department undertook a more extensive analysis of TV over a six-month period and analysed content from dramatic fiction, news and current affairs, documentaries, and light entertainment programmes (BBC, 1972). Unlike Halloran and Croll, the BBC's researchers did not follow the Gerbner method precisely, although in general terms, their analysis was conceptually of the same type. Violence was treated essentially as an explicit form of interaction between human beings. However, because the BBC's study sampled materials from a broader spectrum of programme types than did Gerbner's, it was considered necessary to expand the definition of violence to include unintentional injurious acts and acts of vandalism against property to code incidents of the sort often reported or depicted in non-fictional programmes.

Each of these British investigations indicated that although a common feature of programming, violence was not as prevalent on British TV as on American TV. In fictional drama, the only category of programming in which direct comparisons between American and British findings was possible, Halloran and Croll found that nearly 56 per cent of programmes coded contained violence — compared with a reported 80 per cent of fictional programmes on American TV (Gerbner, 1972). In nearly 48 per cent of fictional programmes, a major character was involved in violence either as aggressor or victim. The rate of violence on British TV drama was 2.8 incidents per programme or just over four incidents an hour, again substantially less than an average rate of over seven incidents per hour reported by Gerbner (1972) for American prime-time TV drama.

In their more extensive analysis of British TV content, BBC researchers found a somewhat greater prevalence of violence in fictional drama in terms of the number of programmes containing at least one major violent incident (63 per cent), but somewhat less violence in terms of the rate at which violent incidents occurred; average numbers of just under two violent incidents per programme or just over two per hour were recorded.

The prevalence and rate of violent incidents was also found in both studies to vary considerably across different forms of drama programme. Thus Halloran and Croll noted that the most violent type of programme in the fiction category was the cartoon. All cartoons coded by them contained some violence and the rate of incidents per hour in such shows was nearly 34. None of the cartoon incidents was fatal, however. Violence was also prevalent in feature films; 80 per cent contained some violence, and incidents averaged over four per hour. This contrasted with plays, of which 50 per cent were violent, but even then, with an average incident rate of less than one per hour, were unlikely to be very violent programme by programme. After cartoons, the most violent programmes coded by Halloran and Croll were crime, western, action—adventure shows. All programmes in these categories contained violence, and an average rate of nearly eight incidents per hour.

Turning to the BBC's (1972) analysis of the prevalence of violence for different programme forms or 'Themes', once again agreement with Halloran and Croll was not complete. Feature films contained at least one major violent incident in 86 per cent of cases which compares quite well with Halloran and Croll's 80 per cent figure, whereas the category of programmes labelled as 'TV series' by BBC researchers, which consisted largely of crime—detective, western and action—dramas, contained violence in only 75 per cent of cases, as contrasted with *all* such programmes monitored by the Leicester researchers. Inconsistencies across the violence measures produced by these two studies for the same areas of TV content become even more pronounced when consideration is given to mean rates of violent incidents per programme type. The BBC team coded an average of just over three incidents per hour for feature films, one per hour less than Halloran and Croll. But even more significantly, they coded 2.2 incidents per hour for 'TV series', a little over 25 per cent of the average rate of incidents per hour recorded for the crime, western, action—drama categories by the Leicester team. Even when examining particular themes or particular series, BBC violent rate statistics remained lower than those reported by Halloran and Croll. Thus, the BBC reported that westerns contained a higher rate of violent incidents than any other type of TV series, but at 3.9 incidents per programme, this was still only about half the rate reported by Halloran and Croll for crime—western—action categories.

This provides an illustration of the fact that even slight variations in the categories or criteria of violence employed in a coding scheme can give rise to substantially discriminant assessments of the volume of violence on TV. In the following sections, a more detailed discussion is presented on this and other problems associated with a programme-based analysis of violent TV content.

Problems with programme-based assessments of TV violence

The overall picture of the world of TV drama revealed by content analytic investigations is that it is a violent one. But how much credence can be given to this observation? The data derived from any system of monitoring are only as good as the methods used to generate them and doubts have been raised as to whether content analysis of the kind used to produce the violence profile represents a valid and meaningful measure of TV violence. To elucidate on this further, the following discussion will focus on methodological and conceptual problems identified for Gerbner *et al*'s violence profile. The latter analytical framework is perhaps the most widely cited source of data on current levels and brands of violence on TV, and has served as a model for assessments of TV violence around the world. Most of the criticisms levelled against the violence profile therefore are applicable or relevant to other research projects which have employed similar techniques of TV violence measurements.

Methodologically, the main problems surrounding the violence profile centre on the following points:

1   The definition of violence employed.
2   The programme sample.
3   The weighted items of which the Violence Index is composed.
4   The interpretation of Risk Ratios.

First of all, let us look at the definition of violence employed and its consequences for identifying violent content. The definition of violence for coding purposes stated by Gerbner (1972) focuses on behaviour and events but ignores context. Thus comedy shows may be scored as violent along with such events as accidents and natural disasters in action-adventure dramas. The reason for this is that violence is defined normatively and is measured wherever it occurs. Gerbner would claim that whether or not comedy programmes are 'violent' is an empirical issue, and that accidents or disasters are deliberately included in TV drama and if they fit the definition cannot justifiably be ignored. Yet one could argue that neither comedy nor natural disaster is equivalent to the inter-personal attacks usually thought of as TV violence.

Disagreement has been reported over the programmes identified as violent in one year by Gerbner's data and by other analyses of violent content in the United States by the 'Christian Science Monitor' and the National Association for Better Broadcasting, even though the latter two were in close agreement (see Coffin and Tuchman, 1973). During 1968, for example, Gerbner and the 'Monitor' analysed adjacent weeks of programming using similar techniques in which coders viewed episodes of programming and counted acts of 'violence'. Of 53 programmes which were included in both studies, there were 20 programmes which both agreed were violent and 14 programmes which both agreed were non-violent. However, there were a further 19 programmes which Gerbner classified as violent, but which the 'Monitor' regarded as non-violent. This disagreement resulted largely because the 'Monitor' recorded incidents from contexts normally perceived as violent while Gerbner tabulated violence wherever it occurred, regardless of context. In particular, Gerbner considered humorous acts and accidents in his violence count whereas the 'Monitor' did not.

In another comparison of Gerbner's violence scores with those produced by TV critics and members of the general public, rating consensus was again absent (Coffin and Tuchman, 1973). Greenberg and Gordon (1972a) developed violence ratings on a five-point scale based on the judgement of a sample of professional critics and a sample of ordinary viewers. An average violence score was computed for each programme based on the 'violence rating' scale responses of each group of judges. To facilitate comparisons between Greenberg and Gordon, and Gerbner, Coffin and Tuchman also obtained continuous—variable scores for programmes studied by Gerbner.

While Greenberg and Gordon employed two quite disparate sample groups to rate TV programmes on a violence scale, there was very close agreement in the ratings by the two groups: a Pearson product-moment correlation of 0.80 for all programmes and 0.97 for those programmes studied in common with Gerbner. However, while the public and critics agreed very closely with each other, they did not agree with Gerbner in classifying programmes as violent; a correlation of only 0.48 between Gerbner and the general public, and 0.56 between Gerbner and the critics in terms of Gerbner data on the number of violent acts per half hour. This lack of really strong correlation between the two studies reflects the fact that comedy programmes were rated as more violent by Gerbner than by either the public or critics in the Greenberg and Gordon study. To conclude, therefore, the use of a normative definition of violence requires some qualification in interpretation, and programmes identified as violent by its use conform more perfectly to the normative perception when comedy or other formats normally considered inconsistent with violence are excluded.

Secondly, the programme sample monitored by Gerbner has been criticised for its time-span and for what it excludes. The sample typically consists of one autumn week of prime-time and weekend morning programming each year and is, according to Gerbner, intended to reflect the character of each season's TV fiction for general and child audiences, and is appropriate for that purpose (Gerbner and Gross, 1976). However, such is the variation in programming throughout each season today that it is unlikely that any one week alone can prove representative of the whole year's output (Blank, 1977a). Another more important reason why Gerbner's sample does not reflect the nature of TV as a whole is because it excludes news, current affairs, documentaries, 'specials', sports and variety programmes from the main networks and all independent stations and non-network broadcasting, which often take up a large proportion of the average viewer's TV viewing time.

Thirdly, the Violence Index has doubtful validity as a direct measure of the amount of violence on TV because of the arbitrary way in which it combines programme features without justifying the necessity for the inclusion of any component. We saw earlier that the formula through which the Violence Index is obtained consists of summing over five items:

1 the percentage of programmes containing an occurrence of violence.
2 double the rate of violent episodes per programme.
3 double the rate of violent episodes per hour of programming.
4 the percentage of leading characters involved in violent acts, either as perpetrators or as victims.
5 the percentage of leading characters involved in killing, either as perpetrators or victims.

Gerbner's Violence Index thus attempts both to quantify and to aggregate a number of disparate and rather unusual observations. The resulting index number is a summary of the frequency with which violence occurs (counted three different ways), of the roles assigned to victims and aggressors, and of the relative frequency with which a violent act results in death. The complexity of the process is compounded by the fact that some numbers constitute percentages while others are straightforward numerical sums. The index thus becomes a composite figure whose validity and usefulness rests on a host of controversial assumptions, which in turn ultimately rest on Gerbner's broad, undiscriminating definition of violence. Shifts in the index are not readily interpretable unless the index is accepted as synonymous with violence. Even if the definition, the time sample and the rules of programme inclusion and exclusion are accepted, any difference of opinion about the kind of violence that should be emphasised would render the index an imperfect indicator. As Blank (1977a, 1977b) has pointed out, it is unlikely that the Violence Index is truly a measure of the amount of TV violence in a sample of programmes because among the components which it weights are included such (essentially non-violent) factors as leading characters involved in acts of violence. Thus, while the number of violent scenes on TV may decrease over a period of time, an increase in the number of characters involved in violent episodes during the same period could be sufficient to produce a higher overall violence score in the Violence Index. Gerbner and Gross (1976) argue that indices, by definition are arbitrary correlations and that their index serves them as a heuristic device leading to the analysis of the shifts in components behind the trend in the index. However, the index requires more general acceptance before the figures generated can be taken as representative of the level of seasonal change in TV violence. The exclusion of important programme features such as the physical, social and moral contexts in which portrayals occur, which are related to the judgement of acts as violent in everyday life, precludes the acceptance or acceptability of the Violence Index in its current form.

Fourthly, there are problems with the interpretation of the 'victimisation' or Risk Ratios. In a theory of the social function of fictional TV drama, Gerbner argues that TV violence helps to maintain the existing social order by reinforcing beliefs in the likelihood of risk and danger. This 'cultivation' perspective led Gerbner and his associates to calculate 'victimisation ratios' for various demographic categories that purport to indicate the relative degree of risk portrayed. These consist of the ratio of perpetrators to victims of violence in each category, omitting all those not involved in violence. Groups found to have quite high ratios (i.e. risks of being victimised) include women, the poor, and elderly (Gerbner and Gross, 1976). In accord with Gerbner's theory, TV would be especially likely to cultivate insecurity among such viewers.

The problem with the victimisation ratio is that it is an entirely arbitrary indicator. Other measures, such as the actual number or percentage of persons in a given category who are victims, would generally reverse the pattern toward greater victimisation of groups with less social power because of the predominance of white males in action drama. While it is quite possible that focusing on patterns of dominance among those involved in violence may provide insight into a means by which TV drama affects its audience, it is also essential to supplement this data with evidence of audience awareness of the messages supposedly conveyed by the victimisation or risk ratios.

In addition to these methodological problems, the Violence Profile is conceptually limited insofar as it does not have any facility for the measurement of audience assessment of content. Indeed, Gerbner and his associates (1977) have argued that this type of measure does not logically belong to their system of content analysis. Yet this contention is not consonant with the inferences they have made about audience response to patterns of TV content, especially in relation to Risk Ratios data. This attitude towards content measurement, however, is not only conceptually limited, but also likely to lead to ecologically invalid assessments of TV violence. The author believes that insofar as real concern about the amount of violence shown on TV can be traced ultimately to concern about the potentially harmful (cognitive, affective or behavioural) effects of that content on the audience, then it would be both more meaningful and empirically useful to base a system of content analysis on viewers' responses to programme materials. Although a technique such as message system analysis may be able to provide a *reliable* indicator of the frequency of certain (narrowly defined) occurrences on TV, it does not offer any information about the way those occurrences are encoded and interpreted by viewers. Analysis of the modes of coding and appraisal of various types of TV episodes by viewers may be essential if content profiles are eventually to be linked in a direct and meaningful fashion to certain types of audience responses such as, for example, those investigated in cultivation analysis (Gerbner and Gross, 1976).

But there is another important reason for recommending that measures of TV violence are derived from viewer assessments of programme episodes. Recent research has shown that individuals tend to define aggressive episodes in a multi-dimensional way, in terms of the various physical, emotional or ethical contexts in which they have been personally experienced. (Forgas, Brown and Menyhart, 1980). These results imply that it may be totally unrealistic to expect a single, normative definition of violence to have the same (or even any) salience for all individuals across different programme contexts. In the next chapter we turn to the subject of the perceptual salience of TV violence for viewers, and its significance as a concept in terms of which viewers in general, or certain types of viewers, evaluate programmes.

3 The audience and the salience of violence on television

Content analytic studies of TV violence have typically consisted of counts of selected types of events occurring during a specified period of TV output, but in general have little to say about audience response to programmes. In Gerbner's analysis of violent TV content, for example, a few 'expert' raters were employed to record normatively defined occurrences of violence. Although this procedure provided reliable frequency ratings for specific kinds of incidents in programmes, these incidents may have relevance only for coders who are trained to look for them, and may lack any real significance for ordinary viewers.

From these simple frequency counts, Gerbner and his colleagues have derived more complex descriptions of the ways in which units of content occur together in TV drama programming to form recurring profiles or 'messages' concerning the structure and dynamics of contemporary society. These profiles seldom provide an accurate reflection of social reality, but tend instead to emphasise or exaggerate certain events or groups in the social milieu at the expense of others, and may thus cultivate among viewers who watch a great deal of TV, distorted impressions of the way things really are (Gerbner *et al*, 1977, 1978, 1979). However, no evidence is presented to show whether or not 'messages' identified through content analysis are actually perceived and learned by viewers.

Problems arise when generalising from statements about or descriptions of TV content and 'messages' about the social milieu they purportedly symbolise, to how that content is received and interpreted by the audience. As an important first step it is essential to establish the degree of equivalence or conformity between the categories of violence defined by objective content coding frames and the meanings attributed to these categories by ordinary viewers. To what extent do the images and messages defined by content analysis share the same universe of meanings as viewers' perceptions of these entities in fictional TV drama programming? With incidents such as shootings or fights, it may be relatively easy to achieve correspondence between programme structures as they are objectively defined on an *a priori* basis by a system of content coding and as they are subjectively perceived by the audience. But it may be far less accurate to infer the reception amongst viewers of subtle messages concerning norms of social conduct or relationships in the absence of direct tests of their awareness of the programme profiles purportedly conveying this information.

Literature on the nature of violence has indicated that the concept is so broad that the task of deriving a definition of violence that is acceptable to and utilised by people in general may not be practically feasible. Nevertheless, there is evidence to show that viewers' perceptions on the nature of TV programmes are not always strongly in accordance with objective content counts. The next two chapters will examine an alternative approach to the assessment and classification of TV violence in terms of viewers' perceptions of programme content. The need for an audience-based assessment procedure will be elaborated and made apparent through examination of three types of research evidence.

1   Research on the salience of violence as an attribute in terms of which TV programmes are evaluated and otherwise responded to by viewers. How aware are viewers generally of the violence depicted in programmes? Is the level of violence in a programme reflected in audience response towards it?

2   Research on the varying reactions of viewers to different forms of violence, or to violence depicted in different contexts or settings. To what extent and along how many attributes are violent forms differentiated by viewers? Which types of violence are judged as most serious?

3   Research on differences between viewers in their responses to TV violence in general, or to violence of one type or another which are associated with gender, age, social background or personality. Do certain types of viewer consistently exhibit more serious reactions to TV violence than do others? Are some viewers especially sensitive to

certain forms of violence?

The salience of TV violence

Research has shown that structures such as those monitored in
Gerbner's message system analysis or similar models of programme
assessment are not always perceived by ordinary viewers as salient
attributes of programmes. For example, a content analytic study of
British prime-time TV using the Gerbner model found that the rate of
violent incidents per hour was four times as great for cartoon shows as
for any other type of programme (Halloran and Croll, 1972); while a
study of audience perceptions of TV violence with a British sample
indicated that cartoons were not rated as particularly violent by
viewers themselves (Howitt and Cumberbatch, 1974).

Even in TV programmes featuring human characters, violent
portrayals may not be perceived as important or significant aspects of
content. The level of awareness of violence in programmes may be
quite low and viewers may often fail even to mention the violence contained in TV programmes shortly after viewing unless specifically asked
about such content (BBC, 1972).

Further important questions about the salience of violence as an
attribute of programmes are raised by studies of relationships between
violence and liking for programmes. One reason for the inclusion of
violent portrayals in programmes is the belief that there is a strong link
between violence and the degree of enjoyment for viewers. What
evidence is there, however, that programmes which contain violence
are better liked, or that even if they are, that it is their violent content
which necessarily contributes to enhanced appreciation?

Diener and De Four (1978) looked at 71 episodes from major
prime-time broadcasts on US network TV and coded each for
frequency of occurrence of such events as suspense, emotion, sex,
humour, action and violence over a period of three-and-a-half months.
Each episode's score on these categories of content was related to
programme popularity as indicated by the A.C. Nielson index. None of
these features, violence included, emerged as good predictors of a
show's popularity in terms of the size of audience it attracts. Of course
in this study the data base on which programme popularity was estimated was quite independent of that used to define the nature of programme content. Violence, as coded by Diener and De Four, may not
have corresponded with violence as defined by the audience. However,
even when viewers' subjective impressions of the degree of violence
normally featured in TV series are related to their appreciation ratings,
little evidence has emerged to indicate that violence is a salient aspect

of programmes in this context (Himmelweit, Swift and Biberian, 1980).

Perceptions of specific programmes

The above studies indicated that the salience of violent portrayals to viewers is not as significant as their prevalence in programmes might lead one to assume. Unfortunately, the measures of actual or perceived levels of violence in programmes lack the precision to make sound statements about relationships between programme content and viewers' perceptions of that content. Subjective ratings were made to programme titles only, rather than to actual programmes. The content of specific episodes of a TV series can vary considerably from week to week, and from ratings given to its title alone it is impossible to say whether a respondent based his or her impressions of a TV series on the series as a whole or on just one or two episodes from it — perhaps the one(s) most recently seen. For more precise correspondence between viewers' ratings and programme content, it is essential, at some stage, that researchers obtain and measure perceptual responses to actual programme materials. Several such studies were done prior to the author's research. These looked both at a range of perceptions and specifically at appreciation in relation to the amount of violence contained in programmes.

In an exploratory field study conducted by researchers at the BBC's Audience Research Department, viewers were asked to fill out a questionnaire about specific programmes shortly after they had been broadcast, in which reactions to violent episodes and other aspects of programme content were probed (BBC, 1972). *It was found that perceptions of programmes as 'violent' did not depend on the actual number of violent incidents.* Nor was there any strong relationship between perceiving a programme as violent and verbally-reported emotional arousal. Assessment of violence as unjustified, however, was associated with negative evaluation of the programme. Most respondents also claimed that 'realism' was an essential element in their perceptions of violent TV scenes, with violent real life events reported on news bulletins or shown in documentaries generally noted as more violent than violent events portrayed in fictional settings.

In the United States, Diener and his colleagues conducted a series of experiments which examined relationships between levels of violent content in programmes and how much they were liked by viewers. In the first of these experiments, viewers were shown either an uncut version of *Police Woman* or the same episode minus all violent scenes. The uncut version was perceived as more violent than the cut version, and in general was liked somewhat more too. However, among individuals who saw the violent version, those who perceived it as *more* violent liked it less (Diener and De Four, 1978).

In a later experiment with 62 families in their own homes, in which complete programmes from situation comedy and crime—detective series were rated on dimensions such as action, realism, violence and liking, Diener and Woody (1981) found, in contrast to the above study, that high violence programmes were generally liked *significantly* less than low violence programmes, but only by light viewers. There was no difference in liking of violent and non-violent shows among heavy viewers. Viewers in general, however, did rate high violence shows as *significantly more violent* than low violence shows, while other ratings such as action, realism, humour and romance proved to be poor discriminators.

On the question of the salience of violence as an attribute along which viewers evaluate TV programmes Diener's studies of programme appreciation provide equivocal evidence. The *amount* of violence in a programme does not appear to significantly affect programme liking, although it does seem to relate to how violent a programme is *perceived to be*. In Diener's experiment with De Four there is a question mark hanging over the interpretation that the amount of violence alone effected differential evaluations of the violent and non-violent TV materials. It is possible that ratings differences occurred as a result of other uncontrolled or unrecognised variations in programme content. Whilst more adequate controls were employed in this respect by Diener and Woody, even here there was a tendency to treat violence in gross terms only. No attempt was made in any of these studies to examine the effect of different kinds of portrayals on perceptions of programme content.

Viewers may not spontaneously refer to the violence in a programme in post-viewing question and/or discussion sessions, but this does not rule out the possibility that their feelings about a programme are influenced by the presence of violence *per se*, certain forms of violence or by other attributes of content in ways of which they are not always aware. In the remaining sections of this chapter, the variability of violent forms or the settings in which they occur in TV programmes are considered and a number of factors which may mediate viewers perceptions of violent portrayals are examined.

The variety of violence

In the previous section, research evidence was reported which indicated that the level of violence in programmes, as measured by frequency counts of violent portrayals in dramatic storylines, may relate only poorly or not at all to its salience as an important attribute of pro-grammes for viewers. Either viewers actual awareness of violence relative to other aspects of programmes is relatively low during normal viewing conditions (e.g. BBC, 1972) or even where they are able to distinguish its presence, the significance of violent content to their enjoyment of programmes seems to be rather weak (Diener and De Four, 1978; Diener and Woody, 1981).

However, violence occurs in a variety of different forms and different settings. Content analytic frames of TV violence assessment or measurement have been criticised for defining violence normatively and largely intuitively without any recourse to viewers and their perceptions of TV portrayals. At the same time, however, researchers working within this perspective have elaborated TV influences on public conceptions of social reality in a series of sweeping generalisations from data on content profiles alone, and without testing directly the extent to which these profiles are actually assimilated by the audience. Whilst studies on the salience of violence did measure audience responses to programmes, even so violence was treated as a single, wholistic concept. The salience of violent portrayals on TV may however depend crucially on the forms they take or on the contexts or settings in which they occur. This section will look at the variety of forms and settings of violence in an attempt to identify some of the attributes or characteristics of portrayals which may mediate viewers reactions to TV violence. Five types of features will be considered, for some of which evidence already exists on their power to effect different reactions to violent content amongst viewers:

1   The type of programme or dramatic setting in which violence is portrayed.
2   The types of characters portrayed as perpetrators or as victims of violence.
3   The physical form or weapons of violence employed in a portrayal.
4   The degree of observable harm inflicted on victims during a violent attack.
5   The physical—environmental setting in which a violent portrayal takes place.

This will set the scene for the experiment to be reported in later chapters, which focused each in turn on the importance of each of these features to viewers' perceptions of violent content on fictional TV.

Programme type and dramatic setting

The type of programme or particular dramatic theme or setting in which a violent portrayal is depicted has been shown to play an important mediating role in determining how viewers will react to it. Research on behavioural and emotional reactions to TV or film violence has provided a number of important findings on the functional distinction between watching portrayals from different categories of programming whose settings vary in their degree of realism or proximity to everyday life.

Early field research indicated that children found televised violence in realistic settings more uncomfortable or frightening than the stylised encounters that typically occurred in fictional programmes whose settings were far-removed from everyday reality (Himmelweit *et al*, 1958). More recently, Belson, (1978), reported that violence occurring in certain types of programmes appeared to be more potent than violence from other types releasing serious aggressive behaviour in adolescent boys. In particular, programmes presenting fictional violence of a realistic kind, including many contemporary crime-detective series and westerns, were highlighted as powerful facilitators of aggression amongst young male viewers, whilst violence occurring in cartoons or science fiction and comedy settings showed little or no relation to violent predispositions. In laboratory research also, in which the nature of the material shown to viewers can be carefully manipulated and controlled beforehand, significant variations in behavioural and emotional responses to film sequences have been reported for children and adults according to whether portrayals are interpreted as occurring in real life or fantasy contexts. These findings indicate implicitly the need to take into account the setting of violent portrayals as defined by the type of programme from which they are taken when assessing the nature and extent of violent content on TV.

Several experimental studies have shown that post-viewing aggressiveness in viewers is more likely to be enhanced, and to a greater degree amongst those who are predisposed to so react, when film violence is interpreted as realistic rather than as fictional. This difference has been observed amongst nine to eleven year old children shown a common piece of footage of a student campus riot, described to some as an extract from a Hollywood movie, and to others as a newsreel film, (Feshbach, 1972). This finding was replicated among young adults shown the same clip from a war film which was described to one group as an extract from a World War II documentary and to the others as a feature film sequence (Berkowitz and Alioto, 1973). Subsequently repetitions of this design with adult groups produced further reinforcement for the original results (e.g. Geen, 1976, Thomas and Tell, 1974).

Variations in emotional reactions to TV or film portrayals have provided further evidence of viewers' discriminations between portrayals in fantasy and reality contexts. In laboratory research, emotional reactions to media content have been operationalised in several ways: Changes in physiological arousal, changes in the degree of imagination or creativity shown in play behaviour, and variations in facial expressions during or following a film sequence.

Physiological arousal: To measure changes in physiological arousal induced by watching aggressive TV or film portrayals, experimenters have used a highly sensitive technique called the galvanic skin response (GSR) which monitors changes in electrical conductivity of the skin with increases in surface moisture levels which normally accompany emotional arousal.

In a study which manipulated the reality—fantasy set of viewers, whilst holding content constant, Geen and Rakosky (1973), found that viewers who saw a videotape of a prize-fight staged by two professional actors and who were told that the fight was not real, exhibited less emotional arousal (as measured by the GSR method) than others who were led to believe that the fight was real. Among children too, realistic TV portrayals have been found to elicit more profound emotional reactions than fantasy content. Osborn and Endsley (1971) reported that children as young as four or five years registered stronger emotional responses (GSRs) to violence portrayed by human characters than to violence depicted in cartoon film. Unlike Geen and Rakosky, however, Osborn and Endsley did not prime their viewers to perceive one film item as realistic and the other as fictional, hence variations in response to these items may have been due to factors other than the perceived degree of realism. One possibility is that changes in skin conductivity signified greater enjoyment derived from watching cartoon characters relative to human characters.

Imaginative play: Early researchers reported that televised violence may frighten some children, but that anxiety responses more often accompany realistic portrayals than those that are clearly performed in the realms of fantasy (Himmelweit *et al*, 1958; Schramm *et al*, 1961). Out of an interest to discover, through objective, experimental means, whether some forms of violence make children more anxious than others, Noble (1970) showed groups of young viewers either a war documentary or a puppet film, both of which depicted aggressive activity. Anxiety responses were measured in terms of children's play behaviour that was observed before and after exposure to a film portrayal. Previous writers had demonstrated that when frustrated or emotionally upset, children tend to regress in their play and show much less imaginative and sometimes more destructive behaviour (Barker, Dembo and Lewin, 1941). Noble found that watching filmed violence could affect levels of elaborateness or continuity in subsequent play. Children who had seen the war film talked less amongst themselves afterwards and showed less interest and constructiveness in playing with toys provided. Watching the stylistically-portrayed puppet film subsequently resulted in more activity among youngsters, however. Although there was little indication of increased aggressiveness after viewing a violent sequence, this study suggested that anxiety may be an alternative form of response to film portrayals and one that also serves as a useful discriminator between one type of aggression and another.

Facial expressions: According to some investigators, observation of the facial expression of viewers, especially with children, while viewing TV can provide an accurate measure of their emotional reactions to televised violence (Ekman and others, 1972). This technique has been used to examine the differential emotional reactions of children to different forms of televised violence. Lagerspetz, Wahlroos and Wendelin (1978) evaluated the facial expressions of pre-school children while watching TV scenes which included portrayals of physical violence in a fantasy context, physical violence in which suffering of the victim was shown, verbal threats and non-violent incidents. Results showed that scenes of realistic physical violence which portrayed the reactions of the victim evoked the most fear and worry and produced facial expressions coded as signifying seriousness, tenseness and anger. Fantasy human or cartoon violence, however, elicited expressions coded as joy and understanding and produced greater attentiveness and involvement with the action portrayed.

On the evidence of behavioural and emotional measures then, viewers may exhibit quite disparate reactions to violent media portrayals depending on the dramatic settings in which such portrayals occur. These results are not inconsistent with the assumption that viewers can and probably do interpret and discriminate between violent portrayals on the basis of dramatic setting. The consistency of findings so far, albeit with a somewhat restricted range of materials, indicates the need to conduct a more extensive analysis of programme contexts as mediator of viewers' perceptions of TV violence. In Chapter Six, two experiments are reported which examined the extent of variation in viewers' subjective judgements of violent TV scenes from five different types of programmes, and showed that dramatic setting could have a significant effect upon how serious violent portrayals were rated by the audience.

Character type and the impact of TV violence

One of the fundamental ingredients of TV violence measurement within the content analytic perspective is the extent of involvement in violence among different types of characters. Two of the five components of the Violence Index measure of the Cultural Indicators team for American prime-time TV drama consist of the extent of character involvement in violent episodes either as aggressors or victims, killers or killed. According to Gerbner (1972), the distribution of characters in TV drama programmes and the extent to which different types of characters become more involved in violence and the nature of their involvement (i.e. as aggressors or victims) carry important meanings concerning chances and risks in real life for different kinds of people. 'Who commits and who suffers violence of what kind is a central and revealing fact of life in the world of television drama that viewers must grasp before they can follow, let alone interpret, the play ... who gets (and gives) what, how, and why delineates the social structure of the world of television drama. The distribution of roles related to violence, with their different risks and fates, performs the symbolic functions of violence, and conveys its basic message about people'. (Gerbner, 1972, pp.44—45).

Content analysis of the involvement of characters in violence on TV has indicated that more leading characters than not perpetrate or become involved in some form of aggression. On American network TV Gerbner *et al*, (1978, 1979) reported that over 60 per cent of major prime-time TV characters were involved in some type of violence. There were more victims than aggressors, signifying that the character's involvement in violence was more likely to result in that character being injured than escaping unharmed, although the extent to which this was the case varied from one character type to another.

Involvement in violence may be prevalent amongst major TV characters but characters vary considerably in the personalities they portray and in their reasons for committing violence. So, to what extent do audience judgements about violent scenes depend on the types of characters involved in them? Perceptions of violent portrayals may vary according to whoever perpetrates or is the victim of violence. To illustrate the effect of differential involvement of character-types on viewers' judgements of violence, two sets of comparisons will be made here: (1) Between violence perpetrated by law enforcers or 'good' guys, against that perpetrated by law breakers or 'bad' guys, and (2) between violence performed by male characters and that performed by female characters.

Legal versus criminal violence

Perhaps the most consistent theme in serious action—drama programmes on TV is the conflict between good and evil, between the forces of law and order and criminal elements. Content analysis of programming designed to explore the goals of TV characters and the methods usually employed to attain desired ends has indicated that non-legal methods tend to be used as often as legal methods in TV action—drama shows, (Larsen, Gray and Fortis, 1963). In summing up their findings, one of the main conclusions reached by Larsen and his colleagues was that there is a strong tendency for TV to project content in which socially-approved as well as unapproved goals were most often achieved by methods that would not in normal everyday life, be regarded as socially acceptable. This observation drew attention to the frequent and rapid deployment of violent measures, often to an extreme degree, by agencies of law enforcement in TV series when tackling problems of criminality.

Subsequent TV monitoring indicated that whilst bad characters are most involved in violence and killing, it is a prevalent feature of TV drama programming that both good and bad characters use violence. Gerbner *et al* (1979) reported that between 1969 and 1978, on American prime-time TV, just over 58 per cent of good characters and 88 per cent of bad characters were involved in some form of violence.

Content analysis of programming on British TV during the early 1970s did not elaborate on patterns of character-involvement in violence to the extent that American research has done. Nevertheless, a few consistent patterns have emerged from the relatively limited analyses in this respect of the BBC and Leicester research teams. Instigators of violence were usually portrayed as belonging to the wrong side of the law, although a substantial minority of good characters also used violence. About three-quarters of bad or villainous characters were violent, and this was about three times as high as the proportions of good characters or heroes who were violent. Also bad characters were three times as likely to kill their victims as were good characters (BBC, 1972; Halloran and Croll, 1972). To what extent, however, does the prevalence and nature of a particular character type's involvement in violence on TV generally accord with viewers' perceptions of portrayals featuring that type either on the giving or receiving end of violence? Whilst in some programme types, in terms of quantitative measures of actual extent of use of violence, law enforcers and criminals may differ very little, on a qualitative-judgemental level, the reasons and justifications each of these character-types may have for employing violent methods may differ considerably, and so too therefore, might viewers' perceptions of the violence performed by them.

Surveys of public opinions towards various kinds of violence have indicated that legitimised violent actions are usually not perceived as violence. Officially sanctioned violence for example as employed by the police is justified because it is violence, designed to protect the public, to prevent the destruction of property rioters and looters, to deter potential law-breakers. Evidence of a public mandate for official violence of this sort from general social survey studies has indicated that the process of legitimisation is so powerful that even extreme forms of violence may sometimes be regarded by large numbers of ordinary people as acceptable. Gamson and McEvoy (1972) reported in a 1968 survey that 57 per cent of a national American sample agreed with the statement 'Any man who insults a policeman has no complaint if he gets roughed up in return' (p.336). In 1969 roughly half of another national sample in the United States thought that shooting was the best way to handle student protests on campus (Kahn, 1972). This tolerance of official violence may explain the persistent public perceptions of riots and rioters as violent despite the fact that the number of people killed by authorities during civil disorders consistently exceeded the number of people killed by rioters by approximately ten to one. (Couch, 1968.)

Public support for official violence is so pervasive that the definition of violence is itself affected. In one survey, for example, again conducted in the United States, 30 per cent of a national sample said that 'police beating students' was *not* an act of violence, and an astonishing 57 per cent said that 'police shooting looters' was *not* an act of violence (Blumenthal *et al*, 1972, p.73). The semantics of the label violence, therefore clearly reflect the perceived legitimacy of the actor and not merely the nature of his or her act.

In Chapter Seven two experiments are discussed in which comparisons are made of viewers' perceptions of scenes from several types of fictional drama series and which depicted violence perpetrated either by law enforcers or criminals, or 'good guys' or 'bad guys'. Results indicate significant differences in the way violence instigated by these character-types was perceived.

Male versus female violence

The extent to which violence is employed differs more markedly for male and female TV characters than it does for law enforcers and criminals. In general, men are much more likely to use violence than women. The latter are more often characterised as romantic, emotional and dependant than men whenever there is trouble, either of a personal or professional nature (Butler and Paisley, 1980; Tuchman, 1978). Content analysis has indicated that just under half of leading female characters become involved in any violence, whilst as many as four-fifths of leading male characters do so (Gerbner and Gross, 1976). However, when they are involved, women are portrayed more often as victims of violence and less often as aggressors compared with men. Similar patterns of male and female involvement in violence were found also on British TV (Halloran and Croll, 1972).

To what extent however, do viewers' judgements of violent portrayals on TV vary according to the differential involvement in them of men and women?

Women are traditionally considered as being the gentler sex, and violence is not an attribute normally associated with this sex. Not only is involvement in violent or criminal activity less prevalent among women than among men in fictional TV but in the real world also. Female crime rates (and murder rates) do exhibit a tendency to approach closer to those for males in countries where women have greater freedom and equality, such as in Western Europe and North America, (Hoffman-Bustamente, 1973; Sutherland and Cressey, 1974). The sex rates for crime and violence has also changed with time.

Police reports in the United States have indicated that violent crime by women is increasing at a faster rate than that for men.

Another aspect of the way women are customarily conceptualised is the dichotomy of the female character into 'good' versus 'bad'. Some writers have referred to a cultural polarisation of women as either 'mothers' or 'whores'; 'the gentler sex' or 'the more deadly species'.

According to this scheme, those who conform to the idealised attitudes of 'femininity' — gentleness, purity, passivity, maternity — would never commit a violent crime. Any woman who turns to criminality or violence by definition is deviant and bad, since in so doing she has abandoned her natural feminine role. With respect to murderesses particularly, their crime is not seemingly that of killing another human being, but more significantly of having betrayed their womanhood. Buckhart (1973) reported how this dichotomy can directly affect women who have committed a crime. At first the femininity of a woman may prejudice police, judges and jurors in favour of leniency toward her, as she is considered less dangerous and less evil than a male counterpart. However, a woman who has stepped far enough out of line to be convicted can no longer expect the 'protections' of her femininity which she has by virtue of her criminal guilt discarded. Such women may often receive harsh judgement.

The observations ensuing out of these analyses of women, criminality and legal judgements are reinforced by data on individuals' perceptions of violent crimes committed by men and women. McGlynn, Megas and Benson (1976) read college students a summary of a violent murder case in which an insanity plea was entered. In one version the hypothetical defendant was a male and in the other female. Respondents rated the female accused of the violent crime as more 'sick' than an equivalent male person, though all other details about the case were exactly the same in both versions. But are women who commit violent crimes necessarily insane, or at least more so than men, or are they simply judged to be so by others? The picture emerging from evidence on this matter seems to point to the fact that women who murder or perpetrate violent crimes are perceived as deviating more from the 'norm' than their male counterparts, and their actions are judged to be more serious and their personalities as more disturbed.

The discussion so far has looked at judgements of male and female violence in real life. Is there any evidence to show that male and female TV characters who become involved in violence are judged differently by the audience? One recent study bears directly on this question. Reeves and Lometti (1978) asked groups of eight and twelve year-olds to provide descriptions of a selection of well-known male and female characters. In order of importance four main attributes emerged: humour, strength, attractiveness and activity. One dimension in particular, physical strength — was found to discriminate significantly between male and female characters. There was no tendency to spontaneously distinguish between TV men and women in terms of how violent they were.

However, whilst violence may not feature as a salient distinguishing attribute of female and male TV characters, viewers judgements of a violent portrayal may nevertheless be affected by types of character involved and the nature of their involvement. For example, the victimisation of a female character may be perceived as more violent than the victimisation of a male character, other factors such as context, setting and consequences of violence held constant, perhaps because men are generally perceived to have greater physical strength than women and thus are more able to cope with an attacker. In Chapter Seven, two further studies are reported which compared viewers' perceptions of male-perpetrated and female-perpetrated violence from several types of fictional programming to reveal the significance of such character-involvement variations for audience reaction to TV violence.

Physical form and techniques of violence

Violent portrayals depicted in dramatic TV programmes take on many different forms and involve many different kinds of instruments and techniques. Can any one particular instrumental form of violence be classified as more 'violent' than another instrumental form? Once again, the question of how to weight various types of violent episodes on TV may be considered in terms of direct frequency measures or according to audience responses to programme content.

Prevalence and the distribution of different forms of violence

Although not included as a vital component of the Violence Index, Gerbner and his Cultural Indicators team monitored the extent to which weapons characterised violent episodes in drama programming on American prime-time TV. Early reports indicated that over half of violent incidents involved the use of weapons and that the distribution of incidents featuring weapons varied from one type of programme to another. Weapons were generally more prevalent in cartoons (64 per cent of all violent incidents) than in non-cartoon shows (50 per cent) (see Gerbner, 1972).

Content analyses of dramatic entertainment programming on British TV during the early 1970s elaborated further on American findings in cataloguing a number of different kinds of physical violence. BBC researchers found that shootings featuring hand-guns and rifles (39 per cent of violence) and fistfights (37 per cent) were the most commonly occurring forms of violence. These were followed in decreasing order of prevalence by stabbing instruments (12 per cent), domestic items such as chairs or vases (8 per cent), specialised instruments such as traps or poisons (8 per cent), hitting or lashing instruments (7 per cent) and finally military equipment and explosives (6 per cent). Although these data are a decade old, more recent observations of prime-time fictional TV output have indicated that the nature, levels and distribution of violence have remained fairly stable over time and that a range of forms and varieties of violence still characterise these programmes today (Gerbner *et al*, 1979, 1980).

Some forms of violence are more *prevalent* than others on TV. But does the *prevalence* of different varieties of physical violence correspond with their *salience* and *perceived seriousness* for the audience? As we saw in earlier sections of this chapter, viewers perceptions of the salience of violence, *per se* or of the seriousness of particular kinds of violence on TV do not always accord with frequency count data on the extent to which violent incidents occur in programmes. With respect to the different physical forms or techniques of violence, is the most prevalent form also to be considered the most 'violent' because it occurs more often? Perhaps the more frequently occurring forms of violence afford extra opportunity for imitative learning or for the cumulative build up of desensitization with respect to those particular portrayals.

Or, should relatively infrequent styles of violence be taken as most violent because their unusual character makes them stand out as particularly unpleasant and disturbing for viewers? The latter questions concern audience response to TV content and require analyses of viewers' reactions to violent episodes. Is there any evidence of differential sensitivity amongst viewers with respect to different forms or techniques of violence?

Audience response to different physical forms of violence

The range of violent forms and techniques shown in feature films or TV drama series is wide, but as yet no systematic examination of differential audience reactions to these various physical forms has been attempted by any researchers. The extensive literature on the effects of TV violence on human aggression deriving from experimental laboratory work, for example, has actually analysed only a very small number and range of violent portrayals.

Although evidence has emerged that individuals can be triggered into behaving more aggressively after viewing violence of several distinct physical varieties, no comparisons of the realistic impact of these different forms have been conducted. Instead comparisons have customarily been made between one type of violent portrayal and a non-violent portrayal.

Following up on a real life incident in which two high school youths re-enacted a knife-fight scene from the film *Rebel Without A Cause*, resulting in one boy being seriously injured, a group of researchers at the University of Toronto conducted a series of experimental investigations with the same knife-fight from the movie to test its aggression-stimulating properties further (Walters, Thomas and Acker, 1962; Walters and Thomas, 1963). They found that watching this scene increased the punitiveness of adult viewers relative to a non-violent scene from another source. In a more recent experimental study, Liebert and Baron (1972) showed groups of five to nine year old children either an exciting sports sequence or a short extract from the crime-drama series *The Untouchables* which contained a chase, two fist-fights, two shootings and a knifing. Each child was subsequently placed in front of a large box that had wires leading into the next room. On the box were two buttons, a green one labelled 'HELP' and a red one labelled 'HURT'. The experimenter explained that the wires were connected to a game another child was playing in the next room. The child viewer could either help or hurt the other child by pressing the appropriate buttons. Children who had been shown the episode from 'The Untouchables' pressed the HURT buttons more frequently and for longer durations than those who watched the sports sequence.

Whilst this study indicates different strengths of behavioural reaction of viewers following exposure to a non-violent sequence and a violent one containing a variety of forms of physically violent activity, it offers no indications of any different degrees of impact for different physical forms of violence.

The 'weapons' effect

Imitation and disinhibition effects are undoubtedly influential but another element of concern over the impact of different instrumental forms of televised aggression relates to their capacity to 'trigger' aggression among viewers. Some writers have suggested that media portrayals may be particularly likely to evoke aggression in viewers when they contain specific features which have come to be strongly associated with violence through cultural learning processes (Berkowitz, 1970; Berkowitz and Le Page, 1967).

Among the features that are presumed to have this powerful aggression-eliciting property are weapons. Several experimental demonstrations of the so-called 'weapons' effect have shown that antagonised individuals are more likely to behave in an aggressive manner and/or to show stronger aggression when they subsequently perform their aggression in the presence of a weapon rather than in a weapon-free situation (Berkowitz and Le Page, 1967; Tannenbaum, 1971). Only one study of this kind made any attempt to vary the levels of violent content shown to individuals. Leyens and Parke, (1975), compared viewers' behavioural aggressive reactions under a mood of anger and frustration, following exposure to photographic slides which they defined as high, moderate or low in aggressive content (depicting a revolver, a whistle and a box of chocolates respectively). Whilst exposure to the revolver slide elicited most aggression from viewers, the definition of a photograph of a whistle as moderately aggressive seems highly dubious.

Another point to be noted about 'weapons' effect experiments is that the presence of weapons, or photographs of weapons usually elicits aggressive responses only amongst individuals who have been annoyed, whilst little impact has been observed amongst non-angered respondents. From the perspective of measuring distinctions made by viewers between different types of weapons of violence, however, the 'weapons' effect research offers no useful indicators. Does this mean that whilst the presence of weapons in the environment *per se*, whether in actuality or on film, may facilitate aggressive responding amongst angered individuals, that there is very little in the way of differentiations between physical forms of violence and 'observer' reactions to them? Certainly, at a purely behavioural level of measurement this would seem to be true. But on a perceptional level, a preliminary study carried out for the Surgeon General's Scientific Advisory Committee on Television and Social Behaviour in the United States in the early 1970s indicated that viewers do make discriminating judgements between different physical violent forms. Greenberg and Gordon (1972b) examined young boys' perceptions of selected programme scenes of differing kinds and degrees of violence. Some of these scenes involved the use of weapons, others did not. Results showed that scenes of violence involving weapons such as hand guns or rifles were rated as more violent, less real and less acceptable than weaponless scenes depicting for example hand-to-hand combat. This study indicated that on the level of viewers' perceptual judgements about violence, the physical characteristics of that violence may be an important mediator of its perceived seriousness. In Chapter Eight two experiments are reported which examined this issue further and in which a broader range of physical violent forms were assessed.

Degree of observable harm

In the previous sections of this chapter the nature of violent portrayals has been differentiated along a number of attributes including the setting, the types of characters who perpetrated a violent attack, and the physical form of violence. Each of those attributes has been found to have some effect on audience reactions to media violence and may therefore provide valid and meaningful dimensions in terms of which to classify violent TV content. The nature of character involvement either as an attacker or as a victim of violence may have a particular effect on the way in which violence is perceived. Related to this factor however is another different feature of violence − the degree of harm and suffering caused to a victim by a violent attack, and it is the significance of this feature to audience judgements about violent portrayals that we now turn.

TV characters deal out a lot of violence but they also extensively suffer the punitive and injurious consequences that accompany this involvement. In the content analytic model of the Cultural Indicators group the relative probabilities of being hurt or killed, as manifested in their victimisation ratios are interpreted as a dramatic demonstration of the power structure of the TV's fictional world (Gerbner and Gross, 1976, Gerbner, *et al*, 1978, 1979). Analyses of the outcomes of violence on prime-time drama output indicated that a substantial proportion of aggressive episodes resulted in injurious or painful consequences for some of the characters involved. On American TV nearly 40 per cent of violent incidents resulted in casualties, and 38 per cent of all casualties were fatal (Gerbner, 1972). On British TV around the same period, content analyses showed that 77 per cent of all violent episodes resulted in some pain or suffering, and one-third of these casualties were fatal (BBC, 1972). Clearly, harmful consequences are a prevalent feature of televised violence. What effects do they have on audience reactions to violent portrayals?

Behavioural research has shown that the expression of pain by a victim can have profound effects on the subsequent behaviour of that person's attacker. When one person attacks another, a frequent consequence is an expression of discomfort or annoyance by the victim. When this expression is perceived by the aggressor, it conveys certain information to the latter about the impact of his attack (e.g. that it has achieved a desired or undesired effect) and may affect the probability of his attacking again. Two hypotheses have been proposed concerning the effects of pain on further aggression against a victim by an attacker which predict violent outcomes. According to one hypothesis the suffering of the victim may lead to the vicarious arousal of similar unpleasant emotional feelings on the part of the aggressor. Such empathic arousal may then act to inhibit subsequent attacks against the suffering victim. The second hypothesis argues that the pain cues emitted by the victim may serve as reinforcing stimuli for the aggressor, and thus may facilitate attacks against this victim.

Empirical investigations of these hypotheses have produced evidence to support both the facilitating and inhibitory effects of a victim's suffering on his attacker's aggressive behaviour. However, research has also indicated that the likelihood that one of these effects will occur rather than the other depends a lot on other aspects of the context in which the aggressive display takes place and upon the mood of the aggressor. Most of the studies in this area have examined the effects of observing the suffering of a live victim on a person's aggressive behaviour, and only one or two have explored the impact of the consequential nature of filmed violence on viewers' reactions. Nevertheless, in setting the context for the experiments reported in this chapter it will be of interest and relevance to review both of these sources of evidence.

The impact of watching a 'live' victim's suffering

Experiments concerned with the behavioural effects of watching a victim's pain and suffering on the attacker's further aggression have generally employed the same technique for measuring aggression — the 'aggression machine' method designed by Buss (1961) — in which an individual is led to believe that he is assisting in an experiment concerned with the effects of punishment on learning and problem solving. In this situation the experimental participant is asked by the experimenter to deliver an electric shock via a special apparatus to which another person is wired up, every time this person makes a mistake on a learning or problem-solving task. Aggressiveness is assessed in terms of the magnitude and duration of electric shocks administered. The victim is in actuality an accomplice of the experimenter and only pretends to be hurt when the shocks are applied. Prior to this performance, however, manipulations are carried out with some experimental participants in an attempt to unwittingly annoy and anger them. Thus some individuals are primed to behave aggressively whilst others are not, prior to being given the opportunity to display aggression themselves against a helpless victim. Usually, the source of the annoyance is the attacker's eventual victim, thus providing additional incentive to the attacker to make his target suffer.

Using this experimental procedure, Geen (1970) found that when the victim of an aggressive attack (actually an experimental accomplice) pretended to suffer a great deal of pain when an unwitting (and non-angered) participant delivered an electric shock, the latter more often became inhibited against aggressing further and made his attacks less severe than when the victim suffered in silence. In subsequent studies, Baron (1971a, 1971b) found that male college students showed less aggression than a victim who had earlier annoyed them, when he exhibited pain and suffering following their initial attack on him, than when he showed no pain. Non-angered attackers showed the same patterns of conduct. Indeed, as the magnitude of pain showed by the victim increased, the strength of attacks (intensity and duration of electric shocks) delivered against him decreased. These results suggested that signs of suffering on the part of the victim may act as an effective deterrent to further attacks against this person, even when aggressors have been previously made angry.

Film portrayals and the impact of victim's suffering

As with 'live' victims' pain reactions, research has shown that when viewers are made aware of the painful aftermath of an aggressive film portrayal, they are subsequently less willing to behave aggressively against another person in contrived laboratory settings. Goranson (1969) found that the effect of unpleasant consequences for the victim of violence in a film portrayal is to reduce the level of aggressiveness in angered viewers compared to a film portrayal with a more pleasant ending. In his experimental demonstration of this effect, Goranson showed individuals a boxing-fight sequence from the feature film *Champion*, in which one fighter was savagely beaten by another. After seeing this fight sequence viewers next listened to a tape-recorded synopsis of events supposedly following the fight involving the loser. In one version of the story, the loser (or victim) was described as eventually dying from his injuries, whilst in another version he went on to another successful career. Afterwards, viewers took part in another experimental task in which their propensity towards aggressiveness was assessed with the 'aggression-machine' technique described above. Results showed that subsequent aggressiveness among viewers was stronger among those who had heard the synopsis describing pleasant consequences for the defeated fighter. Hearing that the injuries from the fight resulted in the defeated fighter's death, had the effect of inhibiting viewer aggression against another person.

Goranson's findings were reinforced by those of another study by Hartmann (1969) who showed adolescent delinquent boys three versions of a film sequence depicting two boys playing basketball. Prior to seeing the film, half of the boys were made angry and then angered and non-angered boys were each divided equally into three groups. One group saw a non-violent version of the film sequence simply depicting two boys about their own age playing basketball. A second group saw a version in which the boys in the film played happily enough to begin with, but then quarrelled and had a fight. In this version, the camera focused on the instrumental acts of aggression of the boy who won the fight. A third group also saw the fight sequence that ensued between the two boys after their quarrel but on this occasion camera shots emphasised the painful reactions of the defeated boy as he was hit. When subsequently allowed to punish an experimental accomplice for his mistakes in a learning task by administering electric shocks to him, it was found that previously angered boys who had watched the pain consequences version of the film portrayal became more aggressive than those who had watched the instrumental aggression version. Boys who had not been made angry earlier on, however, became more aggressive after watching the version focusing on the actions of the aggressive film actor than after seeing the version focusing on the painful reactions of the film victim.

Hartmann interpreted these findings as showing support for the empathy hypothesis described earlier. Under conditions of no anger arousal, intense pain reactions on the part of a victimised film actor produce powerful emphatic feelings in viewers which inhibit their tendencies to behave violently themselves. Anger, however, would appear to raise the threshold beyond which disturbing film portrayals give rise to these feelings in viewers and in turn inhibit their aggression.

Studies of behavioural aggression have indicated that the consequences of involvement in violence for the victim affect the way viewers respond to portrayals behaviourally. This in turn implies some degree of differential interpretation of violent portrayals in terms of the degree of harm to victims depicted in them. The significance of this attribute of violent content to audience *perceptions* has been more directly supported in an experiment reported earlier, by Greenberg and Gordon (1972b). They obtained young male viewers' judgements of violent scenes which differed along a number of dimensions including the degree of harm inflicted on victims. Scenes in which actors physically harmed themselves or another were perceived as more violent and less acceptable than scenes in which harm was overtly intended but unsuccessful (e.g. shooting at someone and missing). The latter portrayal in turn was rated in more serious terms than scenes depicting physical damage to an inanimate object (e.g. smashing furniture). In an extension of this research, two experiments were carried out by the author and are reported in Chapter Nine which provided a further examination of the importance of the depicted harmfulness of televised victims to audience appraisals of televised violence.

The physical setting of violence

The occurrence of violence on TV can, as we have seen, be coloured by a variety of characteristics, which can have independent and interdependent effects on viewers' reactions to violent portrayals. One aspect of violent scenarios that has not been considered to any extent in relation to audience response, and yet is an intrinsic ingredient of any portrayal, is the physical environment in which violence occurs. Previous content analytic models have examined the physical locations of violent actions in so far as they occur in urban, rural or uninhabited settings. Published findings in the early 1970s indicated that more violent incidents occurred in remote settings than in heavily populated areas. However the past ten years has seen a growth in popularity of the crime-detective genre and in the prevalence on prime-time TV of violence in urban settings.

Two fundamental types of physical-environmental conditions in which violence occurs, which may mediate viewers' responses to violent portrayals, are whether the action occurs during *daylight* or *after dark*, and whether it occurs *indoors* or *outdoors*. Neither of these features has been investigated previously in relation to viewers' reactions to televised violence, but in Chapter Ten two experiments are reported which indicate small effects of physical setting, particularly of location (indoors versus outdoors), on audience perceptions.

4 Individual differences and the perception of television violence

In the previous chapter we saw that public definitions of violence, whether in real life or on TV, vary considerably and can be determined to a significant degree by characteristics of actions themselves, by the individuals involved in them and by the settings or contexts in which they occur.

However, just as the characteristics of violent episodes can vary widely so too can the characteristics of the individuals who observe and make judgements about them. What is 'violent' or 'disturbing' to one person may be dismissed as harmless by another. Research has indicated that individuals' viewing habits and reactions to TV content can vary with sex, age, social background, attitudes and personality. Consequently, an important area for consideration by any system of programme assessment is that of individual variations between viewers in their perceptions of TV content. Consistent and significant idiosyncratic variations in the perception or definition of televised violence among different groups of viewers should be incorporated into any analytical framework which aims to provide a comprehensive classification or assessment of violence in terms of audience response.

There are many characteristics along which people differ and an exhaustive review and analysis of these in relation to audience responses to TV content is beyond the scope of this research. However, several facets of individual differences have been found by previous research to have particularly strong mediating influences on the way people use, interpret and react to TV content and some of these will be explored here.

Gender and self-perceptions of masculinity and femininity as potential mediators of TV violence perceptions

Content analysis of dramatic TV programming has indicated different degrees of involvement in violence of male and female characters. Once involved, the outcomes of violence for males and females tend to differ significantly too. Women tend to be more often depicted as victims than men and some writers have suggested that such patterns of portrayals engender stereotyped beliefs about the relative competence and roles of the sexes in society. But do men and women react differently to the portrayals they see on TV, especially to those involving violence? With respect, specifically, to aggression, researchers have reached a fairly general consensus of opinion that aggressive conduct is more characteristic of males than of females. Studies of human aggressive behaviour have revealed that sex is a major determinant of propensity to use aggression. Research with children has shown consistently that boys exhibit more aggressive behaviour than girls (Lansky, Crandall, Kagan, and Baker, 1961; Levin and Sears, 1956), particularly with respect to physical violence. Girls, however, may often exhibit verbal hostility. It has been found that boys often react differently than girls to TV portrayals of aggression. Bandura (1965) reported that boys were more likely to imitate a violent TV portrayal than girls. Liebert and Baron (1972) found not only that boys were more aggressive at play than girls, but also that viewing a violent TV portrayal produced a greater increment in levels of aggression subsequently during play among boys than among girls.

The above studies indicate sex differences in the behavioural reactions of viewers to violent portrayals, but do men and women also perceive TV violence differently? Fenigstein (1979) conducted a study to find out whether levels of personal aggressiveness affect preferences for viewing TV violence in which comparisons of male and female preferences were also made. He found that given a choice to watch violent or non-violent film clips, the films chosen by men contained more violence than those chosen by women.

The question of androgyny

In recent years, one of the major approaches to the study of sex differences has been the measurement of the *masculinity* and *femininity* of individuals. Masculinity is a concept that is usually associated with such characteristics as independence, assertiveness, dominance and aggressiveness, whilst femininity is typically defined by dependence, passiveness, sensitivity and emotionality. However, the simple division of males and females into masculine and feminine types respectively has been challenged by some researchers on the grounds that an individual's masculinity or femininity is not constant and can be influenced and does change over time. Furthermore, appropriate sex roles or characteristics are not rigidly assigned to each biological sex and some individuals may be characterised, and many indeed characterise themselves, in terms of both masculine and feminine attributes, (Bem, 1974; Spence and Helmreich, 1978). The concept of androgyny asserts that both masculine and feminine traits may co-exist in the same person, and those individuals who exhibit a relatively high degree of both are labelled 'androgynous'.

Research on androgyny has shown that biological sex alone may not be sufficient to indicate whether a person will exhibit typically masculine or feminine attitudes and behaviours. The extent to which a person feels or perceives himself or herself to be characterised by masculine or feminine traits may also be vitally important. How important is androgyny as a mediator of viewers' perceptions of TV violence? So far only one published study has related measures of masculinity and femininity to audience ratings of TV programmes. Diener and Woody (1981) investigated possible effects of androgyny on degree of liking for high violence and low violence programmes but found no differences in appreciation of either programme type associated with viewers' ratings of how masculine or feminine they perceived themselves to be.

Sex of characters — androgyny and perception of TV content

The nature of male and female viewers' reactions to TV portrayals, however, may depend significantly on the type (i.e. sex) of characters involved in them, and upon the perceived sex-appropriateness of the actions depicted. Children learn during the early years of their lives that some behaviours are socially more acceptable or tolerable when performed by boys, whilst others are regarded as more appropriate for girls. This in turn is reflected in the kinds of characters and behaviours on TV that each sex pays most attention to. There is evidence that elementary school children selectively recall media content that is congruent with traditional sex-roles (Maccoby and Wilson, 1957). Children generally recall more of the behaviour of actors of their own sex than of actors of the opposite sex. However, when sex-inappropriate behaviour is involved, such as when female characters act aggressively, or males act affectionately, children tend not to recall the counter-stereotypical behaviours of their own sex. This tendency may carry through into adult years. Maccoby, Wilson and Burton (1958) found that male viewers in their late teens and early adult years paid most attention to male leads in films, whereas female viewers in the same age-group were most attentive to female leads.

There is conflicting evidence as to whether it is the sex of the character in the portrayal or the sex-appropriateness of the behaviour depicted (regardless of the sex of the performer) that is most critical to differential attention, retention or imitation of the portrayal by viewers. Early observational learning studies indicated that boys imitated male actors more than female actors, while the opposite was true of girls (Bandura, Ross and Ross, 1963; Bandura, 1965). More recent research found a tendency for male and female viewers to imitate male and female actors equally (Maccoby and Jacklin, 1974). One reason for these equivocal findings, suggested by some writers, is that viewers pay more attention to the behaviour of the characters than to the characters themselves. But even on this point, research evidence has not provided an unambiguous solution. Barclay and others (1977) found that girls tended to imitate feminine behaviour more than masculine behaviour regardless of the biological sex of the model. The behaviour observed in this case was physically assertive or aggressive play. Relatively weak corresponding tendencies were observed among boys; but it is possible that they were less convinced by the staged aggression shown to them because of the fantasy context in which play took place. (They were asked to imagine themselves to be a GI in their play, and this may not have been regarded as a particularly masculine thing to do).

In contrast, Wolf (1975) demonstrated that the sex of a character is more important than sex tendencies of behaviour. Wolf found that boys imitated a sex-inappropriate behaviour (playing with a toy oven) more from a male actor than a female actor.

All of this research, of course, has adopted a strict dichotomy of sex-role behaviours into either masculine-types or feminine-types and assumed that boys are characterised entirely by propensities towards the former, and girls by propensities towards the latter. However, some audience members may have non-traditional sex-role preferences in the way they behave and hence may learn more from non-traditional models than viewers with traditional sex-role preferences. Perry and Perry (1975) found that children who showed strong preferences for masculine-type behaviours tended to recall a male actor's behaviour better than a female actor's, even though the actions performed were neither masculine nor feminine.

A more important predictor of the amount of attention paid to male and female TV characters and of the impact on viewers of these characters' involvement in violence may be self-perceived sexuality, rather than biological sex. As we shall see in Chapter Twelve, viewers' perceptions of male-perpetrated and female-perpetrated violence on TV vary according to whether they perceive themselves in primarily masculine or feminine terms, and that these self-perceptions were often more closely related to judgements of different forms of TV violence than actual gender.

Social background and social beliefs as potential mediators of viewers' perceptions of TV violence

The effects of media content on audience attitudes and behaviour have generally been found to be more immediate and pronounced when the audience regards the content as true-to-life. Thus, a televised report about actual violent events such as might occur on a TV newscast or in a documentary film may produce more extreme perceptual, emotional or behavioural reactions from viewers than similar events portrayed in an obviously fictional context. A highly dramatic and authentic portrayal of violence in a convincing, realistic fictional programme, may be evaluated or responded to in a different way than a violent portrayal of a similar instrumental form in an animated cartoon setting (e.g. Feshbach, 1972; Lagerspetz, Wahlroos and Wendelin, 1978; Reeves, 1978; Thomas and Tell, 1974).

However, the perceived degree of realism of TV content does not simply depend on the nature of that content *per se*, but on a comparison by viewers of the event portrayed with events they have experienced in real life. A portrayal which appears realistic to one viewer may not be so judged by another whose real life experience, presumably differing from that of the former, informs him that such events do not occur in actuality. The perceived reality of TV portrayals then is to a large extent a patterned function of the specific social and cultural background of the viewer, and of the beliefs about social reality which the viewer holds.

A relevant theoretical basis for this assertion is found in Mead's symbolic interactionist theory, in which the individual's self-image develops out of interactions with and accompanying perceptions of events and situations existent in his or her social environment (Strauss, 1964). People develop conceptions of themselves and their place in the world through interaction with others, in the context of the social system in which both they and relevant others are participants (Reeder, Donohue, and Biblarz, 1960). Among the perceptions that are taken from others are the goals and the normative structure of the social system, along with a perception of goals and behaviours that deviate from those norms. These perceptions have been labelled 'social ideals' and include ideals for self and ideals for others (Tichenor *et al*, 1976). Maintenance of the social order depends on the extent to which these ideals are internalised by the individual. Mass media content, including that of TV programmes, is assumed to be representative of such norms. However, different sub-cultures exist within society whose norms differ not only from each other but also in the case of minority or non-dominant groups, from the norms displayed on TV – which tend to be consonant with or reinforce the dominant cultural norms. So to what extent do individuals from different social or cultural backgrounds vary in their perceptions of violent portrayals and associated characterisations on TV?

Greenberg and Dominick (1970) found that disadvantaged, minority adolescents living in deprived neighbourhoods, perceived the TV they chose to watch as more realistic than did white, middle-class adolescents living in more affluent areas. Thus TV may provide disadvantaged adolescents with a source of knowledge about life other than that provided by the immediate environment in which they live.

Greenberg and Gordon (1972b) investigated social class and racial differences in the perceptions of TV violence of adolescent boys for the Surgeon General's Scientific Advisory Committee on Television and Social Behaviour. Ratings were obtained on four violent and two control scenes that had been videotaped from actual broadcasts. The writers assumed that social class and race (black versus white) might differentiate perceptions of violence on the supposition that black and lower-class youths are more familiar with violence in their immediate environment and thus might be more accustomed to high levels of violence, which would result in their rating violence in less extreme terms. Results provided some support for these assumptions showing that both race and socio-economic status were related to perceptions of the violence. In general children from lower income families, both black and white judged the behaviour in the violent scenes as more acceptable, realistic and enjoyable than children from higher income families.

Fear of Victimisation.

This social belief factor represents persons' perceptions of how much danger there is in the world for themselves and others from violent and criminal attack and their fear of this danger. Previously, research carried out in the United States has shown that fear of personal attack is related to amount of TV viewing, and that heavy viewers generally exhibit more fearfulness than light viewers. Whilst a consistent finding among American TV viewers, so far no support for a relationship between weight of TV viewing and fear of victimisation has been found amongst British samples (Wober, 1978; Wober and Gunter, 1982). However, these studies examined only how much TV people

62

watch and not their reactions to actual programme materials. There is evidence to show that individuals faced with a threat to personal safety in their immediate environment tend to choose to watch violent media material over non-violent material (Boyanowsky, 1977; Boyanowsky *et al*, 1974). Consequently, fearful individuals may also tend to evaluate violent portrayals differently than less anxious people.

Anomia. The relatively rapid development of industrial economy brought with it a migration of people from stable rural communities to the cities where they lived as strangers among strangers. Many of these people who were accustomed to living in an environment surrounded by relatives, friends, tradition and a general sense of belonging, felt a sense of having no roots and of being alone in an indifferent, impersonal world. Added to this, constant exposure to reports of organised crime, violence,and corrupt public officials accentuated these feelings of isolation and alienation and cultivated among many an extreme cynicism or 'anomia' — the feeling that one lives in a kind of human jungle where no one can or should be trusted.

As with fear of victimisation, research has shown a tendency for feelings of mistrust and a generally cynical view of the world to be stronger among heavy than among light TV viewers (Gerbner *et al*, 1977, 1978) and these social perceptions have been interpreted as reactions to TV cultivated in particular by violent programming. However, anomia may be a deep-seated response to the existing social structure, of which TV forms but a single part, rather than simply to TV alone. Social cynicism supposedly cultivated by an impersonal environment has been hypothesised to affect individuals' reactions to real life violent incidents (Latane and Darley, 1970) generally producing an apathetic response of lack of concern for victims. Whether anomia also mediates individuals' perceptions of televised violence, however, is a question researchers have not yet tackled.

Locus of control. In an influential theory of human behaviour, Rotter (1965) proposed that the social environment played a predominant role in shaping the dominant behavioural tendencies of individuals. He believed that through their experiences in different social situations people build up patterns of expectancies concerning their abilities to attain goals and effect changes in their social environment. According to Rotter, people can be reliably differentiated into those who believe that their actions can and do affect the course of their life — internal locus of control — and those who believe their life is controlled by luck, fate and chance, or other forces beyond their personal influence — external locus of control.

In 1965 Rotter produced the internal—external control scale to indicate the strength of these contrasting beliefs in individuals and this scale has since been used extensively as a measure of personality. Wober and Gunter (1982) reported that external control or strong belief that fate determines events in one's life was significantly related to heavier viewing of fictional and of informational output on TV. External controllers also held more fearful beliefs about society. This opens up the possibility that an individual's position along the internal—external locus of control continuum may relate also to that person's perceptual responses to TV programmes.

Belief in a just world. This concept was discussed by Rubin and Peplau (1975). Research with this scale has indicated that many people believe that the world is a place where good people are rewarded and bad people are punished. Believers in a just world have been found to be more likely than non-believers to admire fortunate people and to derogate victims, thus permitting the believers to maintain the perception that people in fact get what they deserve.

Some writers have argued that in order to maintain the fit between happiness and goodness (and between punishment and wickedness), people will exert considerable effort to alleviate the suffering of another — but only when they believe that the sufferer does not in fact deserve his fate. In an analysis of contributions to a *New York Times* '100 Neediest Cases' appeal, it was found that the largest proportion of contributions went to victims of child abuse who clearly were not responsible for their suffering, whilst the fewest were received by those people with psychological illnesses or moral blemishes — cases in which the victim might be considered blameworthy and hence deserving to suffer. In an experimental demonstration of this, Rubin and Peplau (1973) found that young adult men, who listened to the live broadcast of the US 1971 national draft lottery, reacted sympathetically towards those of their number who unfortunately (in their opinion) were drafted, unless they were also high scorers on the Just World Scale. The latter tended to react favourably towards those who avoided being drafted but were unsympathetic and resentful towards draftees. Lerner has attempted to explain this kind of reaction by stating that 'all of us need to believe that we live in a world in which we and others like us can get what we deserve — and deserve what we get' (1973, p.51). As a result of this need we tend to believe that even ostensibly random rewards and punishments must in fact reflect an underlying moral order.

Among the perpetuators of the belief in a just world are the mass media. Virtually all TV dramas have the same predictable storyline with the good guy finally triumphing over the bad guy as justice prevails. It has also been shown experimentally that people rate scenes of physical force or coercion by actors as more or less aggressive depending on the perceived justification for the perpetrator's behaviour (e.g. Brown and Tedeschi, 1976), but it is clear also that the perceived justification of an aggressor's use of coercion may not be the only important factor determining how a violent incident is evaluated by an observer; whether or not the victim deserved what he got may also be a crucial variable, and this perception may be more likely to occur among those observers who hold strong 'just world' beliefs.

One published study which has examined empirically belief in a just world and its relations with TV viewing, by Gunter and Wober (1983), found that viewing of action—adventure programmes and of American programmes of this type in particular, was related to belief in a just world amongst a sample of British viewers, indicating that those who devoted proportionately more of their viewing time to these kinds of programmes exhibited stronger beliefs that the world is a just place. Unfortunately, these correlational data cannot indicate the direction of causality in this relationship. It could be that heavy viewers of action—drama programmes are assimilating from those programmes the message that justice typically triumphs over evil in the end, and believe this to be true of real life. However, this result may also reflect the tendency of people who already believe that the real world is a just place to turn to dramatic story-lines for further reinforcement and clarification of their beliefs. If belief in a just world is associated with differential TV viewing patterns and preferences, it may also be related to varying judgements about different kinds of violent or coercive behaviour in programmes, especially in contemporary settings in the context of conflict between the agencies of law and order and criminal elements.

Personal aggressiveness and the perception of TV violence

Some individuals are naturally more aggressive than others; not only do they show a greater propensity to use aggression themselves, but they also evaluate the violence performed by others differently than less aggressive persons. The main interest here is how individual levels of aggressiveness are related to viewers' reactions to violent TV content.

A series of correlational studies carried out for the Surgeon General's Committee on TV violence indicated that viewing televised violence is significantly related to aggressive behaviour. McLeod, Atkin and Chaffee (1972, 1976) found a strong positive correlation between viewing violent programmes and ratings of aggressiveness among pre-teenage children.

Dominick and Greenberg (1972) found a relationship between extent of violent programme viewing and willingness to endorse the use of violence by nine to eleven year old boys. In a more extensive analysis of children's viewing preferences and their relationship to personal aggressiveness, Greenberg and Atkin (1977) found among 9—13 year old boys and girls that heavy viewers of violent programmes tended to select aggressive solutions to problem situations considerably more often than light viewers of these programmes. These findings have usually been interpreted to show that watching TV violence may cause enhanced propensity towards aggression among young viewers, but their correlational nature leaves them open to the reverse interpretation that youngsters who are already aggressive in nature tend to prefer watching violent programmes.

Aggressiveness and preferences for TV violence

Virtually all of the research concerned with media violence has attempted to determine whether the viewing of violence is associated with or more crucially causes aggression. Little experimental research has been directed at understanding why people watch violent programmes. Recent investigations, however, have indicated that one reason for the consistent finding of a strong association between levels of violence viewing and personal aggressiveness among viewers may be that people who are already aggressive or angry tend to prefer violent programming.

Attempts to experimentally manipulate temporary aggressive dispositions by angering respondents have proved successful in demonstrating a link between mood and preference for violent film material (e.g. Freedman and Newtson, 1975). Generally, angry people prefer violent movies. Fear as well as anger has been found to have a similar effect on movie performances. Boyanowsky, Newtson and Walster (1974) found that attendance at a violent film increased markedly following a brutal local murder, whereas no such increase occurred for a non-violent, romantic movie.

Several experiments have employed a strategy of sensitising individuals to think aggressively before giving them an opportunity to choose between watching violent or non-violent films. Goldstein (1972) invited respondents to read one of three prose passages; one of which contained aggressive material, another sexual material and a third neither aggressive nor sexual content.

These people were then asked to indicate from a list of violent, erotic or neutral movies which one they would prefer to watch. Results showed that individuals who had read the aggressive passage preferred aggressive movies to all others.

In a series of experiments concerned with personal aggressiveness and preferences for violent TV programmes, Fenigstein induced young men and women to have what he termed aggressive or nonaggressive fantasies. Each respondent was given a list of words and asked to make up a story including all the words provided. For some respondents the list contained words describing instruments of violence or violent behaviours that were designed to induce aggressive thoughts (or fantasies). Afterwards, they were asked to choose from a list of films the one they would most like to watch. It was found that aggressive fantasies in men only, compared to nonaggressive fantasies, increased the preference for viewing violence.

All of the studies discussed above manipulated temporary aggressive dispositions of individuals. However, people may vary on a more deep-seated and permanent basis in their propensities towards aggression. This sort of personality dimension may have more substantial influences on viewers' long-term programme preferences and viewing habits, and also on their responses to TV violence. In a two-wave panel study of young people across a one-year lag, Atkin, Greenberg, Korzenny and McDermott (1979) explored the relationship between attitudes towards verbal and physical aggressiveness and programme preferences over time. They used measures of dispositions towards aggression at one stage of measurement to predict TV viewing patterns at a second stage of measurement and found in the presence of controls for other important variables, that tendencies towards physical aggressiveness were strongly related to preferences for a number of violent programmes the following year. Physical aggressiveness was a good predictor of future preferences for violent TV programmes among boys only, whilst verbal aggressiveness was a strong predictor for girls only.

Clearly, convincing evidence is accumulating that aggressive pre-dispositions can have important effects on viewers' preferences for TV violence. Why should this be so? One reason why aggressive people may seek out violent TV content is that they seek reinforcement for their anti-social behavioural tendencies from seeing attractive TV characters behave in the same way. Johnson, Friedman and Gross (1972) have suggested that it is not violent content *per se* that account for preference differences between aggressive and non-aggressive youngsters, but the social role of the leading male character. Young boys in particular seek out appropriate 'models for manhood' and the active, aggressive personality presented by many of TV's leading heroes offers a very attractive role-model. This, if true, is itself a matter for serious concern, but it does call for a change in the way the impact of TV violence is analysed, so as to take into account individual differences between viewers in their selectivity of viewing.

Aggressiveness and reactions to TV violence

The correlational data reported above suggests the possibility of differences in preference for violent TV content among aggressive and non-aggressive viewer-types, but to what extent do these types differ in their reactions to televised violence? Behavioural evidence has indicated that the anti-social effects of violent TV portrayals are strongest and are most likely to occur among individuals who are already aggressive, thus lending some support to the notion that aggressive types may seek reinforcement for their own behaviour from televised violence.

In a series of field studies with institutionalised delinquents in the United States and Belgium, Parke, Berkowitz, Leyens, West and Sebastian (1977) manipulated the TV diet of these boys and monitored variations in their everyday behaviour which occurred as a function of the types of content they were shown. Different groups received either five violent films or five non-violent films over a period of one week. It was found that those boys who watched the violent films exhibited greater increases in their verbal and physical aggression against other boys than those who saw the non-violent content. However, it was those boys who were usually classified as more aggressive who were most likely to show these adverse reactions to violent film material.

It is the aim of the research reported in this volume to examine the feasibility of developing a technique for the assessment of televised violence using viewers' perceptions of actual programme content to define more and less serious forms of violence. Personal aggressiveness would seem to indicate the behavioural impact of violent TV or film material; to what extent does it affect viewers' perceptions of this content?

Searle (1976) studied adolescents' perceptions of filmed violence in the James Bond film 'Goldfinger' and the film 'The Comedians' based on the Graham Greene novel. She differentiated her subjects in terms of their responses on two measures of aggressiveness: (a) Rosenzweig's Picture-Frustration Study Form; and (b) Self-reported Levels of Personal Aggressiveness.

After watching one of the two full-length films, subjects' evaluations of the major characters were compared. There was no simple tendency for highly aggressive youths to view filmed violence or characters as being less violent than low-aggressive youths. Aggressive film characters tended to be rated as more aggressive by low self-rating subjects than by high self-rating subjects, thus apparently confirming the view that individuals accustomed to violence in real life rate filmed violence as less violent than those from non-violent backgrounds. Taking into account projection-test data it emerged, however, that a rather more complicated psychodynamic explanation was needed to understand the relationship between aggression and perceptions of film heroes or villains as aggressive.

Although there was no simple correlation between either the aggressiveness of an individual or his self-perception of being aggressive and his ratings of the aggressiveness of film characters, there was evidence of an interaction effect between actual (projection-test rated) aggressiveness and self-perception of film characters. Individuals who, by the objective picture-frustration test measure, were found to be aggressive but tended not to have a self-concept as aggressive, rated film characters as more aggressive than did those who were equally (objectively) aggressive and who also admitted it. To generalise from these findings it could be suggested that individuals who are unable to come to terms with their own aggressiveness are also most sensitised to violence on film.

The Eysenckian Personality Model and Perception of TV Violence

In their book, *Sex, Violence and the Media*, Eysenck and Nias (1978) suggested that Eysenck's three-dimensional model of personality could serve as a useful conceptual and methodological framework with which to assess individual differences in reactions to TV violence.

The constituent factors of this model are extraversion, neuroticism and psychoticism. The extraversion dimension is concerned with the degree of sociability of an individual and represents a continuum ranging from characteristics such as outgoing, impulsive, uninhibited and sociable at one end (extravert) to quiet, retiring and introspective at the other (introvert). The neuroticism dimension concerns the emotionality of an individual. Some people differ from others in the ease with which they can be aroused emotionally and in the extent to which they get worried and depressed about things. This dimension is defined by attributes such as anxiety and emotional instability at one end (neuroticism) versus calmness and emotional stability at the other. The psychoticism dimension is one that is characterised by tough-mindedness at one extreme and tender-mindedness at the other. People who score high on this dimension are often found to be selfish, aggressive, suspicious, emotionally cold and not uncommonly somewhat anti-social.

None of these dimensions has been related to individuals' use of or reactions to TV. However, given the extensively empirically substantiated claims by Eysenck that these dimensions represent fundamental defining aspects of human personality, it is not unreasonable to assume that individuals who differ in their positions along these continua may also exhibit different reactions to TV programmes and more specifically to particular kinds of (violent) portrayals in programmes. Eysenck (1967) has indicated, for example, that neuroticism interacts with extraversion to determine personal levels of aggressiveness, and that unstable or neurotic extraverts tend to show stronger propensities to exhibit intense anger and violent or unruly behaviour than do other personality types.

This opens up the possibility that neurotic extraverts also perceive the aggression of others, including violence perpetrated by characters in fictional TV settings, in a fashion that is distinct from the perceptions of individuals with a different blend of these characteristics. Similarly following from Eysenck's theory of crime and personality (Eysenck, 1964) which suggests that criminals and delinquents tend to score highly on all three (E, N and P) scales, it might be expected that people with high scores are not only more likely to engage in anti-social acts, but are less likely to perceive TV portrayals as violent, disturbing or anti-social than are people with lower scores on all three variables.

5 A framework for the perceptual analysis of television violence

The previous chapter has shown that the traditional methods of assessing TV violence, programme-based and audience-based, are not satisfactory in isolation. Studies of public perceptions of real life violent scenarios have indicated that people ordinarily make often highly refined, multi-faceted judgements about violence (Forgas *et al*, 1980). This fact has important implications for the analysis of televised violence because most people will experience a far greater number and variety of violent forms via TV than they are ever likely to encounter in their normal, everyday lives. They may therefore develop and exhibit a range and subtlety of judgements about violent episodes on the TV world which are at least as complex as those made for violence in the real world.

In Chapter Two and Chapter Three two perspectives on the assessment of TV content were critically examined, and both, in isolation were found wanting. In the first of these perspectives, labelled *programme-based* because of its detailed analytical paradigms concerned solely with the assessment of content profiles within programmes in terms of *a priori* objective definitional frames, involved compiling catalogues of narrowly-defined violent incidents in terms of their frequency of occurrence. The second perspective, labelled the *audience-based* approach, focused on viewers' subjective judgements about programmes. Neither perspective was judged to provide an adequate framework within which to produce ecologically valid and practically useful measures of TV violence.

The fundamental problem with content analysis is that it normally provides no indication of the meaningfulness of its content categories for the audience. Although it is possible to construct increasingly complex descriptions of TV programmes using content analysis techniques, major problems arise when moving from statements about what the content *implies*, as assessed by objective analysis of its inherent structures, to how it is actually *perceived and interpreted* by the audience. Analysis of the ways that viewers ordinarily differentiate between TV portrayals (e.g. between very violent and not very violent) is essential in this writer's opinion, if content profiles are eventually to be linked in a direct and meaningful fashion to audience reactions to TV programmes. An empirical framework needs to be explored which can provide an analysis of TV violence which corresponds both with the content of programmes and with the way the public perceives that content.

Studies within the audience-based approach have attempted to derive classifications of TV content from the viewers themselves, but all too often the methods employed have not examined individuals' perceptions of specific sequences or portrayals. Most typically, viewers' perceptions of actual programme content were not assessed at all; only their perceptions of programme titles. Therefore any evaluative or descriptive responses from viewers about the programmes in question could not be related directly to content (e.g. incidents, events or relationships) depicted in programmes. Then, even when actual programme sequences have been used as stimulus materials, seldom has there been any attempt to compare and contrast viewers' perceptions across a series of specific portrayals of violence whose features were varied systematically in order to find out if particular attributes (e.g. types of weapons used, character-types involved, seriousness of harmful consequences for victims, physical or dramatic setting, etc.) have any effects on the way televised violence is appraised by viewers.

Exceptions to this were two studies carried out by Greenberg and Gordon (1972) for the Surgeon General's Scientific Advisory Committee in the United States in which adolescent viewers from different social backgrounds rated short TV scenes that differed in terms of the forms of violence they portrayed (e.g. fist-fights, shooting, car-crashes etc.). This research found marked differences in viewers' perceptions of the seriousness of different physical forms of violence. Curiously though, this sort of experiment was not followed up and developed further to assess audience perceptions of a wider range of televised violence, and among a broader population — until now. In this book new research is reported which explored two methodologies for the assessment of TV violence from fiction programming in terms of direct audience response. Perceptions of violence portrayals were also related to differences among viewers themselves with respect to their self-perceptions, social beliefs, aggressive predispositions and personality characteristics. Within two quasi-experimental frameworks, small samples of viewers made a variety of perceptual responses to selected violent excerpts from a range of fictional TV output. The content of these excerpts was varied systematically along certain critical dimensions of content whose significance as factors in terms of which viewers discriminated between violent portrayals was assessed. In the remainder of this chapter details of these methodologies will be given, together with a brief account of the conceptual, social psychological framework within which this research was founded.

Social psychological foundations

Conceptually, the perspective adopted in this research to assess and classify TV violence in terms of the way it is publicly perceived, was influenced by recent work in social psychology on the perception of social episodes or social situations (e.g. Argyle, Furnham and Graham, 1981; Forgas, 1979). The broad aim of social situations research has been to discover the perceptual dimensions used by people to discriminate between different types of incidents or events in various social contexts. Social episodes have been defined as units of interaction which represent 'any sequence of happenings in which human beings engage' and which 'have a beginning and an end which can usually be identified' (Harre and Secord, 1972, p.10).

Perceptions of relationships between social encounters or situations which characterise a particular cultural (or sub-cultural) milieu can be described in terms of an episode space. However, episodes also represent cognitive models of behaviour sequences typical of certain social situations housed in the minds of individuals, and meaningful taxonomies of episodes are obtained by measuring, for specific individuals, their subjective perceptual discriminations between episodes comprising a particular episode space. A very similar model for classifying and assessing social events in an ecologically meaningful way was outlined many years earlier by symbolic interactionist theory. A basic assumption of this theory is that people create symbolic social environments where physical objects and actions assume more or less importance in terms of what they mean to observers. Because the social meaning of objects and events in this symbolic environment is contained in the minds of individuals these entities must be described in subjective terms from the standpoint of the perceiver. For symbolic interactionists as well as for social structure analysts, the quality of objects and events occurring in different social contexts can be properly defined only in terms of the way they are subjectively perceived and interpreted by individuals.

Turning to the problem of analysis of TV violence, the work on social episodes or social situations offers a useful conceptual and methodological background against which to develop an empirical framework in which to assess the salient and definitive attributes of violent portrayals on TV.

TV programmes represent an extremely complex and often ambiguous stimulus domain which cannot be adequately classified or otherwise assessed using normative objective definitions or descriptions of content. Social situations research has shown that people may construe social events of the same type in many different ways which are partly determined by the context or environment in which events occur and partly by enduring personality characteristics of the individuals themselves. With reference particularly to perceptions of aggressive or violent episodes, recent research, carried out within this social—psychological perspective, has shown that people classify aggressive acts in terms of not one but several distinct factors, and furthermore, that the relative salience of particular features of violence varies across individuals who hold different beliefs or values (Forgas *et al*, 1980). If people distinguish between personally experienced, real-life violent episodes in this multi-faceted way, the same may be true of the way in which they classify and define violent episodes in TV programmes. The research reported in this volume was designed to find out whether and to what extent this is the case. The following sections describe the methods employed in the research.

Research methods

Selection of TV materials

Logistically, this research began with the selection of TV materials for perceptual analysis by viewers. This initial stage of the research involved video-recording more than 90 hours of fictional TV content broadcast on all three TV networks in the United Kingdom over a six-month period during the second half of 1980. This content carried a wide array of different kinds of violent episodes. Programmes were selected for video-taping on the *a priori* expectation, gauged from British and American content-analytic studies, that they would contain some violence, and indeed in many cases that they would be likely to depict high frequencies of violent incidents. The types of programmes focused on most were those that had been identified by content analysis as the most violent on TV, that is, in terms of the prevalence of violent incidents.

A limiting feature in the selection of materials was to find violent episodes whose characteristics exemplified attributes which had either been previously recognised by content analysts and indicated in their coding schemes and/or manipulated to a limited extent by 'effects' researchers who had shown such features to mediate audience reactions to TV violence. The current research focused on the following five major categories of content attributes in terms of which violent portrayals could be grouped, and which had either primarily been referred to by content analysts or manipulated by 'effects' researchers:

1   *Programme genre or type* (i.e. the realism or authenticity of violence as determined by the dramatic setting in which it is portrayed).
2   *Character involvement* (i.e. the types of characters featured in violent episodes — male versus females; and law enforcers versus criminals).
3   *Physical form* (i.e. episodes in which weapons were used versus those featuring unarmed conflict).
4   *Consequences of violence* (i.e. the outcome of violence for victims, fatal or non-fatal injury, or no observable harm).
5   *Physical setting* (i.e. violence depicted during the day or at night, and in indoor or outdoor locations).

The significance of each of these features on viewers' perceptions of TV violence was systematically and independently examined in a series of twelve quasi-experimental studies.

The rating procedures

Two designs were explored in this 'perceptual analysis' of TV violence. These designs involved two different methods of presentation and audience assessment of violent excerpts, although each drew on the same pool of stimulus materials, employed the same rating concepts, and examined common sets of content attributes.

In the first procedure, programme excerpts were presented one at a time to a panel of viewers who judged each portrayal along eight rating scales: *violent, realistic, exciting, humorous, likely to disturb people in general, suitable for children, frightening* and *personally disturbing*. Each scale had seven response options ranging on the *violent* scale for example from 'not at all violent' (scored one point) to 'extremely violent' (scored seven points). These scales were selected to reflect a variety of different judgements about TV violence other than simply how 'violent' it is or appears to be.

One thing that is of interest for example is to be able to match up emotionally-based reactions of viewers to their perceptions of how violent TV scenes are because a common justification for the inclusion of violence in drama programmes is that it adds to the entertainment value of such programmes. American research on this particular question has indicated that viewers appear not to enjoy violent programmes more than non-violent programmes, and to some extent may even like them less (Diener and De Four, 1979; Diener and Woody, 1981). However, these studies, like so many others, considered violence in a holistic fashion and failed to explore whether different kinds of violence produced different levels of enjoyment. In the experiments reported here, some indication of enjoyment of the TV materials was obtained by asking viewers to rate how exciting and how humorous or amusing they found each scene to be.

Previous research has shown that one of the most important dimensions along which viewers judge TV content is its perceived realism (Howitt and Cumberbatch, 1974). Also, realism is a particularly powerful mediator of audience reactions to televised violence. Violent portrayals judged to be true to life have been shown to evoke significantly stronger emotional and behavioural responses from viewers than those occurring in a fantasy context (Berkowitz and Alioto, 1973; Feshbach, 1972; Lagerspetz, Wahlroos and Wendelin, 1978; Noble, 1975). Hence, viewers sampled here were asked to state how realistic or true to life they perceived each violent portrayal to be, not simply to find out whether the perceived degree of violence in a particular TV scene was associated with its perceived realism (which on the basis of existing research evidence one could predict it very likely to be), but more importantly to see whether one form of violence (e.g. instrumental technique, character involvement, consequences, physical setting) was consistently perceived as more authentic than another — a feature of audience reactions to televised violence that had not previously been examined in such detail.

It was thought to be of interest also to find out whether people are necessarily frightened or disturbed by TV material they also judge to be violent, and whether they believed such material as likely to upset other people and children. It has been shown for instance that people may sometimes choose to watch a violent film rather than a non-violent film, particularly when they are faced with a threatening situation in real life (Boyanowsky *et al*, 1974; Boyanowsky, 1977). It seems that some violent film material can have a comforting effect, when its portrayals resemble events of which the individual is afraid or feels threatened by in real life. By facing up to the same fears vicariously, the individual learns how to cope with and possibly to reduce them. Hence, not all forms of violence, even though recognised by observers as 'violent', may be equally frightening. Furthermore, individuals who are frightened by different things may show widely varying estimations of how frightening a particular violent portrayal appears to them to be.

Whilst violent portrayals may be perceived as personally disturbing, will a viewer necessarily generalise the same reaction to other viewers for all or for particular kinds of violence? Also will a viewer who finds a TV scene personally upsetting prefer that it was not shown to children? In the absence of any factual evidence on these questions elsewhere, it was decided that the opportunity should be taken in this research to find the answers. Hence, panel members were asked to judge how disturbed by each scene shown to them they thought other people in general would be, and whether or not it was suitable for children. It would be of interest here to find out which particular kinds or forms of violent portrayals were judged to be potentially upsetting or unsuitable for others and also whether these judgements exhibited similar scoring patterns to other subjective ratings, especially those concerning how violent and personally disturbing the same scenes were thought to be.

Seven studies were run in which programme excerpts were judged singly. In each study, one of the five categories of content attributes was in focus and was varied across the set of episodes on which judgements in that study were made. The mean scores for each type of portrayal were compared via *post hoc* statistical analyses, which were designed to indicate the extent to which the particular attributes in question (e.g. programme genre, character type, physical form, consequences, or physical setting) had any significant effects on viewers' judgements.

In the second procedure, programme excerpts were presented to a second panel of viewers in pairs. Over a series of five studies, sets of six excerpts were edited into a compilation of fifteen pairs so that each episode was paired with each of the other five from the same set. The same eight rating concepts were employed again, but judgements were made in a different fashion. Instead of judging each violent clip on its own, viewers were required to make discriminative judgements between each member of a pair of scenes. Thus, when judging episodes along the *violent* scale viewers said which one of a pair was the more violent, and by how much. Four response options were available: 'slightly more violent', somewhat more violent', 'moderately more violent', and 'a great deal more violent'. These responses were scored from one to four points respectively, whilst the scene judged to be the less violent received zero points. A points tally was computed for each scene by summing over the points received from each of its comparisons with the other five scenes in the set. Thus, the minimum score possible from five paired-comparisons on each rating scale was zero (i.e. if a particular scene had been rated as the less violent against all of the other five), and the maximum possible was 20 points (i.e. if a scene had been rated as 'a great deal more violent' against each of the others). These raw scores were converted to proportions for each programme episode of the maximum total possible, and this ratio served as an indicator of how violent, frightening, etc. each episode was perceived to be relative to the others against which it was judged. An advantage of this procedure over the first one described above is that it allows viewers to choose directly between portrayals of different types which they think is the more violent, realistic, frightening or whatever, whereas the first procedure relies on *post hoc* statistical comparisons of portrayal that were actually rated singly, and hence is a more indirect method of assessing the salience of certain features for viewers' judgements about violent incidents. Together, however, both techniques could provide powerful indications of which attributes of violent portrayals are important to viewers' perceptions, especially if similar patterns of ratings or rank orderings of certain types of portrayals emerge from each procedure.

The panels

Two groups of viewers were recruited to take part in the studies. Both groups were paid a fixed hourly rate for participation, and each took part in six sessions run over several days during a six-week period in the summer of 1981. These groups will be referred to throughout as Panel One and Panel Two. It should be noted that neither of these groups was representative of the population at large, although each panel consisted of a heterogeneous selection of people from many walks of life including housewives, factory workers, university technicians, schoolteachers, students, retired and unemployed people. The demographic profile of each panel is shown in Table 5.1 and indicates the broad spectrum in demographic terms covered in each of these groups. Panel One consisted of 40 people recruited in the Oxford area of England, who took part in seven experiments in which programme excerpts were judged singly. Panel Two consisted of 34 different individuals from London and Oxford, who took part in five experiments in which programme excerpts were judged in pairs. All members of both panels were asked about their TV viewing habits, and most (over 90 per cent in both groups) claimed to be regular viewers who watched TV on at least three or four days a week.

Individual difference measures

Mention was made in Chapter 1 of research which indicated that the *salience* of violence in TV programmes for viewers may not always match its *prevalence*. It was also seen that different individuals exhibit

Table 5.1

Demographic profiles of panels

		Sex		Age				Class			Terminal age of education		
		Males	Females	15–24	25–34	35–54	55+	ABC_1	C_2	DE	15	18	21+
Panel One													
(n=40)	%	45	55	31	24	25	15	43	43	14	20	35	45
Panel Two													
(n=34)	%	50	50	35	15	32	18	70	24	5	18	38	44

different magnitudes and types of response to violent material. Differences in reactions to TV content have been associated in previous research with sex, age and social class characteristics of individuals, but people can be categorised and differentiated in other ways which may even cut across their demographic profiles.

Individuals' perceptions of themselves, their beliefs about the world around them, and deep-seated, enduring personality dispositions are all important psychological factors which may determine or mediate the way they interpret their experiences. All such variables need to be considered at some stage in relation to viewers' responses to TV content, and no ecologically valid system of content assessment based on audience perceptions can afford to ignore individual difference factors of these kinds.

In the current research, four categories of individual differences measures were obtained from each member of Panel One and were related in a systematic fashion to their judgements of different kinds of televised violence. These four types of measures, which reflect the individual difference mediators of viewers' reactions to TV violence were:

1   Self-perceptions
2   Social beliefs
3   Attitudes towards aggression
4   Personality

The aim of this aspect of the research was to identify characteristics of viewers' psychological make-up which had any marked relationship with their judgements about different forms of TV violence or about TV violence in general. The scales used to define these four categories of individual difference are described briefly below.

Self-perceptions

Measurement of self-perceptions focused on individuals' descriptions of themselves in terms of a number of given attributes which were designed to indicate respondents' positions along a single continuum of masculinity—femininity. Masculinity and femininity have traditionally been presumed to represent opposite poles on a single dimension, with men usually characterised by mainly masculine qualities and women by feminine qualities. More recently, however, some writers have suggested that this dichotomy is too rigid and actually inaccurate. It has become recognised increasingly that some people may exhibit fairly high degrees of masculinity and femininity. Such individuals have been labelled 'androgynous'.

Bem (1974) developed a questionnaire called the Bem Sex Role Inventory (BSRI) to measure these characteristics in people. The typical form of the BSRI consists of 60 adjectives, 20 descriptive of masculine traits, 20 descriptive of feminine traits, and 20 neutral items. The selection and allocation of these adjectives to masculine and feminine categories had been determined by the endorsements given to them by independent samples of judges. The BSRI asks a person to indicate, normally on a seven-point scale, how well each adjective is a description of his or her own subjectively perceived character. On the basis of these responses, each person then receives a masculinity score, a femininity score, and an androgyny score. For the purposes of the current research, a shortened form of the BSRI was used which consisted of 10 masculinity, 10 femininity, and 10 neutral items randomly selected from the original instrument. These items are shown in Table 5.2. From their response to these items masculinity, femininity and androgyny scores were computed for each panel member and were related to his/her perceptions of violent portrayals.

Table 5.2

Sex Role Inventory

Masculinity	Femininity	Neutral
Aggressive	Affectionate	Reliable
Independent	Shy	Sensitive
Forceful	Tender	Truthful
Assertive	Gentle	Happy
Ambitious	Eager to sooth	Helpful
Able to make	hurt feelings	Tactful
decisions	Gullible	Adaptable
easily	Sympathetic	Sincere
Athletic	Understanding	Friendly
Willing to	Sensitive to the	Moody
take risks	needs of others	
Competitive	Fond of children	
Self-sufficient		

Derived from Bem (1974)

Social beliefs

Four scales were used to measure social beliefs, or individuals' percept-ions of their social environment. These scales were:

1   Fear of victimisation
2   Anomia
3   Locus of control
4   Belief in a just world

The items that made up each scale are shown in Table 5.3.

Fear of victimisation. This consisted of a seven-item scale which was designed to assess individuals' perceptions of how much danger there is in the world and their fear of personal risk from violent or criminal attack. These items were taken from scales used previously in research on the impact of TV (Gerbner *et al*, 1977, 1978 in the USA and Doob and Macdonald, 1979 in Canada).

Anomia. This was measured on a five-item scale whose items had once again been used by American researchers interested in the cumulative long-term influences of TV on public conceptions of social reality (Gerbner *et al*, 1977, 1978, 1979). However, the history of this scale goes back to Srole (1957) who developed it to provide a measure of general cynicism and hopelessness that was considered as a reaction to the social environment as a whole rather than to any one specific aspect of it such as TV.

Locus of control. The measure here was a five-item sub-scale derived from the original instrument developed by Rotter (1965). This scale was designed to indicate individuals' expectancies concerning degree of personal influence over events in their lives. Rotter believed that people, on the basis of their experiences of success or failure in attain-ing personal goals and ambitions, could be reliably differentiated into those who were confident that they controlled their own destinies versus those who felt that their lives were controlled by external forces such as luck, fate or chance. To find out whether 'internal controllers' differed from 'external controllers' in their judgements about TV violence, respondents' scores on Rotter items were related to their perceptions of programme excerpts.

Belief in a just world. This was indicated via respondents' scores on a scale developed by Rubin and Peplau (1975) to measure peoples' beliefs concerning the degree of justice in the world. These authors found that it was possible to differentiate people in terms of whether they thought that the world is basically a just place in which the good

Table 5.3

Social belief scales

Fear of victimisation

The chances of one of my family or close friends being the victim of an assault during the next year are remote

I worry about having my home burgled and property damaged

More money should be spent on police patrols in my neighbourhood

I am afraid to walk alone in my own neighbourhood at night

These days it is not safe to let children play alone in local parks

More people should keep firearms in their homes to protect themselves

Women should carry a weapon such as a knife to protect themselves against sexual assault

Belief in a just world

When parents punish their children, it is almost always for a good reason

It is rare for an innocent man to be wrongly sent to jail

In almost any business or profession, people who do their job well rise to the top

Anomia

It's hardly fair to bring children into the world the way things look for the future

These days a person really doesn't know whom he can count on

Most public officials aren't interested in the problems of the everyday man

Nowadays a person has to live pretty much for today and let tomorrow take care of itself

The people in Parliament are out of touch with the rest of the country

Locus of control

People's misfortunes result from the mistakes they make

Getting a good job depends on being in the right place at the right time

People's lives are controlled by accidental happenings

I feel that I have little influence over the things that happen to me

---

are rewarded and the bad are punished. A three-item sub-scale was drawn from Rubin and Peplau's longer original version. The selected items had been used elsewhere in research on the impact of TV (Gunter and Wober, 1983). The latter work had indicated a positive correlation between amount of TV viewing time devoted to crime—detective series in which the good usually triumph over those who break the law, and the belief that the world is really a just place. It was of interest in the current research to find out whether responses on the just world belief scale would relate to perceptions of different kinds of portrayals from crime—detective series.

Attitude towards aggression

Personal dispositions towards aggression have been found to mediate behavioural responses to media violence, and may to some extent also underlie preferences amongst some people for violent-action programmes (see Gunter, 1983 for review). Such predispositions might also therefore relate to judgements individuals make about different kinds of TV violence. Self-endorsed propensities towards aggression were obtained on a series of items taken from the Buss—Durkee Hostility Inventory (Buss and Durkee, 1957). This instrument was designed to measure individuals' enduring propensities towards different forms of aggression — verbal and physical. The complete inventory consists of seven sub-scales, of which four were used in the current research.

1   *Assault*. This sub-scale was designed to measure individuals' self-endorsed use of physical violence against others, including fighting but excluding the destruction of property.
2   *Indirect hostility*. This sub-scale measured aggression as manifested in forms such as malicious gossip, practical jokes, and temper tantrums.
3   *Irritability*. This sub-scale indicated readiness to show anger including having a quick temper and rudeness.
4   *Verbal aggression*. This sub-scale was designed to indicate personal tendencies towards behaviour such as arguing, shouting, screaming, cursing or swearing and issuing verbal threats.

The items on each of these sub-scales are shown in Table 5.4. Each sub-scale was treated as a separate measure of aggressive predispositions and each was related to panel members' perceptions of programme excerpts.

Table 5.4

Buss—Durkee hostility inventory

Assault

Once in a while I cannot control my urge to harm others

I can think of no good reason for ever hitting anyone

If somebody hits me first, I let them have it

Whoever insults me or my family is asking for a fight

People who continually pester me are likely to get a punch on the nose

I seldom strike back even if someone hits me first

If I have to resort to physical violence to defend my rights, I will

There have often been times when people pushed me so far that we came to blows

Irritability

I lose my temper easily but get over it quickly

I am always patient with others

I get irritated a great deal more than people are aware of

It makes my blood boil to have somebody make fun of me

If someone doesn't treat me right, I don't let it annoy me

Indirect hostility

I sometimes spread gossip about people I don't like

I never get angry enough to throw things

When I am angry, I sometimes slam doors

I never play practical jokes

When I am angry, I often sulk

I often get annoyed when I don't get my own way

I can remember being so angry that I picked up the nearest thing and broke it

I often show my anger by banging my fist on the table

Verbal aggression

When I disapprove of my friends' behaviour, I let them know it

I often find myself disagreeing with people

I can't help getting into arguments when people disagree with me

Even when my anger is aroused I don't use strong language

If someone annoys me, I am apt to tell them what I think of of them

continued

85

Table 5.4
(continued)

Irritability (continued)	*Verbal aggression* (continued)
People often bother me just by being around	When I get angry, I often say nasty things
I often feel like a powder keg ready to explode	When people yell at me, I often yell back
I am often rude to people I don't like	I could not put someone in his/her place even if they needed it
I never let a lot of unimportant things irritate me	I often make threats I don't really mean to carry out
	I generally cover up my poor opinion of others
	I would rather concede a point than get into an argument about it

Personality

Social psychologists have found that individuals differ in their preferences for different social situations and that such preferences may exhibit consistent patterns of relationships with certain enduring personality characteristics (Argyle, Furnham and Graham, 1981; Furnham, 1982). Reactions to particular situations may vary too according to personality. Research into responses to stressful situations, for example, has revealed that the degree of anxiety shown by a person under stress can vary considerably from one individual to the next. One significant distinction made by early writers was between trait anxiety and state anxiety (Cattell and Scheier, 1958). State anxiety was defined as a transitory condition of the individual that changes over time and from one set of circumstances to another. Trait anxiety, on the other hand, represents a relatively permanent personality characteristic of the individual (Spielberger, 1966). Several researchers have reported that under stressful conditions high and low trait anxiety people behave quite differently (Rappaport and Katkin, 1972; Spielberger and Smith, 1966). If different kinds of violent episodes on TV are regarded as potentially stressful or disturbing situations into which the individual enters, albeit vicariously, it is not unreasonable to assume that different personality types will exhibit different reactions to these episodes.

In their book *Sex, Violence and the Media* (Eysenck and Nias, 1978) the authors suggested that the original three-dimensional model of personality developed by Eysenck (Eysenck and Eysenck, 1969) could be useful in this context. Later work by Furnham (1982) indicated that Eysenck's personality dimensions differentiated between individuals and their *preferences* for different (stressful and non-stressful) situations. The question here was: Would these dimensions reliably discriminate between individuals *responses* to potentially stressful situations vicariously experienced via the TV screen? To answer this, each member of Panel One filled out the Eysenck Personality Questionnaire (Eysenck and Eysenck, 1975), a 90-item yes/no questionnaire which provided scores for each person on neuroticism, extraversion, and psychoticism (see Table 5.5).

Table 5.5

Eysenck personality questionnaire

1	Do you have many different hobbies?	YES	NO
2	Do you stop to think things over before doing anything?	YES	NO
3	Does your mood often go up and down?	YES	NO
4	Have you ever taken the praise for something you knew someone else had really done?	YES	NO
5	Are you a talkative person?	YES	NO
6	Would being in debt worry you?	YES	NO
7	Do you ever feel 'just miserable' for no reason?	YES	NO
8	Were you ever greedy by helping yourself to more than your share of anything?	YES	NO
9	Do you lock up your house carefully at night?	YES	NO
10	Are you rather lively?	YES	NO
11	Would it upset you a lot to see a child or animal suffer?	YES	NO
12	Do you often worry about things you should not have done or said?	YES	NO
13	If you say you will do something, do you always keep your promise no matter how inconvenient it might be?	YES	NO
14	Can you usually let yourself go and enjoy yourself at a lively party?	YES	NO
15	Are you an irritable person?	YES	NO
16	Have you ever blamed someone for doing something you knew was really your fault?	YES	NO
17	Do you enjoy meeting new people?	YES	NO
18	Do you believe insurance schemes are a good idea?	YES	NO
19	Are your feelings easily hurt?	YES	NO
20	Are *all* your habits good and desirable ones?	YES	NO
21	Do you tend to keep in the background on social occasions?	YES	NO
22	Would you take drugs which may have strange or dangerous effects?	YES	NO
23	Do you often feel 'fed-up'?	YES	NO
24	Have you ever taken anything (even a pin or button) that belonged to someone else?	YES	NO
25	Do you like going out a lot?	YES	NO
26	Do you enjoy hurting people you love?	YES	NO
27	Are you often troubled about feelings of guilt?	YES	NO

28	Do you sometimes talk about things you know nothing about?	YES	NO
29	Do you prefer reading to meeting people?	YES	NO
30	Do you have enemies who want to harm you?	YES	NO
31	Would you call yourself a nervous person?	YES	NO
32	Do you have many friends?	YES	NO
33	Do you enjoy practical jokes that can sometimes really hurt people?	YES	NO
34	Are you a worrier?	YES	NO
35	As a child did you do as you were told immediately and without grumbling?	YES	NO
36	Would you call yourself happy-go-lucky?	YES	NO
37	Do good manners and cleanliness matter much to you?	YES	NO
38	Do you worry about awful things that might happen?	YES	NO
39	Have you ever broken or lost something belonging to someone else?	YES	NO
40	Do you usually take the initiative in making new friends?	YES	NO
41	Would you call yourself tense or 'highly-strung'?	YES	NO
42	Are you mostly quiet when you are with other people?	YES	NO
43	Do you think marriage is old-fashioned and should be done away with?	YES	NO
44	Do you sometimes boast a little?	YES	NO
45	Can you easily get some life into a rather dull party?	YES	NO
46	Do people who drive carefully annoy you?	YES	NO
47	Do you worry about your health?	YES	NO
48	Have you ever said anything bad or nasty about anyone?	YES	NO
49	Do you like telling jokes and funny stories to your friends?	YES	NO
50	Do most things taste the same to you?	YES	NO
51	As a child were you ever cheeky to your parents?	YES	NO
52	Do you like mixing with people?	YES	NO
53	Does it worry you if you know there are mistakes in your work?	YES	NO
54	Do you suffer from sleeplessness?	YES	NO
55	Do you always wash before a meal?	YES	NO
56	Do you nearly always have a 'ready answer'		

	when people talk to you?	YES	NO
57	Do you like to arrive at appointments in plenty of time?	YES	NO
58	Have you often felt listless and tired for no reason?	YES	NO
59	Have you ever cheated at a game?	YES	NO
60	Do you like doing things in which you have to act quickly?	YES	NO
61	Is (or was) your mother a good woman?	YES	NO
62	Do you often feel life is very dull?	YES	NO
63	Have you ever taken advantage of someone?	YES	NO
64	Do you often take on more activities than you have time for?	YES	NO
65	Are there several people who keep trying to avoid you?	YES	NO
66	Do you worry a lot about your looks?	YES	NO
67	Do you think people spend too much time safeguarding their future with savings and insurances?	YES	NO
68	Have you ever wished you were dead?	YES	NO
69	Would you dodge paying taxes if you were sure you could never be found out?	YES	NO
70	Can you get a party going?	YES	NO
71	Do you try not to be rude to people?	YES	NO
72	Do you worry too long after an embarrassing experience?	YES	NO
73	Have you ever insisted on having your own way?	YES	NO
74	When you catch a train do you often arrive at the last minute?	YES	NO
75	Do you suffer from nerves?	YES	NO
76	Do your friendships break up easily without it being your fault?	YES	NO
77	Do you often feel lonely?	YES	NO
78	Do you always practise what you preach?	YES	NO
79	Do you sometimes like teasing animals?	YES	NO
80	Are you easily hurt when people find fault with you or the work you do?	YES	NO
81	Have you ever been late for an appointment or work?	YES	NO
82	Do you like plenty of bustle and excitement around you?	YES	NO
83	Would you like other people to be afraid of you?	YES	NO
84	Are you sometimes bubbling over with energy and sometimes very sluggish?	YES	NO

85	Do you sometimes put off until tomorrow what you ought to do today?	YES	NO
86	Do other people think of you as being very lively?	YES	NO
87	Do people tell you a lot of lies?	YES	NO
88	Are you touchy about some things?	YES	NO
89	Are you always willing to admit it when you have made a mistake?	YES	NO
90	Would you feel very sorry for an animal caught in a trap?	YES	NO

6 Programme genre and the perception of television violence

Perhaps the most salient discriminating feature of televised violence for most viewers is the type of 'genre' of programming in which a portrayal occurs. There are of course many ways in which one genre of programming can be distinguished from another, but perhaps the most important characteristic is the degree of realism of a particular portrayal or of the setting in which it occurs. Empirical studies of a variety of behavioural and emotional reactions of viewers to TV and film material have indicated with some consistency that realistic content is likely to have more profound and lasting effects on viewers than content that is clearly fictional (Berkowitz and Alioto, 1973; Feshbach, 1972; Noble, 1975; Reeves, 1978).

Thus, researchers have found that young viewers shown film footage depicting violence labelled as real-life action, exhibited significantly more aggressive behaviour subsequent to exposure than did matched youngsters for whom the footage was labelled as fiction (Feshbach, 1972). In the United Kingdom, corroborative evidence for the importance of reality—fantasy differentiation of another kind emerged from work by Greenberg (1974) who found that perceived veracity of TV programmes among teenage schoolchildren was significantly related to their holding aggressive attitudes and to tendencies to watch violent shows regularly. In particular, those who watched a great deal of violent programming and believed that it was realistic were also more likely to believe that violence was the most effective way to resolve interpersonal conflicts.

Unfortunately, in many studies directed primarily at an analysis of the behavioural or emotional impact of TV content, researchers conceptions and operationalisations of the reality of TV have been oversimplified. Thus, portrayals have been labelled as realistic or fictional in a very general sense. Research on the perceptual responses of viewers to TV programmes has indicated, however, that viewers' judgements can be influenced by a complexity of sometimes quite subtle variations in the characteristics of programme content.

In the broadest terms, it has been found that when considering the nature of programme genres such as crime—detective shows, viewers, young and old, discount the 'realism' of TV dramatisations or characterisations of the police and the work they are seen to do because these portrayals are recognised purely and simply as fictional entities. On this basis alone, the events depicted in such dramatic genres are not accepted as holding any direct correspondence with the way things are in real life (Dominick, 1974). However, distinctions between reality and fantasy may become less clear-cut at different levels of content abstraction.

Greenberg and Reeves (1976) have found that as the frame of reference in terms of which TV content was judged narrowed, so the confusion between fictional portrayals and reality became more acute. When youngsters were asked whether or not the events shown on TV action—drama series were like events that happened in real life, most denied the similarity. But when questions focused first on specific series and then on particular characters or families in these series, the reality—fantasy distinctions became blurred. Anecdotal evidence has been cited by some writers to suggest further that adults as well as children can be taken in by some fictional characterisations and settings on TV. A good example of this phenomenon was reported by Gross and Jeffries-Fox (1978) who noted that during the first five years of his appearance in the series *Marcus Welby M.D.* actor Robert Young received over a quarter of a million letters from viewers, mostly seeking medical advice. One explanation for this may be that even quite sophisticated viewers have considerable gaps in their knowledge, particularly of specialist fields with which they rarely if ever come into direct contact in real life.

In summary then, it appears that most viewers can and do make broad distinctions between the nature of TV portrayals on the basis of the programme contexts or settings in which they occur. At a fairly generalised level distinctions between fictional settings and real life are usually quite clear-cut and unambiguous, and are learned by viewers by middle childhood. Typically, portrayals that are perceived to be fictional have a less profound impact on viewers than do realistic portrayals. In contrast, as the level of perceptual analysis or interpretation or programme content becomes more specific, even so far as focusing on particular characters or events in programmes, many more viewers appear to find the reality—fantasy distinction less easy to make. In this chapter two studies are reported which examined viewers' perceptions of violent portrayals from five different categories of programming whose settings varied in their degree of proximity to everyday reality.

Experiment One

The aim of this experiment was to determine to what extent violent portrayals in programmes whose fictional settings vary according to their closeness to contemporary reality are differentially judged by viewers? In order to examine this issue empirically, the first study analysed viewers' perceptions of televised violence taken from five categories of fictional programming. By controlling as far as possible the physical features of the violent actions themselves, this study aimed to demonstrate the significance of fictional setting, and of its proximity to real life, for viewers' judgements about violent portrayals.

Method

Design and materials. This experiment consisted of four sessions of about 40 minutes' duration run on two separate days two weeks apart. Over these sessions 45 programme excerpts were viewed and rated by the members of Panel One. The programme materials had been edited from five genres or TV programming:

1   British-produced crime—drama series (e.g. *The Professionals, The Sweeney, Wolcott*);
2   American-produced crime—drama series (e.g. *Kojak, Mannix, Starsky and Hutch*);
3   a Western film (*Cannon for Cordoba*);
4   science-fiction series (e.g. *Buck Rogers, Star Trek*);
5   cartoon shows (e.g. *Mighty Mouse*).

All excerpts were taken from programmes broadcast on the (then) three major TV networks in the United Kingdom (BBC1, BBC2, and ITV) between three and six months before the experiment.

Excerpts were 30—70 seconds long and each was selected in accordance with Gerbner's (1972) normative definition of violence. There were nine scenes representing each programme genre, of which five featured gunfights and shootings and four depicted fist-fights. Each scene was rated along eight, seven-point unipolar scales: violent, realistic, exciting, humorous, likely to disturb people in general, suitable for children, frightening, and personally disturbing.

The materials were played on a Sony VHS video-cassette recorder and relayed in monochrome over three TV monitors placed about two metres apart at the front of a small lecture theatre. The order of presentation of the scenes was randomised to avoid extensive clustering of scenes from the same programme type or which consisted of the same physical form of violence (i.e. shootings or fist-fights).

Subjects and procedure. The excerpts were rated by Panel One, run as a single group in a small lecture theatre and seated so that each individual could clearly view one of the three TV monitors. The volume and picture clarity of each monitor were adjusted at the beginning of each session so that all panel members could comfortably hear any dialogue and clearly see what was happening in the scenes. At the beginning of the first session on each test day, panel members were told that they would be shown a number of short clips from several different types of TV programmes that had been broadcast on British TV during the previous year. They would judge each excerpt along eight scales. They were asked not to dwell too long when making these judgements but to be as honest as possible when doing so. The scenes were played one at a time and after each one the video-tape was stopped and about two minutes allowed for the completion of ratings. Each session was run in two parts with a five-minute break taken when half the scenes had been completed. Pilot work had shown that a break served to refresh the panel's enthusiasm for the rating task. Between ten and twelve scenes were presented per session so that the panel were never required to rate more than six scenes in succession without a break.

Results

Table 6.1 shows the mean ratings for violent portrayals from each programme genre. A series of Wilcoxon matched-pairs, signed-ranks tests were computed on these data to reveal a number of significant differences between viewers' responses to violence depicted in different fictional settings. In general, shootings and physical fighting occurring in contemporary settings such as those found in British and American crime—drama series were perceived in somewhat more serious terms than similar forms of violence occurring in Western settings, and in substantially more serious terms than similar incidents depicted in futuristic science-fiction or in animated cartoon settings. Put more explicitly, violence in contemporary crime—drama settings was rated as more violent, more realistic, more frightening, more personally disturbing, more likely to disturb people in general, and as less humor-

Table 6.1

Mean ratings for televised violent portrayals within five programme genres

Programme genres			Rating scales					
	Violent	Realistic	Exciting	Humorous	Frightening	Personally disturbing	Likely to disturb people in general	Suitable for children
All scenes								
British crime	5.3^a	2.7^a	4.1^a	1.6^a	3.0^a	2.3^a	3.1^a	2.4^a
American crime	5.0^a	3.3	3.7^{ab}	1.8^a	2.9^a	2.2^a	3.0^a	2.8^a
Westerns	4.5	2.5^a	3.5^{bc}	2.0^{ab}	2.3	1.7	2.7	3.0^a
Science-fiction	3.4	1.3^b	3.2^c	2.4^b	1.7^b	1.4^b	1.7^b	3.9
Cartoons	2.5	1.1^b	3.7^{ab}	4.8	1.3^b	1.1^b	1.3^b	5.3
Shootings scenes only								
British crime	5.0^a	2.8^a	3.9^a	2.0^a	3.1^a	2.3^a	3.1^a	2.4^a
American crime	4.9^a	3.2^{ab}	3.6^{ab}	2.2^{ab}	2.8^a	2.2^a	3.1^a	2.8^a
Westerns	5.0^a	2.4^b	3.4^{ab}	2.2^{ab}	2.1^b	1.5^b	3.0^{ab}	2.8^a
Science-fiction	3.5	1.3^c	3.2^b	2.6^b	1.7^{bc}	1.4^b	1.6^{bc}	3.9
Cartoons	2.5	1.1^c	3.9^a	4.8	1.3^c	1.0^b	1.3^c	5.3
Fist-fight scenes only								
British crime	5.6^a	2.8^a	4.2^a	1.2^a	3.0^a	2.2^a	3.1^a	2.4^a
American crime	5.1^{ab}	3.4	3.9^{ab}	1.4^a	3.0^a	2.2^a	2.9^{ab}	2.8^{ab}
Westerns	4.0^{bc}	2.6^a	3.6^{bc}	1.7^{ab}	2.6^a	1.9^{ab}	2.5^{ab}	3.2^b
Science-fiction	3.4^c	1.4^b	3.3^c	2.2^b	1.7^b	1.4^{bc}	1.7^c	4.0
Cartoons	2.5	1.1^b	3.5^{bc}	4.7	1.2^b	1.0^c	1.3^c	5.3

Note: Means with common superscripts are not significantly different at the $p < .05$ level.
    Scale range: Max = 7 Min = 1

ous and less suitable for children than violence in settings more distanced from everyday life.

In a further breakdown of the data, comparisons between programme settings were made separately for scenes featuring shootings and for those depicting fights not involving weapons. Mean scores per scale for each genre following this separation of physical forms of violence are also shown in Table 6.1.

Further Wilcoxon matched-pairs, signed-ranks tests indicated largely similar patterns of significant differences between genres for each type of violent form, although there was a tendency among scenes featuring shootings and gunfights for Western portrayals to receive ratings on many scales which matched those for portrayals in contemporary crime—drama contexts for perceived seriousness of the violence. With regard to the two genres in which violent portrayals generally received least serious ratings, the most powerful discriminations were made on three scales. Science-fiction scenes were perceived as more violent, less humorous and less suitable for children than were cartoon scenes. Violence in neither of these contexts was rated as very frightening or disturbing however.

Experiment Two

Experiment One indicated that violent portrayals from different categories of programming are judged in quite distinct ways by viewers even though other attributes of their content may be very similar. However, these differences emerged from *post hoc* comparisons of viewers' perceptions of different groups of scenes where each scene had been rated independently, and were not the result of one type of scene being directly compared to another in a single judgement by viewers. When viewers are given the opportunity to say directly in what ways and by how much two TV portrayals are alike or different, to what extent do the same attributes emerge as important distinguishing features as appeared following analyses of viewers' perceptual ratings of scenes viewed one at a time?

In order to investigate this question several of the attributes examined in single-scene ratings studies were also examined within the framework of a paired-comparisons design in which viewers were presented with two scenes in sequence and distinguished between them along each of a series of evaluative scales. It was reasoned that if the same attributes emerged as salient distinguishing features of violent TV portrayals within both procedures, together the two sets of findings should provide strong evidence that such features represented important defining characteristics of televised violence for viewers. To begin with then, Experiment Two examined viewers' differential perceptions of violent portrayals from different programme genres using direct comparisons of pairs of scenes presented sequentially one immediately after the other.

Method

This study consisted of exhaustive paired comparisons between six programme excerpts of 40—70 seconds duration and taken from three programme genres: American crime—drama (*Mannix*, *Starsky and Hutch*), Westerns (*Alias Smith and Jones*, *Cannon for Cordoba*) and science-fiction series (*Buck Rogers*, *Star Trek*). Brief synopses of these scenes are presented in Table 6.3. The physical form of violence and the degree of observable harm caused to victims were held constant as far as possible across scenes. In each case, the violence depicted a shooting between a 'good' character and a 'bad' character in which the former shoots that latter in self-defence. (All 'good' guys were popular and clearly recognisable figures known to most viewers.)

The six scenes were edited together in pairs. Exhaustive pairing meant that each scene was paired with and judged against each of the other five. Hence, a fifteen-pair sequence was generated from the six scenes used in this study. As each scene had to be viewed and rated by the panel five times, a number of measures were taken to avoid rapid repetition of the same scene within too short a space of time, for example, the pairs of test scenes were interspersed with ten other dummy pairs. Then ratings were obtained over two sessions of an hour and one-and-a-half hours' duration respectively which took place on two separate days. Each session was divided into half-hour segments, following each of which a ten-minute break was taken. Five pairs only were presented per half-hour segment, of which three pairs consisted of test items and two of dummy items. These pairs were sequenced so that each test pair was separated by a dummy pair.

Each pair of excerpts was judged along eight scales as in Experiment One: violent, realistic, exciting, humorous, frightening, personally disturbing, likely to disturb people in general, and suitable for children. However, instead of saying how violent, realistic, frightening, etc. each particular clip was along a unipolar continuum, viewers were required to make a dissimilarity judgement in which they said how different two scenes were along each scale. Thus, along the violent scale, for example, viewers had to decide which one of the two scenes in each pair was the more violent, and by how much. The latter judgement was made along a four-point continuum, 'slightly more ...', 'somewhat more ...', 'moderately more ...', and 'a great deal more ...'. The scene judged as the less violent was scored zero points, while the scene perceived as the more violent received from one to four points depending on the degree of perceived dissimilarity between them.

Ratings were made by a different group of viewers than those who took part in Experiment One. In this and all subsequent paired-comparisons studies, perceptual judgements were made by Panel Two which consisted of 34 people (17 men and 17 women) from diverse social and occupational backgrounds. Although not a representative sample, the demographic heterogeneity of this panel matched that of Panel One, and within the two different frameworks of TV violence assessment used in this series of studies together provided useful indications of viewers' perceptual reactions to different kinds of fictional violence.

Table 6.2

Synopses of TV scenes used in Experiment Two

	Programme	Scene
1	*Starsky and Hutch*	Starsky chases after two hooded villains trying to escape after holding up a store. One villain turns and aims his gun at Starsky, but the latter fires first and shoots the villain.
2	*Starsky and Hutch*	Starsky is fired upon by a man with a rifle and returns fire, wounding the man in the leg.
3	*Cannon for Cordoba*	A US Marshall is forced into gun-play in a house by a Mexican bandit. The Marshall outdraws and shoots the bandit.
4	*Cannon for Cordoba*	In a street gunfight, a US Marshall shoots several villains who refuse to be arrested by him.
5	*Buck Rogers*	Buck Rogers is challenged by a villainous character in a futuristic night-club, and in the ensuing laser gunfight the villain is stunned by Rogers' laser gun.
6	*Buck Rogers*	Buck Rogers returns fire and stuns a villainous character when the latter attacks him with an electric ray.

Results

Over the five appearances of a scene in a fifteen-pair compilation, it could receive from zero to 20 points per viewer. The raw score for each scene on each scale was converted to a proportion of the total score possible (i.e. a score of 16 points equals 16/20 or .80), indicating the salience of that quality as a characteristic of one scene relative to others against which it was compared. The results reinforced those of Experiment One for the three genres of fictional programming which the two studies had in common. The mean ratings for each scene are summarised in Figure 6.1.

Portrayals from American crime—drama series were rated as the most violent, most realistic and most disturbing, and as the least suitable for children and least humorous. Conversely, science-fiction portrayals were judged to be the least violent, realistic, and disturbing, and as somewhat more humorous and suitable for children. Western portrayals fell in between the latter two genres on all scales, but were generally closer in their ratings to those of American crime—drama materials.

Discussion

The first two experiments indicated that panel members made clear-cut distinctions between violent TV portrayals on the basis of their fictional settings. Previous research had indicated that violence occurring in certain types of programmes could have stronger effects on viewers' emotional responses (Lagerspetz *et al*, 1978) or behavioural responses subsequently (Belson, 1978; Noble, 1975). Belson (1978) reported, for example, that regular watching of programmes presenting fictional violence but of a realistic kind such as crime—detective series, or watching Westerns was most closely related to aggressive tendencies amongst adolescent boys. Viewing of cartoon or science-fiction content, however, showed little or no relationship with violent predispositions. Of course, Belson relied on respondents' self-reports and memories of what they had seen over a period of many years, and a question-mark must lie over the reliability of this information. Nevertheless, at a perceptual level of response measured in the current research, and under conditions in which all test individuals based their responses on the same content, a similar pattern of classification of TV violence by fictional setting emerged.

As the proximity of the fictional setting of violence approached more closely to contemporary everyday reality, portrayals were perceived to be more violent and more disturbing. This pattern of perceptual response was observed for two different forms of physical violence and in the presence of controls for other potentially import-

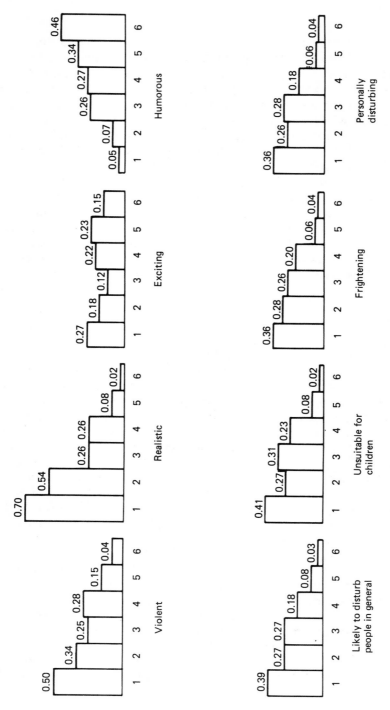

Figure 6.1   Mean paired comparison ratings for violent excerpts from five programme genres

102

ant variations in content (e.g. types of characters involved, degree of observable harm caused by violence). The validity of these findings is reinforced further by the fact that the same patterns of perceived seriousness emerged from two different sets of individuals and under two different methods of rating programme excerpts.

7 Character type and the perception of television violence

One of the fundamental ingredients of TV violence measurement within the content-analytic perspective is the extent of involvement in violence among different types of characters. Two of the five components of the Violence Index measure of the Cultural Indicators team at the University of Pennsylvania for American prime-time TV drama consist of the extent of character involvement in violent episodes either as aggressors or victims, killers or killed. According to Gerbner (1972), the distribution of characters in TV drama programmes and the extent to which different types of characters become involved in violence and the nature of their involvement (i.e. as aggressors or victims) carry important meanings concerning chances and risks in real life for different kinds of people:

> Who commits and who suffers violence of what kind is a
> central and revealing fact of life in the world of television
> drama that viewers must grasp before they can follow,
> let alone interpret, the play ... who gets (and gives) what,
> how, and why delineates the social structure of the world
> of television drama. The distribution of roles related to
> violence, with their different risks and fates, performs the
> symbolic functions of violence, and conveys its basic
> message about people (Gerbner, 1972, pp.44–45).

Content analysis of the involvement of characters in violence on TV has indicated that more leading characters than not perpetrate or become involved in some form of aggression. On American network TV, Gerbner *et al*, (1978, 1979) reported that over 60 per cent of major prime-time TV characters were involved in some type of violence. There were more victims than aggressors, signifying that a character's involvement in violence was more likely to result in that character being injured than escaping unharmed, although the extent to which this was the case varied from one character type to another.

But in counting up the prevalence of violent incidents as a measure of televised violence, using character involvement as a fundamental unit of measurement, content analysis treats each character's use of violence as equivalent. How valid or meaningful is this type of analysis?

Content-analytic studies have reported varying degrees of involvement in violence on TV drama programmes for characters of different types. But whilst character involvement in violence has featured as a major component in measures of the prevalence of violence on fictional TV, to what extent do viewers make differential judgements about televised violence on the basis of the types of characters who are involved? There are two particularly pertinent and fundamental aspects to this question which need to be considered at this point: how violent are TV characters generally perceived to be by viewers; and how credible are their actions?

Are TV characters seen as violent by nature?

To what extent is violence perceived as a salient or typical attribute of different TV characters? Content analysis has shown that a large proportion of major TV characters get involved in violence at some time during a TV series. Some authors have contended that the violent roles they play and the outcomes of involvement in violence for different types of characters represent a symbolic demonstration of the sources of power and vulnerability in the TV world. Through a process of generalisation, this symbolism can in turn influence public perceptions of the real world as well as of the TV world (Gerbner *et al*, 1977, 1978, 1979; Tuchman, 1978). The differential prevalence of involvement in violence of different characters might condition viewers to expect to see certain character types get involved in violent incidents more often than others, and also to be more accepting of violence. However, although violence may be *prevalent* amongst major TV characters, analyses of audience perceptions have not indicated aggressiveness to be a *salient* defining attribute of characters for viewers.

Reeves and Greenberg (1977) asked groups of eight- to twelve-year-old children to say to what extent and in what ways fourteen prime-time and weekend daytime characters from TV drama shows differed from each other using whichever descriptive terms they liked. In order of importance, four main attributes emerged: humour, strength, attractiveness and activity. Using a different sample of children and different TV characters, Reeves and Lometti (1978) carried out a replication study. Among the new characters in the TV sample were three additional women to balance more evenly the ratio of male to female characters. Essentially the same four discriminative dimensions emerged again. The one important difference was that the second dimension from the original study – physical strength – more clearly differentiated TV characters of different sex. It was the only attribute which clearly separated male and female TV characters in the sample. The most interesting aspect of this set of findings is that violence did not emerge among the most salient discriminating features of TV characters for young viewers of different age-bands, even though they were permitted to choose their own descriptive or evaluative terms. Indeed, even when additional female TV characters were supplied in the second study, to reflect the increased presence of leading female actors in American TV series during this spell, there was no tendency to distinguish them spontaneously as less violent than male leads. However, whilst violence may not feature as a salient or recognisable attribute of TV characters (male or female), viewers' judgements of a violent episode may be affected by the types of characters involved and the nature of their involvement. For example, the victimisation of a female character may be perceived as more violent than the victim-isation of a male character, other factors such as context, setting, instrumentation and outcome held constant, perhaps because men are generally perceived to have greater physical strength than women and thus may be more able to cope with an attack. Similarly, violence perpetrated by a law-enforcer is likely to be evaluated differently than similar violence performed by a villain because of the presumed just-ification underlying the actions of each character type.

A second important point is the relative amount of credence attached to the actions of characters by viewers in different contexts offered by fictional programmes. As we saw in the previous chapter, viewers can make distinctions between violent portrayals on the basis of the proximity of their setting to everyday reality. Events shown in fantasy settings were given lower realism ratings by viewers than were events in more authentic, contemporary settings, and were also per-ceived as less violent and disturbing. Consequently, the location and setting of violent TV portrayals could mediate the salience of differ-ential character involvement for viewers when the latter are required to make judgements about violence perpetrated by different kinds of actor.

Previous evidence on the realism of TV characters or of the behaviours they perform is conflicting. The extent to which viewers confuse fact with fiction where fictional characters are concerned seems to depend to some degree on the specificity of the events or character- isations under examination. Anecdotal evidence mentioned earlier implied extensive belief among many thousands of American viewers that the leading character in a popular medical TV soap opera was in fact a practitioner of medicine in real life (Gross and Jeffries-Fox, 1978). Closer to home, when the star of the long-running soap opera *Crossroads* was shown apparently killed in a fire, fans of the serial threatened and vandalised the house of the actor who played the part of the character responsible for starting the fire, apparently believing that the characters were real people and that the fire was a genuine incident at a real motel.

Objective empirical research has shown that such bizarre responses among viewers are probably the result of a rare degree of confusion of the fictional world of TV drama with the real world, and that more usually people make clear-cut distinctions between fictional characters and personalities in reality. Studies with adolescent boys have shown that the events and characters portrayed in popular crime—detective series, for example, are seldom confused with real life. Even boys who have had little direct contact with the police in actuality, usually dismiss TV police as idealised characterisations who do not resemble their professional counterparts in the real world (Dominick, 1974; Rarick, Townsend and Boyd, 1973).

In this chapter, four experiments are reported which looked, with- in two different experimental designs, at the mediating effects on viewers' perceptions of televised violence of two different categories of character-types' involvement in violent portrayals. The first two studies employed single-scene ratings and paired-comparisons designs respectively to examine viewers' perceptions of violence perpetrated by law-enforcers versus that perpetrated by criminals in TV drama. The third and fourth studies used the same designs in turn to compare viewers' judgements of violence perpetrated either by male characters or by female characters. All studies also included assessments of the relative significance of different character perpetrators of violence in different fictional settings.

Violence perpetrated by law-enforcers and by criminals

The most frequently recurring theme of TV's action—drama pro- grammes is perhaps the violent conflict between criminal elements and the forces of law, order and justice. Typically, any conflicts of this sort are fully resolved by the end of a particular programme or series with the triumph of those on the side of law and order and the bringing to justice of perpetrators of criminal or anti-social acts.

Content analysis of programming designed to explore the goals of TV characters and the methods usually employed by them to attain desired ends has indicated that non-legal methods tend to be used as often as legal methods in action—drama shows (Larsen, Gray and Fortis, 1963). Larsen and his colleagues concluded that there was a strong tendency for TV to portray characters aiming to achieve socially approved goals via methods which would not normally be regarded as acceptable in real life. In particular, this observation drew attention to the frequent and rapid deployment of violent measures, often to an extreme degree, by agencies of law enforcement when dealing with criminal behaviour.

The Cultural Indicators team at the University of Pennsylvania has provided data which lend further support to this observation. They have shown that whilst in terms of actual distribution of portrayals in TV drama programmes, more criminal characters become involved in violence than non-criminal types, nevertheless, law-enforcers still appear to use violence a great deal as well, and when doing so, the latter were usually depicted as successful aggressors whose violent behaviour was an effective means of dealing with the activities of criminal elements. Symbolically then, aggression as performed by a law-enforcer is possibly to be seen as more attractive than that displayed by a villain because the former character-type enjoys more success in its use than does the latter. But this interpretation of the symbolic message transmitted by TV drama portrayals is based on untested assumptions about audience perceptions of content. Do viewers perceive violence perpetrated by a law-enforcer on TV drama in the same way as violence perpetrated by a law-breaker?

Whilst in Gerbner-style content analysis a violent act receives the same weighting of intensity regardless of by whom it is perpetrated, this is not true of public definitions of violence, which typically reflect the perceived legitimacy of the act (Brown and Tedeschi, 1976; Kane et al, 1976). People have been found to exhibit remarkable tolerance of legitimised violence, but not for unjustified coercive actions. A number of researchers have reported, for example, that large sections of the public endorse the use of violent methods by the police in the line of duty (Blumenthal et al, 1972; Gamson and McEvoy, 1972; Lincoln and Levinger, 1972). If individuals make these distinctions between violent incidents occurring in real life, it is not unreasonable to assume that perceived legitimacy will mediate judgements about violent portrayals in TV drama. Hence, it may be more ecologically valid to assign different weights to violent incidents on TV that are performed for legitimate and illegitimate purposes. To test this assumption empirically, a study was run in which a panel of viewers rated excerpts from British and American crime—drama series which depicted violence perpetrated either by law-enforcers or by law-breakers.

Experiment Three

Method

The 40 members of Panel One were shown and rated twelve excerpts: six from British crime—drama series (e.g. *The Professionals*, *The Sweeney*, *Target*) and six from American crime—drama series (e.g. *Kojak*, *Mannix*, *Starsky and Hutch*). All excerpts were between 50 and 70 seconds long and depicted violent conflict between law-enforcers and criminal elements. All incidents involved shootings in which the victim was either seriously injured or killed. Half the scenes (three per programme category) depicted violence perpetrated by a law-enforcer, and the rest depicted violence performed by criminals equally drawn from both types of programming.

Each scene was judged along eight, seven-point, unipolar scales: violent, realistic, frightening, personally disturbing, likely to disturb people in general, suitable for children, exciting and humorous. These scales were designed to elicit a variety of judgements about televised violence from viewers which are relevant to programme monitoring.

This study consisted of a single session which took place in a small lecture theatre and lasted for about one hour. Although aware that this study was designed to investigate perceptions of televised violence, the panel was given no indication about the particular aspects of violent portrayals of interest to the experimenter. As a further disguise of the comparisons being made, six dummy scenes were also presented which did not feature violence between law-enforcers and law-breakers. The programme excerpts were played one at a time in a randomised sequence over three monochrome TV monitors situated about two metres apart at the front of the theatre. Following each excerpt, the video-tape was stopped and viewers were given about two minutes to complete their ratings of it. Half-way through the session, a ten-minute break was taken to alleviate any build-up of fatigue or loss of interest in the task.

Results

Tables 7.1 and 7.2 show the mean ratings respectively for violent portrayals according to the character-type who perpetrated the violence (averaged over British and American TV materials) and accord-

Table 7.1

Mean ratings for televised violence perpetrated by law-enforcers or criminals

	Violent*	Realistic	Exciting	Humorous*	Likely to disturb people in general*	Suitable for children*	Frightening*	Personally disturbing*
Law-enforcer violence	5.6	2.9	3.9	1.7	3.1	2.5	3.0	2.3
Criminal violence	5.6	3.3	3.6	1.6	3.2	2.5	3.1	2.4

Note: *Mean ratings not significantly different at $P < .05$ level

Table 7.2

Geographical setting and mean ratings of violent portrayals

	Violent	Realistic	Exciting	Humorous	Likely to disturb people in general*	Suitable for children	Frightening*	Personally disturbing*
Scenes from British series	5.9	2.7	4.0	1.4	3.2	2.3	3.0	2.2
Scenes from American series	5.4	3.4	3.6	1.9	3.2	2.7	3.1	2.4

Note: *Mean ratings not significantly different at $P < .05$ level

ing to geographical setting of the violence (averaged over character-types). Average ratings of between five and six points out of seven indicated that these scenes were judged by the panel as generally quite seriously violent. Consistent with this was the perception of practically no humour in the scenes. However, in spite of this, these materials, which depicted violence typical of that found in peak-time TV action—drama series, were not considered as especially frightening or likely to disturb self or others. At the same time though, the panel did not recommend these scenes as suitable for children.

In relative terms, a series of Wilcoxon matched-pairs, signed-ranks tests indicated significant differences in the perceived seriousness of portrayals associated with the type of perpetrator and the geographical setting of the violence. Table 7.1 shows that there were few differences in perceptions of law-enforcer and criminal violence, averaged over British and American scenes. Criminal violence was perceived as more realistic and less exciting than law-enforcer violence, but these were the only significant differences. There were more differences associated with geographical setting, however, with scenes from British programmes rated as significantly more violent, less realistic, less suitable for children, less humorous and more exciting than those from American series.

In view of previous findings on public opinions towards legitimate and illegitimate violence (Gamson and McEvoy, 1972; Lincoln and Levinger, 1972), it seemed surprising that there should be so few differences between perceptions of law-enforcer and criminal-perpetrated violence here. However, upon examining perceptions of violence perpetrated by these two character-types *within* British and American settings, a different pattern of ratings emerged. Results summarised in Table 7.3 indicate an interesting reversal in direction of relative perceived seriousness of law-enforcer and criminal violence in British and American programmes.

In American settings, British viewers perceived violence perpetrated by criminals as significantly more serious (i.e. more violent, more realistic, more frightening, more personally disturbing, more likely to disturb others, and less humorous) than that performed by law officers. However, for scenes taken from British TV series, law-enforcer violence was rated as more serious on these scales than was criminal violence. Furthermore, law-enforcer violence in British crime programmes was perceived as significantly more violent and less humorous than criminal violence in American programmes of the same genre.

Table 7.3

Character type, geographical setting and ratings of violent portrayals

	Violent	Realistic	Exciting	Humorous	Likely to disturb people in general	Suitable for children	Frightening	Personally disturbing
Law-enforcer violence								
British series	6.3	2.6^a	4.0^a	1.1	3.4^b	2.1	3.1^{ab}	2.3^{ab}
American series	5.0	3.2	3.7^{ab}	2.3	2.9^a	2.8^a	2.8^a	2.2^a
Criminal violence								
British series	5.5	2.8^a	3.9^a	1.6^a	3.0^a	2.4^b	2.9^a	2.1^a
American series	5.5	2.7	3.5^b	1.5^a	3.4^b	2.6^{ab}	3.3^b	2.6^b

Note: Ratings with common superscripts are not significantly different at the $P < .05$ level

Experiment Four

In Experiment Three viewers' perceptions of televised violence perpetrated either by law-enforcers or law-breakers were obtained for programme excerpts rated singly, and the extent to which one type of portrayal was perceived to differ from another type was estimated from statistical comparisons of the individual values obtained by each type afterwards. Because every scene was rated along the same seven-point scales, the range over which discriminations between scenes could be made was limited. Hence, the magnitude of perceived differences between certain of these portrayals may have been influenced to some extent by the limited scale range. One way around this problem is to invite viewers to make direct comparisons between pairs of scenes. Then, each time two scenes are compared, it would be along a scale range unique to that pair. Such judgements might permit more powerful discriminations to be made between portrayals revealing important attributes in terms of which people distinguish between violent incidents which may otherwise have remained hidden with less sensitive rating paradigms.

The paired-comparisons procedure was used in Experiment Two and results there largely reflected patterns of ratings found with similar materials in Experiment One which employed single-scene ratings. When Panel One rated scenes singly in Experiment Three, results indicated that violence perpetrated by law-enforcers was perceived as less violent than that enacted by criminals in American crime—drama programmes, but that in British programmes of the same type, this pattern of ratings was reversed with police and law-enforcer violence perceived as more serious. When given the opportunity to make direct comparisons between pairs of scenes depicting violence instigated by these character-types, however, do viewers make the same kinds of perceptual distinctions? Experiment Four was designed to answer this question.

Method

In this study, Panel Two were shown a sequence of fifteen pairs of scenes generated from a basic set of six programme excerpts. These excerpts were edited so that each scene was paired with each of the others in the set. Table 7.4 contains brief descriptions of the content of each excerpt. As in all the other studies reported in this volume, selection of scenes was made in accordance with Gerbner's (1972) definition of violence.

The six excerpts were taken from three categories of programming: British crime—drama, American crime—drama, and science fiction. There were two scenes from each category, one of which featured violence perpetrated by a law-enforcer and the other of which depicted violence perpetrated by a villain.

Table 7.4

Synopses of TV scenes used in Experiment 4

	Programme	Scene
1	*The Professionals**	Two men attack agents Bodie and Doyle who forcibly subdue their attackers in a fight in a back alley.
2	*Target*	Police ambush fight and eventually arrest a gang of armed robbers as the latter unload stolen money from a van.
3	*Kojak**	Kojak fends off an attack from a villain and in a fight eventually knocks his attacker almost unconscious.
4	*Starsky and Hutch*	Starsky and Hutch intimidate and beat up two heavies who refuse to let them enter a building they wish to search.
5	*Star Trek**	Captain Kirk fights and over-comes an alien who attacks him on a distant planet.
6	*Buck Rogers in the 25th Century*	Buck Rogers fights prison guards in an attempt to escape from captivity.

* Signifies scenes in which villainous characters attacked good guys; the remaining scenes depicted aggression instigated by forces of good against criminal or evil elements.

Each pair of programme excerpts was differentiated along eight scales as described in Experiment Two. Similar precautions to those employed in that experiment were used again here to avoid successive presentation of critical test pairs. The fifteen experimental pairs were interspersed with ten dummy pairs which featured violence that did not involve law-enforcers in conflict with criminals. The study was run in a small lecture theatre in two sessions of one hour and one-and-a-half hours' duration respectively on two separate days. These sessions were divided by ten-minute breaks into half-hour segments in each of which five pairs of scenes (three test pairs plus two dummy pairs) were presented.

The rating and scoring procedures were the same as those described in Experiment Two. Over the five comparisons with the other excerpts each portrayals could attain up to 20 points. This raw score was then transformed for each excerpt into a proportion of the maximum total possible. These proportions indicated how violent, disturbing, exciting, realistic, etc. each portrayal was perceived to be compared with the others against which it was judged. The mean ratings obtained by each excerpt per scale are shown in Figure 7.1.

Results provided support for the findings of Experiment Three in that violence perpetrated by law-enforcers was perceived as more violent, more frightening, more personally disturbing and more likely to disturb people in general, and as less suitable for children than criminal violence among portrayals from British crime—drama series. On the other hand, among American portrayals this pattern of ratings was reversed. It is interesting to note also that within the science-fiction genre, violent portrayals were perceived as much less serious than those from either crime—drama genres, but that even within this fantasy realm of TV fiction, character-type comparisons indicated perceptual distinctions consistent with those for American crime scenes. In general, violence instigated by a 'good' character was rated as less serious than violence performed by a 'bad' character.

On genre differences, British crime—drama scenes were perceived as more realistic and also as more violent and more disturbing than American crime—drama scenes. On the whole, science-fiction scenes were perceived as not at all violent, frightening, disturbing or unsuitable for children. These findings confirmed the genre effects observed in Experiment Two and also illustrate the more highly discriminative judgements that are possible with the paired-comparisons method relative to single-scene ratings. In particular, the latter method indicated more pronounced perceptual distinctions by viewers between British and American crime—drama portrayals which were much less clear-cut in Experiment One.

Discussion

Clear distinctions emerged between perceptual ratings of violence

116

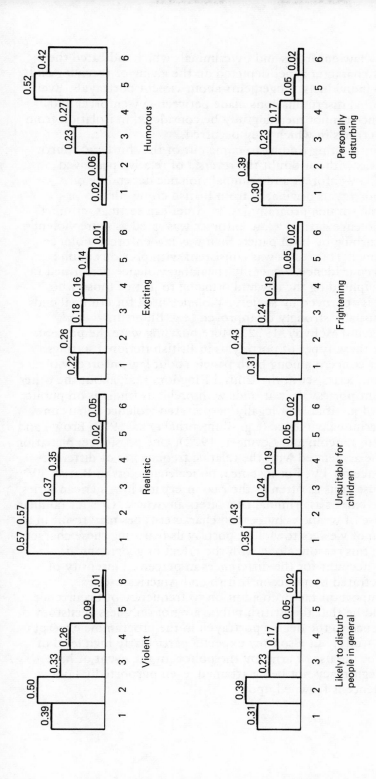

Figure 7.1   Mean paired-comparison ratings for violent excerpts depicting violence perpetrated by law-enforcers and by criminals

117

perpetrated by law-enforcers and by criminals which indicated the importance of character-types depicted on the giving or receiving end of violence to individuals' judgements about violent portrayals. Even so, the perceptual discriminations made between law-enforcer and criminal violence cannot meaningfully be considered in isolation from the fictional settings in which they occurred.

The most interesting finding to come out of the third and fourth experiments was without doubt the reversal of relative perceived seriousness of law-enforcer and criminal violence depending on whether the portrayals originated from British crime—drama or American crime—drama programmes. In American settings, criminal-perpetrated violence against a law-enforcer was rated as more violent and more disturbing by both panels than was law-enforcer violence against a criminal. This result was consistent with previous public opinion research evidence. Generally speaking, violence performed in the service of upholding the law and bringing to justice those who break the law is approved by society. Violence used for criminal ends is conversely usually strongly disapproved (e.g. Blumenthal *et al*, 1972; Gamson and McEvoy, 1972). More puzzling were the percept-ual ratings for these types of portrayals in British fictional settings.

The greater concern among both panels about law-enforcer violence in crime—drama series set in the United Kingdom than about the other forms of violent portrayals is at odds with previous findings on public endorsement of justifiable or legally-perpetrated violence versus un-justifiable or criminal violence (e.g. Blumenthal *et al*, 1972; Brown and Tedeschi, 1976; Lincoln and Levinger, 1972). One possible explanation for this may be associated with the relative frequencies of different kinds of violence on TV. For instance, police characters in British TV series do not use guns as often as their counterparts in American series, or to the same extent as criminal characters anywhere. Greater familiar-ity with the use of weapons by certain character-types may result in a desensitisation of viewers to violent portrayals featuring these charact-ers. Certainly, this reason, along with the effect of geographical location, may account for the differences in perceived intensity of violence perpetrated by police in British and American series.

Another important factor in addition to frequency of occurrence, however, could be that the British public are not only less accustomed to police violence to the degree portrayed in the programme excerpts shown in this study, but also they expect a particularly high level of justification for the use of arms by the police. In the event of high standards of legitimacy not being attained, even purportedly law-enforcing violence is frowned upon.

Violence perpetrated by males and females

Content-analytic studies of the presentation of the sexes on peak-time TV drama programming have indicated pronounced stereotyping and rigidity in the way women are portrayed. Women do not appear as often as men in leading roles, especially in adventure—action series, and when they do appear, they tend to be depicted in only a very narrow range of roles (Butler and Paisley, 1980; Tuchman, 1978).

The Cultural Indicators research of George Gerbner and his colleagues has indicated that women, on the whole, tend to be less involved in violent incidents on TV, but once they are involved, they are more likely to be victims than aggressors (Gerbner, 1972; Gerbner *et al*, 1977; 1978; 1979). The profile of victimisation among male and female TV characters has been interpreted by some writers as a metaphor for the relative incompetence, helplessness and dependency of women in society, especially in spheres outside the home (Tuchman, 1978). The Gerbner group have shown that 'good' female characters seem to enjoy a much better chance of giving than of being on the receiving end of violence (Gerbner *et al*, 1979).

Generally, leading female characters on TV play good or innocent roles rather than evil or criminal roles (although this pattern has been changing somewhat in recent years); hence TV does tend to show women as weaker and less able to cope effectively with problem situations, especially violent ones, most of the time. To what extent though are viewers aware of these patterns of portrayals of the sexes and to what extent is the relative prevalence of violent victimisation amongst males and females on TV reflected in viewers' perceptions of violent episodes?

The particular meanings supposedly conveyed about certain social groups such as women by patterns of portrayals in fictional TV programmes have usually been *inferred* by content-analytic researchers from the extent to which such groups fall victim to violence in these programmes, and depend on the validity of an assumption that viewers draw the same inferences and assimilate them into their conceptions of social reality. Yet seldom are viewers' perceptions of this TV content tested directly. For example, while televised episodes which consist of male-perpetrated violence are far more *prevalent* in fictitious stories on TV than are those featuring female-perpetrated violence, and while female victimisation is relatively more common than male victimisation (*pro rata*), little research has been done to examine the extent to which viewers differentiate between violent portrayals involving male and female aggressors or victims.

The significance of differential involvement of the sexes in violent TV portrayals for viewers' judgements of televised violence is suggested by research with children from which physical strength emerged as the most important attribute in terms of which they discriminated between leading male and female characters (Reeves and Greenberg, 1977; Reeves and Lometti, 1978). Thus, if male characters are generally perceived to possess greater physical strength than female characters, perhaps they might also be conceived by viewers to be better equipped to cope with a violent attack upon them. The belief that women are generally less able to defend themselves against physical attack may mediate judgements that portrayals depicting female victimisation are more violent and more disturbing than are those depicting male victimisation. To test this, the following two experiments compared viewers' perceptions of violent portrayals which depicted either a male attacking a female or a female attacking a male.

Experiment Five

Method

Members of Panel One were shown and rated twelve programme excerpts of between 40 and 70 seconds' duration which featured two categories of violent action. Six scenes portrayed a male aggressor attacking a female victim, while the other six scenes depicted a female aggressor attacking a male victim. These scenes were taken from three genres of programming: contemporary British crime—drama (e.g. *The Professionals*, *The Sweeney*, *Target*); contemporary American crime—drama (e.g. *Kojak*, *Mannix*, *Charlie's Angels*); and futuristic science-fiction series (e.g. *Buck Rogers*, *Star Trek*). Each scene portrayed one of two forms of violence, either a fight of physical struggle, or a shooting, and each of these styles of violence was represented equally among male-perpetrated and female-perpetrated violent incidents.

Each scene was rated along eight, seven-point, unipolar scales: violent, realistic, frightening, personally disturbing, likely to disturb people in general, suitable for children, exciting, and humorous. These scales were the same as those used in previous experiments.

Panel members were run as a single group in a small lecture theatre in a session which lasted approximately 50 minutes and was split into two parts by a five-minute break. The purpose of this break, as in other experiments, was to alleviate the build-up of fatigue or loss of interest with the rating task. Although aware that this study was designed to investigate audience perceptions of televised violence, no indication was given to the panel that the feature of critical interest to the researchers was the sex of aggressor and victim in violent scenarios. In order to disguise further this comparison six additional violent scenes not featuring any direct conflict between male and female characters were interspersed and rated with the twelve test scenes. In all then eighteen scenes were rated in this study.

The scenes were played on a Sony U-matic video-recorder and presented over three monochrome TV monitors placed about two metres apart at the front of the viewing theatre. Panel members were seated so that they had a comfortable, unobscured view of one of the monitors. The excerpts were presented one at a time, and at the end of each one the video-tape was stopped and the panel were given about two minutes to complete their ratings for that scene along the eight scales. Panel members were instructed not to dwell too long in making their judgements, but to be as honest as possible in their ratings of each portrayal.

Results

Statistical comparisons of mean ratings of violent episodes featuring male victimisation by a female attacker and female victimisation by a male attacker were computed separately for each scale using Wilcoxon's matched-pairs signed-ranks test. Table 7.5 summarises the mean ratings and indicates levels of statistical significance between the scores for male- and female-perpetrated violence.

These results indicate that whilst there were a number of fairly well-marked variations in ratings of male and female violence, the difference between viewers' perceptions of how violent these two kinds of portrayal were seen to be was negligible. Male violence on a female victim was perceived as significantly more realistic, more frightening, more personally disturbing, and more likely to disturb other people than was a female character attacking a male victim. Scenes showing female victims were rated as significantly less suitable for children, less exciting and less humorous. Thus, Panel One members were apparently less entertained by TV portrayals showing men attacking women, which they also perceived as more true to life, disturbing to themselves and unlikely to be enjoyed by others.

The programme excerpts shown to respondents in this study were taken from three categories of programming, and further pairwise comparisons between perceptions of male-perpetrated and female-perpetrated violence were therefore computed within each programme genre, again using Wilcoxon tests. The results of these analyses are summarised in Table 7.6.

Although no significant differences in the perceived level of violence in male-perpetrated and female-perpetrated violent portrayals emerged over all materials, marked distinctions on this scale did occur within different programme settings, and not always in the same direction. Thus, male violence on a female victim was perceived as more violent than female violence on a male victim, but only in con-

121

Table 7.5
Mean ratings for televised violence perpetrated by males and females

	Violent*	Realistic	Exciting	Humorous	Likely to disturb people in general	Suitable for children	Frightening	Personally disturbing
Male-perpetrated violence	4.1	2.9	2.9	1.8	2.7	2.8	2.8	2.2
Female-perpetrated violence	4.2	2.4	3.5	2.2	2.3	3.2	2.3	1.7

Note: *Statistically non-significant difference
Mean ratings on all other scales are significantly different at the $P < .01$ level

Table 7.6
Mean ratings for male-perpetrated and female-perpetrated televised violence within programme genres

	Violent	Realistic	Exciting	Humorous	Likely to disturb people in general	Suitable for children	Frightening	Personally disturbing
British crime drama								
Male-perpetrated violence	5.8	3.6	3.4[a]	1.1[a]	4.2	1.8	4.3	3.3
Female-perpetrated violence	4.8	2.8[a]	4.1	2.1	2.6[a]	2.8[a]	2.7[a]	1.8[a]
American crime drama								
Male-perpetrated violence	3.8	3.4	3.1[ab]	1.3[ab]	2.5[a]	3.1[a]	2.7[a]	2.1[a]
Female-perpetrated violence	4.4	3.1[a]	3.4[a]	1.6[b]	2.5[a]	2.9[a]	2.7[a]	1.8[a]
Science-fictions								
Male-perpetrated violence	2.6	1.6	2.4	2.7[a]	1.4[b]	3.9	1.5[b]	1.3[b]
Female-perpetrated violence	3.3	1.2	3.0[b]	2.7[c]	1.6[b]	4.0	1.6[b]	1.4[b]

Note: Ratings with common superscripts are not significantly different at $P < .05$ level

temporary British crime—drama settings. For American crime—drama and science-fiction portrayals, the pattern of responding on this scale was reversed. Female-perpetrated violence was perceived as significantly more violent than male-perpetrated violence. Male violence was rated as more realistic than female violence across all three categories of programming. On the other scales, however, such as how humorous, frightening, personally disturbing, likely to disturb people in general, or suitable for children these two types of portrayal were perceived to be, no significant differences occurred except for violent episodes in contemporary British crime—drama settings. In general, male violence was rated as more serious on a variety of scales than was female violence.

Experiment Six

Method

This study was designed to supplement Experiment Five and offer further analysis of viewers' perceptions of male- and female-perpetrated violence in different TV drama settings. A different group of 34 individuals who constituted Panel Two were shown and gave ratings on six programme excerpts taken two each from a British crime—drama series (*The Sweeney*), an American crime—drama series (*Charlie's Angels*), and a science-fiction series (*Buck Rogers*). One scene per programme depicted male violence on a female victim and the other depicted female violence on a male victim. Each scene was between 40 and 70 seconds long and depicted a single act of violence. Brief descriptions of these scenes are presented in Table 7.7. Selection of each portrayal was made according to Gerbner's (1972) definition of violence.

The principal difference between this study and Experiment Five was that the scenes were judged here in pairs rather than one at a time. Exhaustive paired comparisons meant that fifteen pairs were generated from the basic set of six programme excerpts, so that each scene was paired with and judged against each of the other five. Viewing conditions were the same in this study as in earlier experiments. The study was run in a small lecture theatre in two sessions of one and one-and-a-half hours' duration on two separate days. These sessions were divided into half-hour segments following each of which ten-minute breaks were taken. To avoid successive presentation of scenes within the experimental set, test pairs were intermixed with ten dummy pairs. Thus, 25 pairs of programme excerpts were presented in total, with five pairs presented per half-hour segment — three test pairs in alternation with two dummy pairs.

Table 7.7

Synopses of TV scenes used in Experiment 6

	Programmes	Scenes
1	*Buck Rogers in the 25th Century* *	Buck Rogers fights a girl villain and stuns her with his laser pistol.
2	*Buck Rogers in the 25th Century*	Two girls attack Buck Rogers and stun him with a laser pistol.
3	*Charlie's Angels*	A man shoots at one of Charlie's Angels in an underground car park.
4	*Charlie's Angels*	An Angel shoots at a man who then runs away before she can shoot again.
5	*The Sweeney* *	A villainous character roughly pushes a young woman into her living room and threatens to beat her up unless she does what he tells her.
6	*The Sweeney*	A plain clothes woman detective disarms and forcibly arrests a young villain as he tries to hold up a shopkeeper.

Note: * Scenes in which a male aggressor attacks a female victim. Remaining scenes depicted a female aggressor attacking a male victim.

Results

The scoring system for the paired-comparison design was described in Chapter 3. Briefly summarised, each scene could receive up to four points per comparison or up to a maximum of 20 points over all five comparisons with other scenes in the set. Raw scores were then transformed into proportions by dividing the actual total score received by each scene by the total possible (i.e. 20 points). Mean ratings for each excerpt per scale are summarised in Figure 7.2.

The paired-comparisons technique revealed marked differences

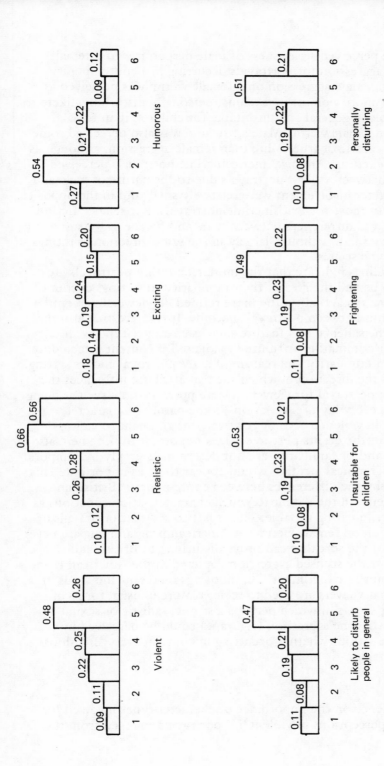

Figure 7.2   Mean paired-comparison ratings for violent excerpts depicting violence perpetrated by males and by females

125

between the perceived seriousness of male-perpetrated and female-perpetrated aggression for portrayals occurring in a contemporary British setting. Male aggression on a female victim was perceived as considerably more violent, frightening, personally disturbing, likely to disturb people in general and unsuitable for children than female aggression on a male victim. Male aggression was also perceived somewhat more realistic or true-to-life than female aggression, although as slightly less exciting. Among American crime portrayals perceived differences between violent portrayals due to the nature of male and female character involvement were relatively small and in the opposite direction than those for British crime portrayals. For science-fiction scenes perceived differences between male and female aggression were generally very small, although largely in the same direction as ratings of British crime scenes.

These findings indicate that the more true-to-life portrayals are perceived to be and the greater their familiarity to settings encountered by viewers in actuality, the more refined do viewers' perceptual discriminations between portrayals become. It is interesting also that not only is the salience of a feature such as character-type as an important discriminating attribute of violent TV content affected by the perceived familiarity and realism of a TV portrayal and its setting, but so too is the direction in which such an attribute influences the meaning of a portrayal for viewers. Where portrayals are seen as being remote from everyday life, variations in the nature of character involvement in violence become relatively insignificant to viewers' perceptions of the events portrayed. It is important to note here also, that realism and/or familiarity are not determined simply by temporal context; geographical location would appear to be as important. This is evidenced by the differences between contemporary British and American scenes in the extent to which characterisation functions as a salient discriminating variable. This is not to say that portrayals of male aggression on female victims in American programming are never likely to be of the sort that can prove disturbing to British audiences. It may be that the stylised aggression depicted in the American crime scenes used in this experiment (i.e. shootings represent the kinds of portrayals that viewers are used to seeing). More unusual forms of aggression or scenes in which perhaps a strong, sadistic or sexual motive underlies the aggression (e.g. rape) could be perceived by many viewers to be serious whether occurring in contemporary British or American settings.

Discussion

Further evidence on the importance of character-types involved for individuals' perceptions of violent TV portrayals emerged from the fifth and sixth studies. Once again, experiments that used two different ratings procedures yielded consistent patterns of response. Both panels agreed on the relative perceived seriousness of violence perpetrated by men on women or by women on men. But as with perceptions of law-enforcer and criminal violence, the precise nature of panel members' ratings varied across fictional settings.

In view of the finding that aggression or violent conduct is associated with men rather than with women (Reeves and Lometti, 1978), it is perhaps not surprising that among excerpts from British programmes, panel members rated portrayals of male characters attacking female victims as significantly more violent and more disturbing than those which featured females attacking males.

What is more difficult to explain is the finding that in American fictional settings, panel members perceived female violence on male victims as more violent and more disturbing than male violence on a female. How can this switch around in ratings across fictional settings be explained? Two hypotheses will be considered.

First of all, content analyses have shown that violence perpetrated by male characters is far more prevalent on fictional TV programming (especially in America) than is violence performed by females. Females, on the other hand, most often feature as victims, when they are involved in any kind of violence on TV (Gerbner et al, 1977, 1978, 1979). Thus, viewers may become more accustomed to seeing male aggressors than female aggressors, and females as victims of males than males as victims of females. Differential degrees of habituation or desensitisation may in turn therefore occur with respect to these different types of portrayal, and more unusual forms of violence may produce more extreme reactions from viewers. On this line of argument, a female attack on a male victim, being a highly unusual type of portrayal, would be expected to elicit fairly extreme responses.

A second possible explanation for the greater perceived seriousness of female violence in American settings may relate to the attitudes towards women who engage in criminal conduct that have been observed by some writers (Buckhart, 1973; McGlynn et al, 1976). These and other writers have pointed to the basic dichotomy of women into essentially 'good' and 'bad' types. Women who conform to idealised notions of femininity — gentleness, passivity, maternity, etc. — are perceived as basically good. Any woman who turns to crime or violence, however, has in so doing abandoned her femininity and is therefore branded as deviant and bad. Such a woman would be perceived in the most extreme and unfavourable terms.

What is more difficult to explain is why one judgemental frame of reference is adopted rather than another in a particular fictional setting. One possible reason could be that the typically normative conception of women as the physically weaker sex is applied most readily in those contexts that most closely approximate the everyday reality of the judges — in the current studies in portrayals occurring in British settings. In more distant fictional locations, other rules become more salient perhaps and are applied instead.

8 Physical form and the perception of television violence

Behavioural research on the 'weapons effect' has indicated that the actual presence of weapons or pictures of weapons or instruments of violence can make an already antagonised person behave more violently against an intimidator than he would do in a weapon-free situation (Berkowitz, 1971; Berkowitz and Le Page, 1967; Leyens and Parke, 1975; Tannenbaum, 1971). However, this work has not demonstrated whether or not certain types of instruments or techniques of violence have stronger aggression-eliciting properties than others, thereby providing a measure of the relative seriousness or intensity of violence represented by different physical forms or actions.

A study carried out for the Surgeon General's Committee in the United States in the early 1970s indicated that at a perceptual level, viewers can and do discriminate between violent portrayals featuring different physical forms of violence. Greenberg and Gordon (1972b) found that violent TV scenes featuring gun-fights or shootings were judged as more violent, less realistic, and less acceptable than were scenes depicting fist-fights or physical, unarmed struggles between protagonists. This study restricted itself to these two forms of violence and provided no indication of the nature and extent of viewers' perceptual discriminations between portrayals involving other kinds of physical violence. No comparisons were made either between perceptions of physical forms of violence in different fictional settings. The studies reported in Chapter 7 indicated that the type of programme setting can function as a mediator of viewers' differential perceptions of violent portrayals involving different character-types as perpetrators or victims of violence. The same might be true also with respect to viewers' judgements about different physical forms of televised violence.

Experiment Seven

Method

Design and materials. Thirty-two programme excerpts were selected, using Gerbner's (1972) definition, from British crime—drama series (e.g. *The Professionals*, *The Sweeney*) and from a Western film (*Cannon for Cordoba*) and a Western TV series (*Alias Smith and Jones*). There were eight scenes representing each of four types of physical violence: shootings, fist-fights, explosions, and stabbings, of which four per type came from each programme genre. All scenes were between 40 and 70 seconds long and depicted a single physically violent incident.

The programmes which provided the scenes had been broadcast on one or other of the three UK TV networks (BBC1, BBC2 or ITV) during peak viewing hours (7 p.m. to 11 p.m.) between three and six months before the study. The programme excerpts were played on a Sony U-matic video-recorder and relayed over three monochrome TV monitors placed about two metres apart at the front of the small lecture theatre in which the study took place. Judgements about each scene were made along eight scales as in the previous experiments.

Subjects and procedure. The subject sample consisted of Panel One. The study was run in two 50-minute sessions, each on separate days. Excerpts were played one at a time, and after each one the video-tape was stopped for about two minutes during which time respondents completed their ratings of it. Each session was divided into two parts by a ten-minute break, and the scenes were evenly distributed throughout the four segments. Although viewers were aware that the researchers were interested in their perceptions of violence no indication was given to the panel that comparisons were to be made between their ratings of different physical forms of violence until all ratings had been completed.

Results

Table 8.1 shows the mean ratings for each physical category of violence averaged over programme genres. Wilcoxon matched-pairs, signed-ranks tests indicated that shootings were perceived as signif-

Table 8.1

Mean ratings for four physical categories of televised violence

Programme genres	Violent	Realistic	Exciting	Humorous	Frightening	Personally disturbing	Likely to disturb people in general	Suitable for children
Average scores								
Shootings	5.6	2.4	3.9ª	1.5ª	2.9ª	2.1ab	3.2ª	2.5ª
Fist-fights	4.7	2.7ª	3.7ab	2.1	2.6	1.9ª	2.8	2.8
Explosions	5.1ª	2.8ª	3.2c	1.5c	3.1ª	2.3b	3.2ª	2.4ª
Stabbings	5.1ª	3.2	3.5bc	1.3	3.3	2.6	3.4	2.4ª
British crime scenes								
Shootings	5.8ac	2.4	4.3	1.3ª	3.1ª	2.3ª	3.2ª	2.3ª
Fist-fights	5.3b	2.8ª	3.9ª	2.0	3.1ª	2.3ª	3.1ª	2.4ª
Explosions	5.7ab	3.1ª	3.8ª	1.2ª	3.7	2.9	3.6	2.0b
Stabbings	6.1c	3.9	3.4	1.3ª	4.1	3.5	4.3	1.7b
Western scenes								
Shootings	5.4	2.5ª	3.6ª	1.7ª	2.7ª	1.9ª	3.2	2.7ª
Fist-fights	4.0ª	2.6ª	3.4ª	2.2	2.1b	1.5b	2.5ª	3.2b
Explosions	4.3ª	2.4ª	3.5ª	1.8ª	2.6ª	1.8ab	2.9	2.7ª
Stabbings	4.1ª	2.6ª	3.5ª	1.3	2.4ab	1.7ab	2.4ª	3.1b

Scale range: Max = 7
Min = 1

Note: Means with common superscripts are not significantly different at the $P < .05$ level

131

icantly more violent overall than were any of the other forms of violence, and that stabbings were rated as the most frightening and personally disturbing, and as most likely to disturb other people. Fist-fights were usually rated as significantly less violent, less personally disturbing, less likely to disturb people in general, and as more humorous than any other form of physical violence.

Table 8.1 also shows the mean scores for different physical forms of violence within each programme genre. Further Wilcoxon tests were computed on these scores to reveal certain differences between genres in the kinds of physical violence perceived as most violent and most disturbing. Within British crime—drama settings, stabbings were perceived as the most realistic, most violent, most frightening, most personally disturbing, most likely to disturb other people, and as the least suitable for children. In Westerns, however, shootings were rated as significantly more violent than stabbings and as slightly more frightening and disturbing.

Experiment Eight

It was apparent from Experiment Seven that viewers differentially perceive violent TV portrayals according to the type or form of physical violence displayed in them. It also became clear that the physical form of televised violence was more salient and important to viewers' judgements in contemporary fictional settings (e.g. crime—detective series) than in settings further removed from everyday life (e.g. Westerns). These results and those from the previous chapter on the importance of character involvement indicate that as the perceived realism of TV content increases so more subtle features of portrayals influence viewers' judgements about the actions displayed. This pattern of judgements for ratings of scenes one at a time was reinforced further by viewers' direct paired-comparisons of programme excerpts. Experiment Eight was designed to examine further the mediating effects of physical form on viewers' perceptions of televised violence within the paired-comparisons procedure.

In Experiment Seven it was found that differences between perceptions of Western portrayals characterised by different forms of violence were fairly small following *post hoc* statistical analyses of the data. However, to what extent does the salience of physical form increase when individuals are given the opportunity to make direct perceptual comparisons of programme excerpts?

As in all other paired-comparisons studies, this study began with a basic set of six excerpts of 40 to 70 seconds' duration. All materials had been selected according to Gerbner's (1972) definition of violence, from a single Western movie called *Cannon for Cordoba*. In all six different physical forms of violence were represented by these scenes: clubbing, knife-throwing, cannon-fire, slashing with a sword, a gun-fight, and a fist-fight (see Table 8.2). These excerpts were exhaustively paired with each other to generate a sequence of fifteen pairs. These pairs were presented with ten dummy pairs to Panel Two, who made dissimilarity ratings on each pair along eight scales as used in all previous studies. All other details of procedure were the same as those described for paired-comparisons studies in earlier chapters.

Table 8.2

Synopses of TV scenes used
in Experiment 8

	Programme	Scenes
1	*Cannon for Cordoba**	Army Captain knocks out the servant of a large Mexican household with a gun-butt.
2		Guard at Mexican fortress is killed by a knife thrown by a member of an invading guerrilla force.
3		Cannon is fired at the gates of Mexican fortress by one of the small guerrilla force.
4		US Army Captain kills Mexican soldier with a sword.
5		US Army Captain in a gun-fight with Mexican soldiers who ambush his men while on their journey into Mexico.
6		Captive American soldier knocks out Mexican prison guard with a single punch to the face in an escape attempt.

* All scenes were taken from this Western film.

Results
Using the scoring method for this design, a total score per excerpt was

calculated by summing over the five individual scores it received from comparisons with the other five scenes in the compilation. Raw scores were then converted to proportions of the maximum score possible. The mean proportions per excerpt are summarised in Figure 8.1.

Results showed that respondents made marked perceptual discriminations between these Western portrayals on the basis of physical form. The following rank order of portrayals emerged on the basis of how *violent* they were perceived to be:

1 Slashing with a sword
2 Knife-throwing
3 Cannon fire at a fortress
4 Shooting in street
5 Clubbing with gun-butt
6 Fist-fight

The same or very similar rankings of the scenes emerged on the other scales, most notably with regard to how frightening, personally disturbing, likely to disturb people in general, and suitable for children excerpts were perceived to be. On degree of perceived realism, low scores across excerpts together with the small differences between them indicate that these portrayals were perceived in a fairly similar fashion as not being very true to life.

Discussion

The physical form or type of violence was found in the seventh and eighth experiments to have a marked effect on panel members' judgements about violent portrayals. Similar patterns of ratings emerged from both experiments. Excerpts that featured stabbings or shootings were perceived as the most violent and most disturbing, and fist-fights were rated as least serious in these terms. In more realistic fictional contexts, stabbings were rated as the most disturbing of all. Explanations for these differences in perceived seriousness can be put forward which relate to the prevalence of each physical category of violence on TV, and to the degree of harm each might be judged by the viewer to inflict on an intended victim.

Content analyses of fictional programming have indicated that the physical forms of violence presented to panel members in these studies occur with quite different frequencies. Shootings and fist-fights are the most common, and each of these occurs three times more often than stabbings, and six times more often than explosions (BBC, 1972). Different degrees of desensitisation to these types of portrayal may therefore develop among viewers and could be invoked to account for different kinds of perceptual reactions to them. Those which occur least often may produce the most severe responses because of the

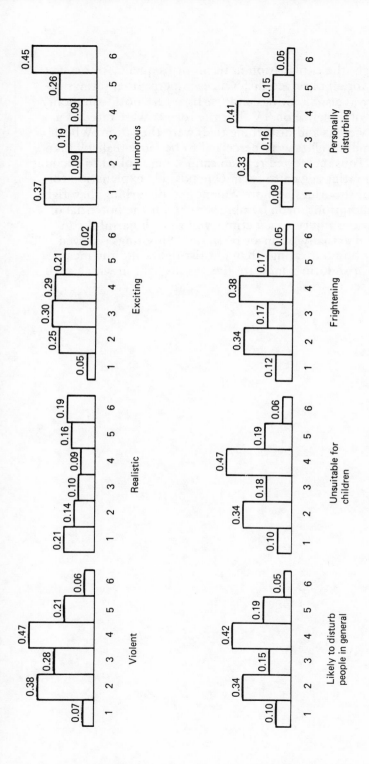

Figure 8.1 Mean paired-comparison ratings for violent excerpts depicting different physical forms of violence

135

unusual quality.

Clearly though, the explanation in terms of frequency of occurrence cannot account for all observed differences in perceptual ratings between these portrayals. Shootings and fist-fights are both commonly occurring forms of violence on TV, but the former were rated as a great deal more violent and disturbing than were the latter by both panels. Furthermore, fights were perceived to be more realistic than were shootings. Thus, perceived realism cannot be invoked to account for the different ratings given to each. One possible explanation for the perception of shootings as more violent and disturbing than fights may lie with assumptions made by observers about the potential of each to cause serious injury to a victim, even though harmful consequence may not actually occur or be shown. Shootings received significant lower humour ratings than did fist-fights and the mean humour scores for shootings indicate the serious light in which such portrayals were seen.

9 Degree of observable harm and the perception of television violence

Important among the characteristics in terms of which violent portrayals on TV can vary is the degree of harm caused to victims by an attacker. Indeed, this factor featured prominently in the definition of televised violence laid down by Gerbner and in those of other researchers for content-analytic violence monitoring purposes (e.g. BBC, 1972; Gerbner, 1972; Halloran and Croll, 1972).

Work done on the behavioural impact of media violence has indicated that the depicted outcome of violence for a victim could function as an important mediator of viewers' overt behavioural responses. For example, non-angered viewers were found to become less aggressive after watching a violent film portrayal with fatal or harmful consequences for a victim than following a portrayal with a pleasant or non-harmful outcome (Goranson, 1969; Hartmann, 1969). Observing intense pain reactions may produce an empathic response on the part of viewers, it seems, which serves to inhibit aggression. Amongst intimidated viewers, on the other hand, anger serves to raise the threshold for developing empathic inhibitory responses so that observation of a victim's suffering enhances rather than inhibits subsequent aggression (Feshbach, Stiles and Bitter, 1967; Hartmann, 1969). In another study, children were more disturbed by violent episodes in which injured victims were seen than by episodes which featured no observable harm to any of the actors (Noble, 1975). Although focusing on behavioural responses subsequent to viewing media violence, these experiments may also indicate some degree of perceptual differentiation of violent incidents by viewers on the basis of the outcome of violence for those who are victimised.

The mediating effect of observed consequences of violence may of course vary in its nature or strength from one type of programme to the next, as was found to be the case for other attributes such as the types of characters involved and the physical form of the violence. Behavioural effects research has indeed already indicated a certain degree of interdependency between the consequences of portrayed violence and fictional context. Noble (1975) reported that whilst filmed violence with sight of the victim produced more anxiety and destructive play behaviour amongst children than did portrayals not showing the victim, the impact of sight of victim was more pronounced still in a realistic setting (as compared with a more obviously fictional one).

Behavioural measures, though indicative, offer only implicit evidence of viewers' perceptual differentiation between violent media portrayals on the basis of degree of observable harm. A more direct assessment of viewers' portrayals is needed. In this chapter, two studies are reported which examined the extent to which viewers can and do distinguish at a perceptual—judgemental level between violent portrayals in which victims are seen to suffer and those in which no harm is depicted. Comparisons were also made of viewers' perceptions of harmful and harmless violence in different programme genres.

Experiment Nine

Method

Design and materials. Eighteen programme excerpts were used in this study. Each scene was between 40 and 70 seconds long and portrayed a single, complete violent action sequence which had been selected in accordance with Gerbner's (1972) definition of violence. The scenes were taken from two categories of programmes, American-produced crime—detective series (e.g. *Kojak*, *Mannix*, *Starsky and Hutch*) and science-fiction series (e.g. *Buck Rogers*, *Star Trek*). Each programme category was represented by nine scenes, three of which depicted fatal violence in which a victim was killed, three showed violence resulting in injury without death, and three portrayed no observable harmful consequences. Other differences between scenes from each genre were kept to a minimum as far as possible. All scenes, for example, depicted shooting incidents between forces of good or law-enforcement and forces of evil or criminality in which 'good' retaliated or reacted in self-defence against violence instigated by 'evil'.

The programmes which served as source materials for excerpts in this study had been broadcast on the three UK TV networks of that time (BBC1, BBC2, and ITV) during peak viewing hours (7 p.m. to 11 p.m.) between three and six months earlier. The scenes were played in a randomly ordered sequence on a Sony VHS cassette recorder and relayed in monochrome over three TV monitors placed about two metres apart at the front of a small lecture theatre. The ratings scales were the same as those used in earlier studies.

Subjects and procedure. The 40 members of Panel One took part in this study which was run in two one-hour sessions in the morning and afternoon of the same day. The procedure was essentially the same as that for previous single-scene ratings studies. Programme excerpts were played one at a time and at the end of each one the video-tape was stopped for approximately two minutes during which time subjects gave their ratings of it. When half the scenes in each session had been viewed and rated in this way, a ten-minute break was taken to alleviate fatigue with the task. During this spell, subjects were allowed to leave the experimental room briefly to obtain refreshments.

Results

A series of Wilcoxon matched-pairs, signed-ranks tests were computed to compare mean ratings for each type of violent scene on each scale. Table 9.1 summarises these results which reveal a number of significant differences in viewers' judgements associated with the degree of harm to victims depicted in a violent portrayal. In general scenes which featured observable harm to victims were perceived in more serious terms (e.g. more violent, frightening, personally disturbing, likely to disturb people in general, less suitable for children and less humorous) than were scenes which portrayed no observable harmful consequences. Overall, there were no differences in the perceived realism of these categories of violence, and no consistent trends were apparent in how serious violent portrayals were perceived to be and how exciting they were rated.

It will be remembered that scenes for this study derived from two genres of programming, American crime—drama series and science-fiction series. The two studies reported in Chapter 3 indicated significant differences between viewers' perceptions of similar physical forms of violence from these two fictional settings. Further studies reported in Chapter 4 and Chapter 5 showed that other factors such as character-types who are involved in the violence as perpetrators or victims and the physical form of violence can mediate viewers' judgements about violent TV portrayals, and also indicated that these factors may be more powerful in some fictional settings than in others.

Table 9.1

Mean ratings of TV violence as a function of degree of observable harm suffered by victims

Consequences of violence	Violent	Realistic	Exciting	Humorous	Likely to disturb people in general	Suitable for children	Fright-ening	Personally disturbing
Fatal	4.4[a]	2.2[a]	3.3[a]	1.6	2.5[a]	3.3[a]	2.4[a]	1.9[a]
Non-fatal injury	4.6[a]	2.2[a]	3.6	2.2[a]	2.4[a]	3.3[a]	2.5[a]	2.0[a]
No observable harm	3.6	2.2[a]	3.3[a]	2.1[a]	2.1	3.6	2.1	1.6

Note: Scale range: Maximum score = 7
          Minimum score = 1

Scores with common superscripts are not significantly different at the $P < .05$ level.

Hence, further comparisons of viewers' perceptions of violence in relation to the degree of observable harm it caused were made separately within each programme category (see Table 9.2).

Experiment Ten

Experiment Nine indicated that viewers' perceptions of televised violence differ for portrayals that depict harmful consequences from those that show no apparent harm to victims. To some extent also, however, the magnitude of differential judgements of harmful and harmless violence varied across programme genres. Studies reported in previous chapters have indicated similar variations in the apparent salience of particular physical attributes of televised violence (such as the characters involved and the physical form of violence) across different fictional settings. Earlier studies also indicated that the subtlety of viewers' differential perceptions of televised violence in terms of these attributes can be emphasised to varying degrees by the nature of the judgements they are required to make.

Studies which employed the technique of direct comparisons of pairs of TV scenes corroborated the findings from those in which *post hoc* statistical comparisons were made of viewers' responses to distinct groups scenes which were rated one at a time. In a further investigation of variations in viewers' perceptions of violent portrayals resulting in harmful and harmless consequences, a paired-comparisons study was carried out in which Panel Two distinguished between pairs of violent scenes which differed in terms of their portrayed outcomes for victims.

Method

This study consisted of direct comparisons between fifteen pairs of programme excerpts, generated from a basic set of six excerpts so that each scene was compared in turn with each of the others. Table 9.3 presents brief descriptions of the content of each excerpt. These excerpts were between 40 and 70 seconds long and were taken from two categories of programmes: American crime—drama series (*Kojak, Starsky and Hutch*) and science-fiction series (*Buck Rogers, Star Trek*). Each programme category was represented by three scenes, two of which per category depicted fatal consequences for victims, two of which depicted non-fatal consequences for victims, and two showed no observable harmful outcome.

The usual procedure for the paired-comparisons design was employed in this study. Panel Two were shown the scenes one pair at a time and compared them along eight scales. In each case, the judgements made were: first, which scene in a pair was the more violent,

Table 9.2

Mean ratings of TV violence as a function of degree of observable harm suffered by victims and programme type

	Violent	Realistic	Exciting	Humorous	Likely to disturb people in general	Suitable for children	Frightening	Personally disturbing
Fatal								
American crime drama	5.5^a	3.2^a	3.8^{ab}	1.2	3.3^a	2.6^a	3.0^a	2.3^a
Science-fiction	3.3^{bc}	1.3^b	2.9^c	1.9	1.7^b	3.9^b	1.7^b	1.4^b
Non-fatal injury								
American crime drama	5.7^a	3.2^a	3.9^a	1.5^a	3.2^a	2.6^a	3.3^a	2.5^a
Science-fiction	3.5^b	1.2^b	3.3^d	2.9^b	1.6^b	4.0^b	1.6^b	1.4^b
No observable harm								
American crime drama	4.0	3.1^a	3.6^b	1.5^a	2.5	3.2^b	2.6^a	1.8^a
Science-fiction	3.2^c	1.2^b	3.0^{cd}	2.7^b	1.8^b	3.0^b	1.7^b	1.4^b

Note: Scores with common superscripts are not significantly different at the $P < .05$ level.

frightening, exciting, and so on; and second, by how much more, 'slightly', 'somewhat', 'moderately', or 'a great deal'. The pairs in this compilation were randomly interspersed with pairs from another compilation and ratings were obtained over two sessions of one hour and one-and-a-half hours. As in previous studies using this design, each session consisted of three parts and although each scene was rated five times against the others, no scene was presented more than once within each 15–20-minute segment of a session.

Table 9.3

Synopses of TV scenes used
in Experiment 10

	Programmes	Scenes
1	*Kojak*	An escaping villain chased by police detectives is shot and killed by a uniformed police officer as he reaches for his gun.
2	*Mannix*	In a gun-fight in a car park Mannix shoots and wounds two men who are trying to kill him.
3	*Kojak*	Two police detectives shoot after a crook as he escapes in his car.
4	*Buck Rogers in the 25th Century*	A group of masked invaders disintegrates unarmed victims as they break into a building.
5	*Buck Rogers in the 25th Century*	In a fight with a villainous character in a futuristic night-club, Buck Rogers stuns the former with his laser pistol.
6	*Buck Rogers in the 25th Century*	Buck Rogers fights off a group of men sent to assassinate him.

Results

The scores for each scene were computed as the proportion of points received out of maximum points possible (i.e. 20 points). Mean scores for each scene per scale are summarised in Figure 9.1. These results indicate that both programme genre and the depicted degree of harm to

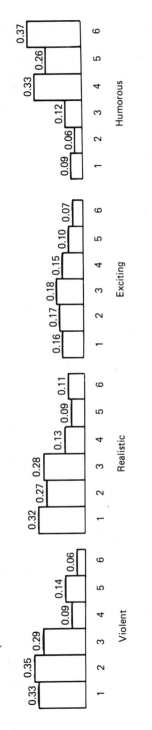
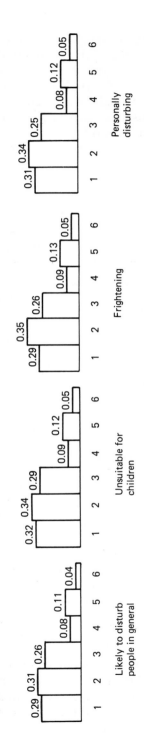

Figure 9.1   Mean paired-comparison ratings for violent excerpts depicting harmful and harmless violence

144

victims were discriminating features. The fictional setting in which portrayals occurred was the more salient attribute and violent incidents from American crime—drama series were rated as considerably more violent, more realistic, more frightening, more personally disturbing and less suitable for children than were similar kinds of incidents from science-fiction series.

Discussion

The ninth and tenth experiments indicated that the consequences of violence for victims provided a further means of perceptual discrimination between portrayals. Patterns of response were again largely in the same direction for both ratings procedures. Scenes which depicted physical harm to a victim were judged to be more violent and more disturbing than were scenes in which no observable harm occurred. This finding was consistent with results reported ten years earlier by Greenberg and Gordon (1972b). The latter writers found that young male viewers perceived scenes in which actors physically harmed each other as more violent and less acceptable than scenes in which harm, though intended, was unsuccessful.

A further discrimination was noted in this research, however, between different kinds of harmful violence. Non-fatal injurious portrayals were judged as more violent and more disturbing than were portrayals resulting in a clear-cut fatality.

Whilst incidents causing fatalities might intuitively seem to be more serious forms of violence than those resulting in non-fatal injuries, the fact that the former were judged by panel members as less serious than the latter probably reflects the relative degree of pain and suffering depicted in these two types of portrayal. Wounded victims suffered much more than fatal victims who, in the scenes presented in Experiments Nine and Ten, were killed quickly and apparently painlessly. Thus, the crucial factor seems to be whether or not victims exhibit pain and suffering rather than simply whether or not their injuries are fatal. It is possible, of course, that among portrayals depicting more or less equal amounts of suffering among victims, those also resulting in fatalities will be perceived as more serious than those showing non-fatal injuries, but this was not investigated in this series of experiments.

10 Physical setting and the perception of television violence

This chapter examines the significance for viewers' perceptions of televised violence of factors not normally given much attention by researchers — the physical setting and location of portrayals. The Gerbner content-analytic model has provided indices of the prevalence of violence on TV in urban, rural or uninhabited settings, but no attempt has been made to investigate the salience of physical setting for viewers in their judgements about or reactions to violent episodes.

Published findings in the early 1980s showed that violent incidents in TV drama occurred more often in remote settings than in heavily populated areas (Gerbner, 1972). However, the past ten years has seen a growth in popularity of the crime—detective genre on prime-time TV and in these series much of the action takes place in urban locations. Two fundamental aspects of the physical setting of violence can readily be identified for incidents occurring in an urban environment: whether the violence occurs during the day or at night, and whether it occurs indoors or outdoors. The mediating effects of these features on viewers' judgements about televised violence are explored for the first time in two experiments reported in this chapter.

Day-time and night-time portrayals

Fear of the dark is a common anxiety among young children and may often remain with them into adulthood, although many would not be prepared as adults to admit openly to such a fear. On TV programmes too, violent portrayals depicted during the hours of darkness may often take on an additional element of suspense or threat that would be missing if they were shown in daylight. What effect then does the presence of darkness have on viewers' perceptions of violent portrayals on TV? Are night-time portrayals perceived to be more violent and more disturbing than day-time portrayals? The next experiment examined these questions by comparing viewers' perceptions of two sets of TV scenes which depicted violence either in daylight or in darkness within the single-scene rating design.

Experiment Eleven

Method

Twenty-four programme excerpts were viewed and rated by Panel One. These clips were 40 to 70 seconds long and represented two genres of programming: American crime—drama series (e.g. *Kojak*, *Mannix*, *Starsky and Hutch*) and Westerns (e.g. *Alias Smith and Jones*, *The Quest*). Twelve scenes (six per genre) depicted violence at night-time and twelve showed action during day-time. These scenes featured either shootings or fist-fights which resulted in either fatal or non-fatal harmful consequences for victims. The latter features were balanced equally between night-time and day-time portrayals. All protagonists — aggressors and victims — were male.

The study was run in two 45-minute sessions, each of which contained one five-minute break. In consequence, respondents were not rating scenes for more than 20 minutes continuously. Day-time and night-time portrayals were randomly intermixed with the restriction that an equal number of each type should be presented per session. The scenes were rated one at a time along eight seven-point, unipolar scales as in the previous studies of this type. The panel was given about two minutes after each scene to complete their ratings of it. Again, although aware of the fact that this study was concerned with perceptions of televised violence, no indication was given to respondents of the precise nature of the comparisons being made.

Results

Table 10.1 shows the mean ratings for day-time and night-time portrayals averaged over programme genres. Wilcoxon matched-pairs, signed-ranks tests revealed significant differences between ratings of these two types of scenario on three scales: exciting, frightening, and personally disturbing. Night-time portrayals were rated as more

Table 10.1

Mean ratings of violent portrayals in day-time and night-time settings

	Violent	Realistic	Exciting	Humorous	Likely to disturb people in general	Suitable for children	Frightening	Personally disturbing
Day-time portrayals	5.1	2.7	3.5	1.6	2.9	2.7	2.8	2.1
Night-time portrayals	5.2	2.8	3.8	1.4	3.1	2.7	3.2	2.4
Significance $P<$	ns	ns	.05	ns	ns	ns	.05	.05

Table 10.2

Mean ratings of violent portrayals in day-time and night-time settings within two programme genres

	Violent	Realistic	Exciting	Humorous	Likely to disturb people in general	Suitable for children	Frightening	Personally disturbing
Westerns								
Day-time portrayals	5.4^a	3.3^a	3.6^a	1.5^a	3.1^a	2.6^a	2.8^a	2.5^{ab}
Night-time portrayals	5.2^{ab}	5.3^a	3.8^a	1.2	3.1^a	2.7^a	3.8	2.5^a
American crime drama								
Day-time portrayals	4.8^{ab}	2.3^b	3.3	1.6^a	2.7	2.7^a	2.7^a	1.8
Night-time portrayals	5.1^{ab}	2.5^b	3.7^a	1.5^a	3.1^a	2.6^a	2.8^a	2.2^b

Note: Scores with common superscripts are not significantly different at the $P < .05$ level

exciting, more frightening, and more personally disturbing than were day-time portrayals.

Table 10.2 presents mean ratings for each type of setting broken down further by programme genre. Wilcoxon tests computed on these data yielded significant differences on all scales. In Western settings, night-time portrayals were judged as more frightening and less humorous than day-time portrayals. In American crime—drama settings, night-time portrayals were perceived as more personally disturbing, more likely to disturb people in general, more violent and also as more exciting. These findings indicate that whether a violent portrayal occurs in daylight or after darkness can have an influence over the way it is perceived by the audience. Furthermore, this influence seems to be somewhat more important in fictional settings that more closely approximate everyday, contemporary reality.

Indoor and outdoor portrayals

In fictional drama programming on peak-time TV today, especially in the popular crime—detective genre whose adventures are generally set in urban locations, there may be frequent switches from indoor to outdoor settings. Whilst this aspect of how and where the action is situated is an important and ever-changing physical element of these shows, no research has been done to investigate its effect on viewers' perceptions of violent content. One of the main differences between indoor and outdoor sequences is that the former can often bring protagonists into much closer proximity than the latter, even when using guns for example to commit violence at a distance. When direct contact aggression is perpetrated, as in fist-fights, the violence may appear more threatening when performed indoors because there is less room to manoeuvre and a greater likelihood of injury to one or other of the protagonists through collisions with furniture, falling downstairs and so on.

To find out whether televised violence portrayed in indoor settings is perceived any differently on average than violence depicted out-doors, when other important features of content such as fictional genre, character-types involved, physical form, and consequences of violence are controlled, a study was conducted in which viewers' perceptions of violence sequences set in these two types of location were compared.

Experiment Twelve

Method

Twenty-four violent programme excerpts of 40 to 70 seconds' duration were selected according to the Gerbner (1972) definition and presented to respondents in Panel One who rated the clips one at a time along eight scales. These excerpts originated from three categories of programming: British crime—drama series (e.g. *The Professionals, The Sweeney, Target*); American crime—drama series (e.g. *Kojak, Mannix, Starsky and Hutch*); and science-fiction series (e.g. *Buck Rogers, Star Trek*). Twelve scenes (four per genre) depicted violence in indoor settings and twelve portrayed violence in outdoor settings. All portrayals involved male characters only who were engaged in either fist-fights or gun-fights and shootings. In all cases of shootings, a victim was non-fatally injured. The study was run in two 50-minute sessions on the same day.

Results

Table 10.3 shows the mean ratings for indoor and outdoor portrayals averaged over programme genres. Wilcoxon matched-pairs, signed-ranks tests yielded significant differences between ratings of violence set in each location on four scales. Amongst the excerpts used in this study, indoor portrayals were perceived as more violent, more realistic, less suitable for children and less exciting than were outdoor portrayals.

Table 10.4 presents the mean ratings for indoor and outdoor portrayals broken down further by type of programme. Wilcoxon tests revealed a number of significant differences between violence in these two locations within genres. First of all, in British crime—drama, indoor portrayals were rated as more violent, more likely to disturb people in general, more frightening, and more personally disturbing than outdoor portrayals. In American crime—drama, indoor portrayals were again rated as more violent and also as more exciting than outdoor portrayals, but also as *less* likely than the latter to disturb people in general. For science-fiction materials, ratings for indoor and outdoor portrayals followed the same pattern as those for American crime—drama materials, with the exception that location made no difference to how exciting a portrayal was perceived to be.

Discussion

Physical setting was found to have mild influences on perceptions of violent TV portrayals. When controlling for differences in features such as fictional setting, character-types, form, and observable harm, few differences emerged between ratings of day-time and night-time portrayals. Violence depicted after darkness was rated as somewhat more violent and more likely to disturb people in general than was that shown during the day. Differences between perceptions of indoor and outdoor portrayals were more numerous and more significant, how-

Table 10.3
Mean ratings of violent portrayals in indoor and outdoor locations

	Violent	Realistic	Exciting	Humorous	Likely to disturb people in general	Suitable for children	Frightening	Personally disturbing
Indoor portrayals	5.2	3.0	3.4	1.6	3.3	2.3	2.7	2.0
Outdoor portrayals	4.9	2.7	3.7	1.4	3.2	2.6	2.8	2.1
Significance $P <$	.05	.05	.05	ns	ns	.05	ns	ns

Table 10.4
Mean ratings of violent portrayals in indoor and outdoor locations within three programme genres

	Violent	Realistic	Exciting	Humorous	Likely to disturb people in general	Suitable for children	Frightening	Personally disturbing
British crime drama								
Indoor portrayals	5.7^a	3.0^a	4.0^a	1.5^{ab}	3.6^a	2.1^a	3.5^a	2.8^a
Outdoor portrayals	5.5^{ab}	3.0^a	3.8^{ab}	1.6^{ab}	3.2^{bc}	2.2^{ab}	3.2^b	2.5^b
American crime drama								
Indoor portrayals	5.4^b	3.5^b	3.7^b	1.4^a	3.4^{ab}	2.4^b	3.5^{ac}	2.7^{ab}
Outdoor portrayals	4.3^c	3.3^b	3.3^c	1.4^a	3.9	2.4^b	3.3^{abc}	2.5^b
Science-fiction								
Indoor portrayals	4.5^c	2.5^c	3.2^c	1.4^a	2.7	3.1^c	2.3^d	1.7^c
Outdoor portrayals	4.0	2.3^c	3.3^c	1.7^b	3.1^c	2.9^c	2.2^d	1.8^c

Note: Scores with common superscripts are not significantly different at the $P < .05$ level

ever, with indoor portrayals perceived in more serious terms than out-door portrayals on most scales.

There were differences in the salience of physical setting as a function of fictional context once again. Comparisons of indoor and outdoor portrayals for British and American crime—drama settings indicated that in the former indoor portrayals were rated as more violent and likely to disturb people generally, but in the latter outdoor sequences were seen as more serious on these scales. Clearly, not only can physical setting features of violent portrayals affect in a mild fashion how such episodes are perceived by individuals, but the relative salience of these features varies across different programme types. Hence it may be more pertinent to take physical setting into account when classifying the perceived seriousness of violence in some fictional settings than in others. It appears from these findings that the more realistic the setting for viewers, the more likely it is that physical setting attributes come into play to influence audience judgements about portrayals.

11 Demographic characteristics, amount of television viewing and perceptions of television violence

The four preceding chapters reported a series of experiments which indicated that individuals can make fine judgements about violent portrayals along a number of different attributes. But in addition to a measure of agreement *across* individuals concerning the relative perceived intensity or seriousness of different forms of televised violence, certain differences *between* individuals also need to be considered.

Four categories of measures of individual differences between panel members were obtained. These were: self-perceptions, social beliefs, attitudes towards aggression, and personality. In the four chapters following this one, evidence on relationships between individual differences and perceptions of TV violence will be examined for each of these measures in turn. In addition to these factors, however, information was obtained from each individual in Panel One concerning sex, age, socio-economic class, terminal age of education, and amount of TV viewing (in days per week). Attention will focus first in this chapter on relationships between these variables and the judgements individuals make about different kinds of violent TV portrayals.

Violence in different fictional settings

In Experiment One, perceptions of TV violence were investigated in connection with the types of fictional programme setting in which portrayals occurred. Violent scenes from five programme genres were judged by Panel One and results indicated that portrayals from contemporary dramatic settings (e.g. British or American crime–drama shows) were perceived as more violent and disturbing on average than were portrayals from more fantastic settings (e.g. cartoons or science-fiction shows).

To find out if demographic characteristics of individuals or their amount of TV viewing were related to variations in this pattern of perceptions, a series of eight canonical correlations were computed (one analysis per scale) in which demographic and TV viewing information were entered as independent variables and perceptual ratings on a particular scale for each category of violent portrayal were entered as dependent variables. These analyses were designed to indicate the extent to which each demographic factor or amount of TV viewing could independently account for variance in ratings of TV portrayals from different programme genres on each scale.

Table 11.1 shows the results of these analyses. Significant canonical variates were found for each rating scale. These variates are interpreted in terms of the strength of loading of each item on them. Items loading highest on a variate represent the defining characteristics of it (Levine, 1977). It can be seen from this table that amount of TV viewing loaded most highly and consistently with perceptions of violence across ratings scales. These findings indicate that lighter TV viewers among the panel members judged violent portrayals from British crime–drama as less violent and realistic, and as less humorous, whilst heavier viewers perceived portrayals from this type of programme as more violent and realistic, and as more exciting. Lighter viewers were also more likely to say that violent portrayals generally were not suitable for children. Perceived suitability for children was also related to sex of rater, with women saying more strongly than men that all violent portrayals shown in this study, with the exception of cartoon material, were not suitable for young viewers.

Violence perpetrated by law-enforcers and criminals

It was noted in earlier chapters that the conflict between the forces of law and order and criminal elements is a prominent theme in fictional storylines on TV. Experiment Three investigated this aspect of TV violence and compared individuals' perceptions of violence perpetrated by law-enforcers with their perceptions of violence perpetrated by criminals. Portrayals were taken from British and American crime–drama series. The initial comparisons indicated that panel members made significant perceptual discriminations between law-enforcer violence and criminal violence, but also that perceptions of these

Table 11.1

Canonical correlations of amount of TV viewing and demographics with perceptions of TV violence from different programme genres

	Violent	Realistic	Frightening	Personally disturbing	Likely to disturb people in general	Suitable for children	Exciting	Humorous
Demographics								
Sex	.10	.13	.24	-.40	-.24	.51	-.24	.30
Age	-.32	-.21	-.02	.03	-.06	-.06	-.30	-.02
Class	-.16	-.09	-.33	-.21	-.14	-.15	.22	.05
Education	.56	-.64	.67	-.79	-.42	-.58	.28	.59
Amount of TV viewing	-.42	-.45	.15	.06	-.47	-.68	.97	-.72
Programme genres								
British crime	-.63	-.68	.02	-.42	-.12	-.25	-.81	-.64
American crime	-.33	-.33	1.05	-.72	-.94	-.69	.21	-.37
Westerns	-.01	.00	.62	.35	.24	-.29	-.03	.16
Science-fiction	.32	.49	-.29	.49	.43	-.55	-.19	.21
Cartoons	-.15	.16	.18	-.35	.19	.01	.20	-.17
Multiple correlation coefficient r_C	.79	.67	.72	.65	.69	.55	.75	.71
Significance level $P <$	.001	.001	.001	.01	.001	.01	.001	.001

portrayals were influenced by their geographical location. In American settings criminal violence was perceived to be significantly more violent than was law-enforcer violence. In British settings, however, law-enforcer violence was judged as the more violent type of portrayal.

A series of canonical analyses was computed to find out if perceptions of these portrayals may be mediated in any way by demographic factors or TV viewing volume. Table 11.2 shows the results from the first of two sets of computations in which background information about panel members was related to their ratings of law-enforcer and criminal violence. The pattern of relationships that emerged here was quite clear. Amount of TV viewing, as stated by panel members themselves, was the highest loading variable with perceptions across all scales. These findings indicated that heavier viewers rated law-enforcer violence and criminal violence as more violent, realistic, and also as more suitable for children. Amount of viewing was related to discriminative ratings of law-enforcer and criminal violence on two scales however. Heavier viewers thought that law-enforcer violence was less likely to disturb people in general, whilst criminal violence was more likely to do so, and also that criminal violence only was more personally disturbing.

The interesting results on perceptions of law-enforcer violence and criminal violence emerged, however, when perceptions of these portrayals from British and American settings were separated out and compared. Further canonical correlations were therefore computed to relate demographic and TV viewing information to perceptions of the two types of portrayal from different programme types. As Table 11.3 shows, significant canonical variates emerged for seven scales out of eight. Amount of viewing was related fairly strongly on several scales to perceptual discriminations of portrayals from different types of programmes. Heavier viewing, together with higher terminal age of education, was associated with perceptions that British law-enforcer violence was more frightening, whereas American law-enforcer violence and criminal violence from both types of programme were less frightening. Heavier viewers with higher education also thought that British law-enforcer violence was more exciting, more humorous and more suitable for children. These individuals rated other portrayals as less exciting and less humorous, but rated British criminal violence as less suitable for children. Sex, age and socio-economic class were only marginally related to ratings throughout.

Violence perpetrated by males and females

Experiment Five investigated the impact of another character division

Table 11.2

Canonical correlations of amount of TV viewing and demographics with perceptions of TV violence perpetrated by law-enforcers and criminals

	Violent	Realistic	Frightening	Personally disturbing	Likely to disturb people in general	Suitable for children	Exciting	Humorous
Demographics								
Sex	-.08	-.07	.35	.56	.11	.45	-.19	-.33
Age	.36	.19	.43	.34	.26	.06	-.39	.10
Class	.13	.06	.13	.14	-.04	.26	.39	.16
Education	.53	.49	.27	.47	.04	.70	.27	.69
Amount of TV viewing	1.41	.58	.22	.16	.74	.47	.85	.50
Character-type								
Law-enforcer	.51	.88	.04	.07	-.48	.70	1.42	.52
Criminal	.50	.12	.96	.94	1.45	.31	.44	.53
Multiple correlation coefficient r_c	.74	.48	.57	.42	.61	.47	.71	.67
Significance level $P <$	.001	.01	.001	.05	.001	.001	.001	.001

Table 11.3
Canonical correlations of amount of TV viewing and demographics with perceptions of TV violence perpetrated by law-enforcers and criminals in British and American settings

	Violent	Realistic	Frightening	Likely to disturb people in general	Suitable for children	Exciting	Humorous
Demographics							
Sex	.02	.09	-.29	.16	-.46	.20	-.33
Age	.39	.01	-.42	.27	-.01	.41	.07
Class	.28	.01	-.07	-.02	.06	-.40	.10
Education	.50	-.46	-.21	.09	.68	-.28	.67
Amount of TV viewing	.26	-.76	-.35	.67	.63	-.84	.57
Character-type							
Law-enforcer violence							
British crime	.23	-.16	.53	-.44	.68	-.78	.30
American crime	.29	-1.19	-.41	.04	.23	.75	.33
Criminal violence							
British crime	.36	-.28	-.39	.58	-.45	.15	.16
American crime	.84	-.59	-.75	.88	.62	.36	.33
Multiple correlation coefficient r_c	.77	.51	.60	.63	.49	.72	.67
Significance level $P <$	.001	.05	.01	.001	.05	.001	.001

on perceptions of TV violence. Violence perpetrated by male characters against female characters and by female characters on male characters was selected from several genres of programming for perceptual comparison by panel members. At a general level, male violence was perceived as more violent and disturbing than female violence, but significant variations in ratings of these two kinds of portrayals occurred across programme types. Whilst male-perpetrated violence was judged in more serious terms than was female-perpetrated violence in British settings, these judgements were reversed for portrayals from American settings.

Ratings of these portrayals in general and more particularly from British and American crime—drama settings were related to demographic factors and TV viewing in two separate series of canonical correlations. The results of these analyses are presented in Tables 11.4 and 11.5.

Table 11.4 shows that significant canonical variates emerged from the first set of analyses for just four scales. These results indicate that lighter viewers from higher socio-economic classes and with better education perceived male-perpetrated violence against female victims as less violent, less likely to disturb people in general, less frightening, and less personally disturbing, and female-perpetrated violence against male victims as more violent, more frightening, and more likely to be generally disturbing to people.

Table 11.5 shows the results from the second set of analyses in which portrayals were divided according to programme of origin as well as sex of perpetrator. Significant canonical variates were found for seven scales here. Results indicate that heavier viewers who finished full-time education relatively early rated male violence in British crime—drama settings as more violent, more realistic, more frightening, more likely to disturb others, and less humorous. Such individuals rated female violence from American settings as less frightening and disturbing, but female violence set in British locations as more emotionally upsetting, though also as less violent.

Interestingly, sex of respondent was associated strongly with perceptions of these portrayals on only one scale. Women on the panel thought more than did men that male and female violence in British settings were personally disturbing, whilst female violence against male victims in American settings was less disturbing to them. This suggests that female viewers do not like any kind of violence between men and women irrespective of who is on the receiving end, particularly when set in a realistic and familiar context.

Table 11.4

Canonical correlations of amount of TV viewing and demographics with perceptions of TV violence perpetrated by males and females

	Violent	Frightening	Personally disturbing	Likely to disturb people in general
Demographics				
Sex	-.22	.06	.37	.33
Age	.89	.14	-.04	-.07
Class	-.38	-.56	-.44	-.67
Education	.41	.98	.63	.84
Amount of TV viewing	-.37	-.48	.01	-.99
Character-type				
Male perpetrator	-2.07	-2.19	-1.70	-1.20
Female perpetrator	1.99	2.25	1.07	1.78
Multiple correlation coefficient r_c	.54	.57	.41	.53
Significance level $P <$	.001	.001	.01	.001

Table 11.5

Canonical correlations of amount of TV viewing and demographics with perceptions of TV violence perpetrated by males and females in British and American settings

	Violent	Realistic	Frightening	Personally disturbing	Likely to disturb people in general	Exciting	Humorous
Demographics							
Sex	-.08	-.11	-.26	.52	.11	.00	.23
Age	.36	.07	-.34	-.02	.28	.29	-.34
Class	.20	.10	-.42	.41	.01	-.15	-.09
Education	-.56	-.46	.53	-.55	.13	-.19	-.56
Amount of TV viewing	.34	.68	-.00	.03	.68	-.97	-.50
Character-type							
Male violence							
British crime	.81	.98	-1.09	.80	.45	-.06	-.71
American crime	-.13	.18	1.05	.35	.11	-.07	.30
Female violence							
British crime	.28	.36	.58	.51	.60	-.95	-.48
American crime	.00	-.78	-1.63	-.87	-1.26	.07	.19
Multiple correlation coefficient r_C	.72	.58	.61	.57	.56	.70	.72
Significance level $P <$	.001	.01	.05	.01	.01	.001	.001

Different physical forms of violence

Experiment Seven examined the effect of physical forms of violence on panel members' ratings of TV portrayals. Four categories of physical violence were presented: shootings, fist-fights, explosions, and stabbings. These were taken equally from British crime–drama programmes and Westerns. Statistical comparisons of perceptual ratings on these scenes for the panel as a whole revealed that stabbings and shootings were judged as the most violent and most disturbing kinds of incidents. Stabbings were rated as most disturbing of all when featured in British crime–drama settings.

These perceptions were related to demographic factors and amount of TV viewing in two series of canonical correlations. The first series related background information about panel members to their perceptions of all scenes; the second series assessed background details with perceptions of excerpts from each programme genre in turn.

Table 11.6 presents the results from the first set of analyses. Significant canonical variates emerged for six scales, and on all these TV viewing was more strongly and consistently associated with perceptions of violent scenes than any demographic variables. These results indicate that heavier viewers, especially female ones, tended to rate all forms of violence as more violent, and shootings and stabbings as more frightening and personally disturbing. Heavier female viewers also judged shootings, stabbings and explosions as less humorous.

Table 11.7 shows the results of canonical correlations of demographics and TV viewing with perceptions of violent scenes from British crime–drama programmes. Significant canonical variates emerged here on all eight scales. Similar analyses with Western materials, however, yielded no significant results.

Interpreting the significant findings here indicates that female, older and heavier viewers amongst the panel tended to perceive shootings and stabbings in British crime–drama as more violent, more realistic, more frightening, more personally disturbing, and more likely to disturb people in general.

Harmful and harmless violence

Experiment Nine looked at the influence on panel members' ratings of TV portrayals of the degree of harm or injury caused to intended victims. Results indicated that harmful violence was perceived as significantly more violent and more disturbing than that which produced no observable harm to victims. This distinction was made irrespective of the kind of fictional setting in which the violence

Table 11.6

Canonical correlations of amount of TV viewing and demographics with perceptions of different physical forms of TV violence

	Violent	Frightening	Personally disturbing	Likely to disturb people in general	Exciting	Humorous
Demographics						
Sex	.15	.40	.74	.24	.40	1.11
Age	-.39	.48	.31	.33	.49	-.05
Class	-.13	.01	.05	.07	.08	.37
Education	.17	-.09	-.04	-.14	-.02	-.10
Amount of TV viewing	1.06	.34	.12	.60	-1.40	.58
Physical forms						
Shootings	1.25	.67	.10	-.60	.25	-.42
Fist-fights	1.10	-.50	-1.01	.20	-.80	.01
Explosions	.22	.31	-.24	-.36	-.92	-1.62
Stabbings	1.90	1.37	1.95	1.66	-.55	-1.77
Multiple correlation coefficient r_c	.52	.52	.51	.54	.54	.57
Significance level $P <$	.001	.05	.05	.01	.01	.05

165

Table 11.7

Canonical correlations of amount of TV viewing and demographics with perceptions of different physical forms of TV violence in British crime—drama

	Violent	Realistic	Frightening	Personally disturbing	Likely to disturb people in general	Suitable for children	Exciting	Humorous
Demographics								
Sex	-.47	.28	-.44	-.54	-.29	.48	-.18	-.34
Age	-1.35	-.68	-.22	-.57	-.43	-.02	-.43	.19
Class	.10	.18	-.16	.17	-.15	-.30	.16	.22
Education	.26	-.38	-.29	.27	-.18	-.78	.17	.71
Amount of TV viewing	-.50	-.45	-.28	-.13	-.31	-.36	1.10	.41
Physical forms								
British crime drama								
Shootings	-2.80	-.87	-.71	-.81	-.31	-1.46	-.19	.10
Fights	.39	1.59	.44	-.95	-.50	.16	1.16	.22
Explosions	-.28	-.20	.26	-1.03	.95	.57	.74	.39
Stabbings	-2.51	-1.38	-1.43	-2.01	-1.09	-.28	-.82	.39
Multiple correlation coefficient r_c	.53	.56	.72	.65	.63	.44	.80	.70
Significance level $P <$	.001	.001	.001	.001	.001	.05	.001	.001

occurred.

Ratings of harmful and harmless violence were related to demo-graphic and TV viewing information about panel members to see if those from different backgrounds or with different viewing experiences varied in their perceptions of these portrayals. Table 11.8 shows that canonical correlations computed on ratings averaged over all pro-gramme materials yielded significant variates on just three scales. These findings indicated that older, heavier viewers rated fatal and non-fatal harmful violence as more violent, more frightening, and more likely to disturb people in general. Harmless violence was perceived as less serious on all these scales. Further canonical correlations were com-puted in which harmful and harmless portrayals from different fictional settings were entered as separate dependent variables. How-ever, no significant or meaningful relationships emerged from these analyses.

Violence in different physical settings

Experiments Eleven and Twelve examined the significance of physical setting on panel members' perceptions of TV violence. The first of these two studies compared perceptions of day-time and night-time portrayals and the second looked at perceptions of indoor and outdoor portrayals. Initial statistical comparisons of ratings indicated that night-time portrayals were perceived as more disturbing than were day-time portrayals. Indoor portrayals were rated as more disturbing than outdoor portrayals.

Canonical correlations were computed on data from both these experiments to relate demographic and amount of viewing information about each respondent to perceptions of each category of violence. No significant canonical variates emerged from these analyses in Exper-iment Eleven, indicating no relationships between demographics or amount of TV viewing, and perceptual discriminations between day-time and night-time portrayals. But in Experiment Twelve, significant variates were found for all rating scales. Findings indicated that better educated and heavier viewing panel members perceived indoor violence as more realistic, more violent, somewhat more frightening, more likely to disturb others, less suitable for children and less humorous than did other panel members. Outdoor portrayals were perceived by the same individuals as less realistic and to some extent as less violent and disturbing than by panel members generally. Women rated indoor violence as more realistic, more likely to disturb people generally, and as less suitable for children than did men. Age and social class were relatively weakly related to perceptions of televised violence as a

Table 11.8

Canonical correlations of amount of viewing and demographics with perceptions of harmful and harmless TV violence

	Violent	Frightening	Likely to disturb people in general
Demographics			
Sex	.05	.41	.20
Age	.79	.66	-.33
Class	.04	-.07	.19
Education	.36	-.11	-.01
Amount of TV viewing	.10	.16	-.69
Consequences of violence			
Fatal	.49	.39	-.79
Non-fatal	1.15	1.85	-1.22
No observable harm	-.76	-.57	1.18
Multiple correlation coefficient r_c	.46	.46	.46
Significance level $P <$	.05	.05	.05

function of its portrayed physical location or setting (see Table 11.9).

Table 11.9

Canonical correlations of amount of TV viewing and demographics with perceptions of TV violence in indoor and outdoor locations

	Violent	Realistic	Fright-ening	Personally disturbing	Likely to disturb people in general	Suitable for children	Exciting	Humorous
Demographics								
Sex	.02	-.54	.39	.31	.58	-.58	-.20	-.47
Age	.31	.37	.27	.31	-.09	.24	-.32	-.07
Class	.01	.20	.22	-.03	.14	.09	.17	.01
Education	.46	.41	.14	-.00	.23	-.65	.29	-.69
Amount of TV viewing	.49	.63	.34	.57	.40	-.70	.98	-.65
Location								
Indoors	1.81	2.83	1.38	.52	1.56	1.46	1.02	.72
Outdoors	-.64	-2.08	-.40	.48	-.60	-.48	-.02	.31
Multiple correlation coefficient r_c	.70	.47	.53	.48	.55	.40	.60	.54
Significance level $P <$	.001	.01	.01	.01	.01	.05	.01	.01

12 Perceptions of self and perceptions of television violence

The previous chapter indicated that amount of TV viewing related with some consistency to respondents' perceptions of different kinds of televised violence. However, few sex differences, age differences, class differences or differences due to education emerged. In this chapter, the discussion turns in more detail to sex differences in judgements about televised violence. However, the focus will not be simply on actual gender as a mediator of panel members' ratings, but on the way an individual *perceives* his or her own sexual characteristics. An individual's self-perceptions in this respect may be just as important as actual sex as antecedents of his or her responses to different social stimuli.

Sex differences are known to be related to different psychological profiles and patterns of behaviours among individuals (see Lloyd and Archer, 1981 for a recent review of the literature). Differential social-isation of girls and boys with regard specifically to the use of physic-ally assertive or coercive behaviours, which results in aggressiveness being regarded as more acceptable among boys than among girls, means that as adults men may hold significantly different attitudes towards violence and aggression than women do, and may also be more disposed than the latter to behave violently themselves. This pattern of social-isation may also mean that men and women react differently to the violence of others and perhaps more specifically to portrayals of violence in fictional contexts on TV.

Whilst actual gender may well be an important mediator of viewers'

171

perceptions of TV violence, it has become increasingly recognised in recent years that sex-appropriate attitudes and behaviours are not so rigidly assigned to each biological sex, and that individuals may often be characterised, and may indeed regard themselves, in terms of both customarily masculine and customarily feminine traits (Bem, 1974; Spence and Helmreich, 1978). The concept of androgyny was introduced into psychological research in recognition of the fact that masculine and feminine traits may co-exist in the same person (or may be perceived to do so either by the individual himself/herself or by others), with those individuals who exhibit (or who perceive to exhibit) a relatively high degree of both being labelled as 'androgynous'.

Little is known as yet to what extent such self-perceptions as well as actual gender are related to (or mediate) reactions to violent TV portrayals. To examine this issue, all respondents in Panel One who took part in studies in which programme excerpts were rated one at a time, were asked to fill out items from Bem's Sex-Role Inventory. This instrument enabled scores to be computed for each panel member on self-endorsed masculinity, femininity, and androgyny (after Bem, 1974).

This instrument consisted of a list of 30 adjectives, of which ten were descriptions of features customarily regarded as masculine, ten descriptions of features customarily regarded as feminine and ten neutral items. Individuals who endorsed a high number of masculine items as characteristic of themselves and a low number of feminine items were labelled *masculine* types. Conversely those high in their endorsement of feminine items were described as *feminine* types. Individuals who perceived large numbers of both kinds of attributes as descriptive of their own character were categorised as *androgynous*. The androgyny score was computed by taking the difference between a person's masculinity and femininity scores and multiplying that difference by 2.322 (after Bem, 1974). According to Bem (1974; Bem and Lenney, 1976), individuals who perceive themselves in androgynous terms are more open-minded and psychologically healthier than more rigidly sex-typed individuals. To see whether variations in these particular self-perceptions mediated differential judgements of televised violence, scores on the more sex-role factors were related to ratings of violent portrayals in each study in which Panel One took part.

Violence in different fictional settings

In Experiment One data were obtained on perceptions of violent portrayals from five different fictional programme settings. To recap briefly, results indicated that portrayals from contemporary dramatic settings were judged to be more violent and disturbing than were portrayals from fantastic, futuristic or animated settings. But to what extent did individuals on Panel One vary in their ratings of violent episodes from these fictional contexts, and in particular, to what extent did their perceptions vary according to self-perceived masculinity and femininity?

To attempt to answer this question, ratings of programme materials were related to panel members' scores on the masculinity, femininity, and androgyny dimensions of the Bem Sex-Role Inventory. Canonical correlations were computed for each rating scale in which demographic factors were entered with sex-role perception scores as independent variables, and perceptions of each category of televised violence were entered as dependent variables. These analyses were designed to indicate the extent to which panel members' self-perceptions were related to (and perhaps could be said to mediate) their perceptions of TV violence in different fictional settings, in the presence of multiple simultaneous statistical controls for the possible effects of demographic factors.

Table 12.1 summarises the results of these canonical correlations and shows that significant canonical variates emerged on seven scales. These variates were interpreted in terms of the loadings of the original variables on them.

Higher masculinity and lower femininity scores were associated with perceptions of violence from all genres, but most of all from American crime—drama programmes, as more suitable for children. Higher masculinity scores also perceived violent portrayals from most genres as less violent than did lower masculinity scores. Individuals who were lower on masculinity and androgyny and higher on femininity perceived violence in British and American crime—drama settings as less realistic.

Violence perpetrated by law-enforcers and criminals

A prominent theme in much TV drama is conflict between the forces of justice and evil or criminal elements. Experiment Three compared viewers' ratings of violent portrayals taken from British and American crime—detective series in which violence was perpetrated either by law-enforcers or law-breakers. In the original comparisons of panel members' perceptions of these portrayals, criminal violence was rated as more violent than law-enforcer violence in American settings only. In British settings, law-enforcer violence was perceived as the more violent. Were differential perceptions of self related to further differences in the way these portrayals were judged? Ratings of these two

Table 12.1
Canonical correlations of self-perceptions and demographics with perceptions of violent TV portrayals from five programme genres

	Violent	Realistic	Exciting	Likely to disturb people in general	Suitable for children	Frightening	Personally disturbing
Demographics							
Sex	.14	-.13	-.23	-.18	-.49	-.25	-.21
Age	-.42	.25	.11	-.17	.25	-.01	.12
Class	-.25	.20	.54	-.29	.34	-.40	-.24
Education	-.59	.62	.43	-.42	.70	-.65	-.64
Self-perceptions							
Masculinity	-.17	-.54	.05	-.26	.90	.11	.51
Femininity	.18	1.27	-.69	-.29	-.63	-.44	-.11
Androgyny	-.00	-.58	-.41	.24	.17	.38	.39
Programme genre							
British crime	-.67	.54	.30	-.31	.32	-.09	-.23
American crime	-.30	.49	.64	-.74	.63	-.98	-.67
Westerns	.02	-.14	-.01	.17	.32	-.53	-.17
Science-fiction	.29	-.39	-.27	.53	.35	-.43	-.91
Cartoons	-.16	-.04	-.02	-.21	.23	-.18	-.09
Multiple correlation coefficient r_c	.79	.72	.72	.72	.57	.76	.72
Significance level $P<$	.001	.01	.01	.001	.05	.001	.001

174

kinds of televised violence were related to viewers' scores on the Bem Sex-Role Inventory to see whether individuals who perceived themselves in highly masculine, feminine or androgynous terms varied extensively in their perceptions of legal or criminal violence.

Canonical correlations yielded significant canonical variates on all eight rating scales. These results are summarised in Table 12.2. High femininity scorers perceived both kinds of violence, but especially that perpetrated by criminals, as more violent. Higher femininity scorers also rated criminal violence as more likely to disturb people in general. Stronger femininity together with weaker masculinity were associated with perceptions of both kinds of portrayal as more realistic, more frightening and more personally disturbing.

High masculinity and low femininity scorers rated law-enforcer violence as more suitable for children, whilst high femininity scorers rated law-enforcer violence as more exciting and criminal violence as less exciting. Androgyny was strongly related to perceptions of televised violence on two scales only. Lower androgyny scorers perceived both law-enforcer and criminal violence as less realistic and less personally disturbing.

To find out if self-perceived masculinity or femininity were related in different ways to law-enforcer violence and criminal violence from different geographical locations, further canonical correlations were computed in which portrayals from British crime—drama and American crime—drama were treated as separate dependent variables. Significant canonical variates emerged on every evaluative scale and these results are summarised in Table 12.3.

Self-perceptions were related most strongly to how realistic, frightening, personally disturbing and suitable for children different portrayals were perceived to be. Lower masculinity coupled with higher femininity were associated with perceptions of law-enforcer violence in British crime—drama contexts as being more realistic, more frightening, more personally disturbing, and as less suitable for children. Higher femininity alone was also related to perceptions of criminal violence in British crime—drama as more personally disturbing and more likely to disturb people in general. Hence discrimination between portrayals from programmes set in different locations was related in a number of ways to individuals perceptions of themselves. Among those for whom designated feminine traits featured prominently in their self-estimations, violent portrayals in geographically proximal locations were judged to be particularly disturbing.

Violence perpetrated by males and females

Experiment Five examined viewers' judgements of televised violence

Table 12.2

Canonical correlations of self-perceptions and demographics with perceptions of TV violence perpetrated by law-enforcers and criminals

	Violent	Realistic	Exciting	Humorous	Likely to disturb people in general	Suitable for children	Frightening	Personally disturbing
Demographics								
Sex	-.16	-.08	-.20	-.38	.13	-.53	.29	.39
Age	.41	.22	-.15	.22	.44	.12	.46	.01
Class	.25	.28	.71	.29	.17	.40	.19	.32
Education	.52	.41	.42	.73	.14	.59	.26	.35
Self-perceptions								
Masculinity	-.11	-.94	-.06	.07	-.27	1.14	-.79	-1.08
Femininity	.51	1.89	.70	-.31	.92	-.78	1.23	1.89
Androgyny	.03	-.79	-.30	.04	-.28	.30	-.41	-.91
Character-type								
Law-enforcer	.30	.68	1.60	.62	.01	1.08	.27	.75
Criminal	.71	.33	-.64	.43	.99	-.08	1.24	1.67
Multiple correlation coefficient r_c	.78	.59	.65	.67	.60	.56	.61	.50
Significance level $P <$	.001	.001	.001	.001	.01	.001	.001	.01

Table 12.3

Canonical correlations of self-perceptions and demographics with perceptions of TV violence perpetrated by law-enforcers and criminals as a function of fictional setting

	Violent	Realistic	Frightening	Personally disturbing	Likely to disturb people in general	Suitable for children	Exciting	Humorous
Demographics								
Sex	-.09	.07	-.23	-.28	.17	-.54	.26	.37
Age	.37	-.15	-.49	.10	.42	.12	.21	-.22
Class	.36	-.27	-.17	-.30	.16	.38	-.65	-.30
Education	.46	-.41	-.24	-.27	.16	.60	-.39	-.71
Self-perceptions								
Masculinity	-.16	-.92	-.93	-1.79	.03	1.07	.07	-.10
Femininity	.47	1.96	1.46	2.96	.50	-.68	-.83	-.30
Androgyny	.09	.90	.49	1.42	-.08	.27	.25	-.05
Scenes								
Law enforcer								
British crime	-.21	.90	.77	1.04	.23	.66	-.49	-.32
American crime	.35	-.97	-.29	-.03	.28	.50	-1.11	-.41
Criminal								
British crime	-.17	.20	.73	1.30	.28	.16	.03	-.23
American crime	1.03	.21	-.74	-.54	.72	.05	.59	-.16
Multiple correlation coefficient r_c	.82	.63	.65	.54	.63	.56	.68	.67
Significance level $P <$	.001	.05	.01	.01	.01	.01	.001	.001

again in relation to the types of characters who were depicted as the perpetrators of violent conduct. On this occasion, characters were differentiated not according to their good or evil qualities, but according to their sex. Comparisons of perceptions of these portrayals initially indicated that male-perpetrated violence was rated in more serious terms than was female-perpetrated violence in British settings, but that in American settings, the latter was perceived to be the more serious.

Viewers' self-perceived masculinity, femininity and androgyny were expected to be particularly relevant to their perceptions of televised violence perpetrated on or by male and female characters. To find out if these perceptions of self were related to viewers' perceptions of violent portrayals distinguishable in terms of differential involvement of the sexes, respondents' Bem Sex-Role Inventory scores were entered along with their ratings of male- and female-perpetrated TV violence into a series of canonical correlations. The results of these analyses are summarised in Table 12.4 which indicates that self-perceptions were related to judgements about male and female televised violence on only four rating scales. Biological sex failed to emerge even on these scales as a prime indicator of viewers' perceptions.

Results indicated that younger people from higher social classes with weak masculinity and androgyny self-perceptions rated male-perpetrated violence on female victims as less violent and female-perpetrated violence on male victims as more violent.

The psychological dimensions of masculinity and femininity were related more strongly to emotional reactions of panel members to violent excerpts. Low femininity with low androgyny was associated with perceptions of male violence on female victims as less frightening and female attacks on male victims as more frightening. Similarly, low masculinity coupled with high femininity was related to perceptions of male violence as more personally disturbing and more likely to disturb people in general. Actual gender of panel members was related to differential perceptions of male and female violence on the latter two scales too. Findings indicated that women perceived male violence on female victims as more personally disturbing and more likely to disturb others and female violence on male victims as less disturbing than did men.

Once again, self-perceptions were related independently to portrayals involving different character-perpetrators of violence from different geographical locations. Table 12.5 shows that further canonical correlations yielded significant variates on seven scales out of eight. Self-perceptions were shown to be related best to differential perceptions of male and female violence according to setting on three scales: realistic, personally disturbing and likely to disturb others.

Table 12.4

Canonical correlations of self-perceptions and demographics with perceptions of televised violence perpetrated by males and females

	Violent	Likely to disturb people in general	Frightening	Personally disturbing
Demographics				
Sex	-.29	.47	.10	.33
Age	-.85	.13	.27	-.08
Class	-.45	-.41	-.39	.38
Education	-.37	-.76	-.86	.48
Sex-role perceptions				
Masculinity	-.24	-.75	.32	-1.10
Femininity	.19	1.60	-.69	1.34
Androgyny	.25	-.98	-.56	-.17
Character-type				
Male perpetrator	-1.79	1.54	2.26	1.56
Female perpetrator	2.10	-1.87	2.16	-.80
Multiple correlation coefficient r_c	.55	.49	.58	.51
Significance level $P <$	.001	.001	.001	.01

Table 12.5

Canonical correlations of self-perceptions and demographics with perceptions of TV violence perpetrated by males and females as a function of fictional setting

	Violent	Realistic	Frightening	Personally disturbing	Likely to disturb people in general	Exciting	Humorous
Demographics							
Sex	-.20	-.12	.07	.41	-.02	-.04	.16
Age	.44	.21	.17	-.10	.34	.04	-.58
Class	.26	.32	.40	.39	.27	.41	-.25
Education	.52	.41	.51	.50	.22	.38	-.71
Self-perceptions							
Masculinity	.17	-.72	.08	-.89	.04	.11	-.16
Femininity	.14	1.59	-.05	1.09	.71	.55	.04
Androgyny	.18	-.58	.41	-.17	-.28	-.08	.05
Scenes							
Male							
British crime	.88	.81	1.28	.75	.70	.21	-.64
American crime	-.28	.30	.04	.64	-.39	.27	.38
Female							
British crime	.21	.40	-.17	.28	.49	.81	-.55
American crime	.12	-.63	-.34	-.84	.14	-.27	.18
Multiple correlation coefficient r_c	.77	.64	.67	.63	.61	.63	.68
Significance level $P <$	.001	.01	.002	.01	.001	.001	.002

Lower masculinity together with higher femininity was associated with perceptions of male violence in British crime—drama settings as being more realistic and personally disturbing, and of female violence in American crime—drama settings as being less realistic and personally disturbing. Higher femininity alone was associated with the judgement that male violence against females in British locations was more likely to disturb people in general. Thus, individuals who perceived themselves in terms mainly of feminine descriptors were more likely to rate male attacks on female victims in familiar geographical settings as especially realistic and disturbing, and such individuals at the same time were much less concerned about female violence against males depicted in geographically remote settings. It was interesting to note throughout that demographic factors were relatively weakly associated with perceptions of these portrayals in the presence of self-perception indicators. Perhaps most surprising was the absence of many relationships between gender of respondents and their ratings of male and female violence.

Different physical forms of televised violence

Violence occurs in numerous physical forms and content analyses of TV output have indicated that certain forms are depicted more often than others in fictional programming. Experiment Seven examined individuals' perceptions of a number of different categories of physical violence and found that some were judged to be more violent and upsetting than others. In particular violent incidents that featured stabbings or shootings were found by panel members to be more disturbing than either explosions or fist-fights. These results of course were from data averaged across the panel for each type of violent scene. But there may also be considerable variations between individuals in their perceptions of different forms of physical violence. Whilst for some individuals, a particular violent sequence may be dismissed as not very violent at all, for others the same sequence may be profoundly disturbing. Such differences may be indicated by the way individuals describe themselves in masculine or feminine terms. To examine this point, panel members scores on the Bem Sex-Role Inventory were related to their ratings of the four physical forms of violence studied in Experiment Seven.

Table 12.6 summarises the results of eight canonical correlations computed on these data. Significant canonical variates emerged on four scales. Results indicated that higher femininity and lower masculinity scorers perceived fights, explosions and stabbings as more violent, more likely to disturb others and as more frightening and

Table 12.6

Canonical correlations of self-perceptions and demographics with perceptions of four physical forms of televised violence

	Violence	Likely to disturb people in general	Frightening	Personally disturbing
Demographics				
Sex	-.42	.01	.18	-.67
Age	.72	-.42	.37	-.20
Class	-.04	-.38	.20	-.06
Education	.43	.09	.22	-.02
Self-perceptions				
Masculinity	-.32	.25	-1.26	.98
Femininity	.71	-.30	1.63	-1.54
Androgyny	.05	-.11	-.24	.62
Physical form				
Shootings	-.10	1.04	-1.75	.23
Fights	1.10	-.90	.37	-.86
Explosions	.63	-.23	.93	.09
Stabbings	.70	-1.21	1.13	-1.77
Multiple correlation				
coefficient r_c	.52	.57	.61	.56
Significance level $P <$	.01	.01	.01	.01

personally disturbing than did other viewers. These individuals in the meantime rated shootings in less serious terms on all these scales. Androgyny was strongly related to viewers' perceptions on only one scale: higher androgyny scorers perceived fights and stabbings as less personally disturbing.

Separate canonical correlations were computed to relate self-perceptions to perceptions of different kinds of physical violence from different programme genres. Table 12.7 summarises the results of these analyses with British crime—drama materials and indicates that significant canonical variates emerged for seven scales. From a parallel set of analyses with Western materials, however, no significant relationships between self-perceptions and ratings of different types of portrayals were found. What did the significant findings for ratings of British crime—drama portrayals show?

Lower masculinity coupled with higher femininity was associated with perceptions of shootings and stabbings as more violent, more realistic, more personally disturbing, more likely to disturb other people, and as less suitable for children. These individuals also rated these portrayals as less exciting. These relationships indicate that portrayals of physical violence, rated by panel members in general as the more violent and disturbing, were rated as even more serious by individuals who perceived themselves predominantly in feminine terms.

Harmful and harmless TV violence

Another important characteristic of violence is the degree of pain and suffering caused to victims. Large numbers of leading characters in TV fiction become involved in violence, and many of these do not escape unscathed. Some characters live to fight again another day; others do not. Experiment Nine compared viewers' judgements of fatal, non-fatal and harmless televised violence and indicated that the degree of harm suffered by those characters who are preyed upon significantly affected respondents' perceptions of violent scenarios. In general, violence resulting in fatal or non-fatal harm to victims was perceived to be more violent and disturbing than was violence resulting in no observable harm.

Some viewers, of course, may be more sensitive than others to the degree of harm inflicted on victims of violence on TV. This differential sensitivity may be indicated by self-perceptions of masculinity and femininity. Thus, respondents' perceptions of programmes excerpts depicting violence that resulted in observable harm or no harm to victims were related to their Bem Sex-Role Inventory scores to find out whether or not this was the case.

Table 12.7

Canonical correlations of self-perceptions and demographics with perceptions of different physical forms of televised violence in British crime drama

	Violent	Realistic	Personally disturbing	Likely to disturb people in general	Suitable for children	Exciting	Humorous
Demographics							
Sex	-.74	-.33	.53	.21	-.63	.07	-.34
Age	1.00	.67	.22	.50	.08	.05	.42
Class	-.11	.03	.17	.22	.19	-.59	.37
Education	.03	.33	.20	.14	.65	-.41	.84
Self-perceptions							
Masculinity	-.57	-.90	-.44	.87	1.88	1.12	-.30
Femininity	.45	1.71	.75	-.80	-1.94	-2.09	.26
Androgyny	.19	-.68	-.14	.43	.97	1.01	.08
Scenes							
British crime							
Shootings	2.48	.74	.25	-.21	2.17	.29	.00
Fist-fights	.18	-1.50	-.55	.85	-1.10	-1.25	-.05
Explosions	.77	.44	.45	-1.29	-.97	-.93	.48
Stabbings	3.18	1.23	1.66	-1.33	.87	1.06	.62
Multiple correlation coefficient r_c	.77	.63	.67	.66	.61	.67	.69
Significance level $P <$	.001	.001	.001	.001	.01	.001	.001

184

Table 12.8 shows that significant canonical variates emerged for five scales. Findings indicated that higher masculinity and lower femininity amongst viewers were associated with perceptions of harmful violence (fatal and non-fatal) as being less realistic, less likely to disturb people in general, less frightening and less personally disturbing. Androgyny was strongly related only to perceptions of how violent these different kinds of violence were. Lower androgyny scores tended to perceive all kinds of violence depicted in this series of scores as more violent than did higher androgyny scores.

Relationships between self-perceptions and perceptions of harmful and harmless portrayals from different programme genres were assessed too. Table 12.9 summarises the results of further canonical correlations which yielded significant canonical variates on seven scales.

Self-perceptions were best related to perceptions of TV violence on four scales: realistic, frightening, personally disturbing, and likely to disturb people in general. Results indicated that lower femininity and higher androgyny were associated with perceptions of most types of portrayal here, but especially with those in science-fiction settings, as being more realistic. Individuals with the latter self-estimates also perceived most of these portrayals as less frightening and disturbing to themselves, but felt that fatal violence in American crime—drama settings would be likely to disturb others. More differentiated or androgynous perceptions of self were therefore related to less concern about personal impact of harmful portrayals, and greater concern about their possible impact on other people.

Violence in different physical settings

Two aspects of physical setting were considered in this research. Experiment Eleven compared respondents' perceptions of violence that were portrayed during the day or at night, and Experiment Twelve looked at perceptions of violence perpetrated either indoors or outdoors. Findings indicated a weak tendency for panel members to rate night-time portrayals as more disturbing than day-time portrayals, and a somewhat stronger tendency for them to perceive indoor portrayals as more violent than outdoor portrayals.

Masculinity, femininity and androgyny scores for viewers were related to their perceptions of violent portrayals in both of these experiments as two series of canonical correlations. No significant canonical variates emerged from eight separate analyses on the data from Experiment Eleven. Table 12.10 shows, however, that significant canonical variates emerged for all eight evaluative scales in Experiment Twelve. Masculinity and femininity related well to perceptions of

Table 12.8

Canonical correlations of self-perceptions and demographics with perceptions of harmful and harmless TV violence

	Violent	Realistic	Likely to disturb people in general	Frightening	Personally disturbing
Demographics					
Sex	.11	-.09	.14	.34	-.31
Age	-.67	-.38	.67	.63	-.33
Class	-.01	-.30	.02	-.07	.04
Education	-.12	.18	.01	-.19	.02
Self-perceptions					
Masculinity	-.02	1.24	-.36	-.83	2.07
Femininity	.08	-1.68	.97	1.19	-2.24
Androgyny	-.64	.17	-.12	-.30	.36
Degree of harm					
Fatal	.56	1.50	.79	.74	-2.24
Non-fatal injury	1.90	.32	.95	1.51	-1.53
No observable harm	.50	-2.53	-.84	-.12	1.39
Multiple correlation coefficient r_c	.57	.44	.48	.49	.54
Significance level $P <$	.01	.05	.01	.02	.02

Table 12.9

Canonical correlations of self-perceptions and demographics with perceptions of harmful and harmless TV violence as a function of fictional setting

	Violent	Realistic	Frightening	Personally disturbing	Likely to disturb people in general	Exciting	Humorous
Demographics							
Sex	-.16	.02	-.30	-.26	.22	-.20	.39
Age	.42	-.30	-.45	.10	.08	.09	-.31
Class	.14	-.14	-.11	-.19	.20	.54	-.12
Education	.55	-.34	-.30	-.61	.42	.38	-.71
Self-perceptions							
Masculinity	-.01	.81	.12	-.03	.22	.28	.01
Femininity	.47	-1.82	-.69	-.55	-.51	.43	-.64
Androgyny	-.01	.84	.57	.58	.65	-.26	.35
Scenes							
Fatal							
American crime	1.05	.17	.03	-.33	1.09	.57	.58
Science-fiction	-.16	1.46	-.42	.09	.29	-.79	.56
Non-fatal injury							
American crime	.27	.49	-.89	-.32	-.09	.24	-.07
Science-fiction	-.01	.81	-1.76	-.88	-.81	.90	-.31
Harmless							
American crime	-.37	.35	-.00	-.28	-.19	-.07	-.38
Science-fiction	.10	.97	-1.74	-1.53	.00	-.36	-.11
Multiple correlation coefficient r_c	.79	.77	.67	.77	.67	.70	.73
Significance level $P <$	.001	.001	.01	.001	.001	.05	.01

Table 12.10

Canonical correlations of self-perceptions and demographics with perceptions of TV violence in indoor and outdoor locations

	Violent	Realistic	Exciting	Humorous	Likely to disturb people in general	Suitable for children	Frightening	Personally disturbing
Demographics								
Sex	-.05	-.37	-.23	-.49	.26	-.65	.42	.54
Age	.42	.49	.00	.15	.45	-.04	.39	-.00
Class	.16	.41	.49	.21	.14	.23	.34	.25
Education	.50	.47	.44	.81	.06	.61	.20	.26
Self-perceptions								
Masculinity	-.19	-1.15	-.24	-.44	-.12	.90	-.55	-.40
Femininity	.63	1.88	.53	.75	.60	-.32	.89	.76
Androgyny	-.07	-.72	-.29	-.07	.10	.15	-.38	.12
Location								
Indoors	1.48	2.34	1.35	-.71	.81	1.08	1.25	1.29
Outdoors	-.50	-1.48	-.38	-.31	.19	-.09	-.26	-.31
Multiple correlation coefficient r_c	.71	.49	.56	.52	.56	.46	.53	.50
Significance level $P <$	.001	.001	.01	.01	.01	.05	.01	.05

indoor and outdoor portrayals throughout all analyses, whilst androgyny was strongly related to differential perceptions of these two kinds of portrayal on only one scale.

Higher femininity and lower masculinity were associated with perceptions of indoor portrayals as more violent and realistic, more frightening and personally disturbing, more likely to disturb people in general, and as less humorous and less suitable for children. The same individuals rated outdoor portrayals as less violent and realistic than did other viewers. Viewers with low androgyny scores concurred with the above individuals on the relative perceived realism of indoor and outdoor portrayals. Further canonical analyses were computed to relate self-perceptions to perceptions of indoor and outdoor portrayals from different programme genres. These failed to reveal any strong relationships and therefore will not be reported.

13 Social beliefs and perceptions of television violence

In continuing the investigation of factors which distinguish viewers and mediate the judgements they make about different kinds of TV violence, this chapter focuses on individual differences, not in the way viewers perceive themselves, but in the way they perceive their social environment. Previous research, mainly conducted in the United States, has indicated relationships between the extent to which people watch TV and particular patterns of beliefs about the real world. Some writers have suggested that TV with its typically exaggerated representation of certain aspects of society at the expense of others, can cultivate distorted beliefs about the real world, especially amongst people who consume a great deal of its content and have no alternative sources of information about the people, places and events it portrays.

Four social belief scales were employed in the current research which each measured factors that have featured previously in research on the social influence of TV. These factors are: *fear of victimisation, anomia, locus of control,* and *belief in a just world.*

Fear of victimisation indicated respondents' perceptions of personal risk from criminal attack which American researchers have shown to be related to TV viewing (e.g. Gerbner *et al*, 1977, 1978, 1979). British research has not replicated these findings (Gunter and Wober, 1983; Wober, 1978; Wober and Gunter, 1982).

191

Anomia indicated respondents' feelings of powerlessness and loneliness in an indifferent, impersonal world where few people can be trusted. Again American research has reported relationships between these feelings and the amount of TV watching (Gerbner *et al*, 1977, 1978), but no such association has been observed among British samples (Wober and Gunter, 1982).

Locus of control is a measure of respondents' belief that they have personal control over events in their lives versus the belief that events are determined by luck, fate or chance. Wober and Gunter (1982) reported that external controllers usually watched more TV than internal controllers.

Belief in a just world indicated how much individuals thought that good people tend to be rewarded and bad people punished. Gunter and Wober (1983) found that respondents who had strong just world beliefs tended also to be heavier viewers of action—adventure programmes, where the good guys usually bring the bad to justice.

Survey research has indicated that certain perceptions or beliefs that people hold about the world around them are related to the amount and type of TV viewing they do. Do these social or societal beliefs mediate their judgements of specific kinds of TV content however? This is a new area for investigation and one in which a few preliminary steps are taken in the current research. This chapter will report results from seven of the experiments discussed earlier in which respondents' ratings of programme excerpts depicting different kinds of violence were related to their scores of the four social belief factors reviewed above.

Violence in different fictional settings

Experiment One examined viewers' perceptions of similar forms of violence in different fictional settings and found that as the setting of a violent incident approached real life the more serious that kind of incident was judged to be. Ratings of the violent excerpts used in this study were related to respondents' social beliefs on four dimensions: personal fear of victimisation, anomia, belief in a just world and internal—external locus of control. Ratings of programme materials on each scale in turn were entered as dependent variables and demographic information on amount of TV viewing and the four social belief factors were entered as independent variables, into a series of eight canonical correlations. These analyses were designed to indicate the extent to which each social belief factor might account for variations in viewers' judgements of violent portrayals from different categories of programmes with the effects of either potentially relevant demographics and viewing variables statistically controlled.

The results of these analyses are summarised in Table 13.1. Significant canonical variates emerged on seven scales. Internal—external locus of control was most powerfully and consistently related to viewers' judgements of the four social belief dimensions. Results indicated that external controllers (i.e. those individuals who tend to believe that events in life are determined by external forces such as fate, luck or chance, rather than by self-determination) rated violent portrayals in the fictional settings of British and American crime—drama programmes as more realistic and also as more violent, more frightening, more personally disturbing, and to some slight extent as less suitable for children.

Such individuals also tended to rate violence in Western and science-fiction settings as less realistic, less frightening and disturbing and as more suitable for children. More fearful and alienated respondents tended to perceive violence in all settings, except for cartoons, as more frightening, personally disturbing and likely to disturb other people, and as less suitable for children. Additionally, respondents who believed that the world is really a just place were less concerned about the suitability of these violent scenes for children.

Violence perpetrated by law-enforcers and criminals

The conflict between agencies of criminal activity and law-enforcement was the theme of excerpts used in Experiment Three. Respondents' perceptions of violence perpetrated by police or detectives and by criminals were compared. How seriously violent or disturbing one type of portrayal was rated relative to the other interacted with the setting in which it occurred. In British crime—drama settings, law-enforcer violence was perceived as the more violent, whilst in American crime—drama settings, more expectedly perhaps, criminal violence was judged as more violent and upsetting. It is not unlikely, however, that the beliefs people hold about the degree of justice there is in the real world, or about their own personal risk of falling victim to crime, together perhaps with the extent to which they perceive themselves to be powerless to do anything about their fate, may function as mediators of their appraisals of legally and criminally perpetrated violence shown on TV. To test this, further canonical correlations were therefore computed in which respondents' scores on the four dimensions of social belief were

193

Table 13.1

Canonical correlations of social beliefs and demographics with perceptions of TV violence from different programme genres

	Violent	Realistic	Frightening	Personally disturbing	Likely to disturb people in general	Suitable for children	Humorous
Demographics							
Sex	.09	-.13	.17	.30	.16	.41	-.30
Age	-.19	-.21	.13	-.36	-.10	-.18	-.31
Class	-.05	-.16	.24	.06	.02	-.39	-.16
Education	-.24	-.29	.61	.56	.13	-.77	.15
Social beliefs							
Fear	-.08	.11	-.44	-.43	-.46	-.41	.46
Anomia	-.05	.10	.17	-.74	.13	-.52	.20
Just world	-.08	.27	.13	.13	-.10	.57	.02
Locus of control	-.45	-.39	-.33	-.78	.09	-.21	-.16
Programme genres							
British crime	-.88	-.47	-.24	-.33	.40	.20	.71
American crime	-.11	-.56	-.86	-.81	.69	.57	.32
Westerns	.04	-.24	-.61	-.46	-.20	.92	.26
Science-fiction	.17	-.44	-.36	-.50	-.38	.53	.10
Cartoons	-.14	.10	.25	.50	.24	.47	.19
Multiple correlation coefficient r_C	.84	.78	.76	.72	.73	.63	.79
Significance level $P <$	.001	.001	.001	.02	.001	.01	.01

related to their perceptions of law-enforcer and criminal violence from British and American crime—detective series.

The results presented in Table 13.2 show that respondents whose beliefs indicated external locus of control, or the tendency to believe in life events determined by fate, perceived law-enforcer *and* criminal violence as more violent than did internal controllers, but rated criminal violence as the more frightening and disturbing. External controllers also perceived law-enforcer violence as more suitable for children, and criminal violence as less suitable than did the average respondent. More fearful respondents rated criminal violence as more frightening and disturbing and as less suitable for children, but thought that excerpts depicting law-enforcer violence were more realistic than those depicting criminal violence.

Experiment Three revealed that the relative perceived seriousness of violence perpetrated by law-enforcers and criminals in TV crime—drama programming depended critically on the location of the action, and that perceptions of these two kinds of violence in British and American locations were reversed. Perceptions of these portrayals in relatively near and distant geographical locations could also depend on respondents' beliefs about the society in which they live, its risks, dangers and its justice. Therefore further analyses were conducted in which ratings of law-enforcer and criminal violence in British and American settings were related as separate dependent variables to social beliefs. The results of these analyses are presented in Table 13.3.

Significant canonical variates emerged for six scales. These indicated that respondents who scored higher on external locus of control, higher on anomia and personal fearfulness, and lower on belief in a just world, perceived law-enforcer violence in British settings as more violent, less humorous and less suitable for children. These respondents tended also to perceive law-enforcer violence in American settings and criminal violence in British and American settings as more realistic. Strong belief in fate (external control) and weak belief in a just world were associated with perceptions of any violence in British settings as more frightening and of violence in American settings, as relatively less frightening. Weaker belief in a just world together with a higher score on anomia were related to the judgement that criminal violence in British locations would be especially likely to disturb other people.

Violence perpetrated by males and females

Investigation of the mediating influences of the types of characters involved as perpetrators or victims of violence on viewers' perceptions of violent TV portrayals was extended in Experiment Five which

Table 13.2

Canonical correlations of social beliefs and demographics with perceptions of TV violence perpetrated by law-enforcers and criminals

	Violent	Realistic	Frightening	Likely to disturb people in general	Suitable for children	Humorous
Demographics						
Sex	-.10	-.05	.24	.03	-.27	-.35
Age	.15	-.24	.06	.13	.14	-.12
Class	.04	-.09	-.12	-.16	.52	.04
Education	.16	-.03	-.08	-.11	.48	.30
Social beliefs						
Fear	.15	.88	.51	.46	-.64	.27
Anomia	.07	-.13	.49	-.07	.32	.06
Just world	.04	.34	-.26	.26	.59	.00
Locus of control	.45	.05	-.28	.21	.79	.40
Character-type						
Law-enforcer violence	.48	.76	.32	-.12	1.44	-.59
Criminal violence	.53	.25	.70	1.11	-.49	-.46
Multiple correlation coefficient r_c	.82	.62	.65	.68	.57	.75
Significance level $P <$	.001	.01	.002	.001	.001	.001

Table 13.3

Canonical correlations of social beliefs and demographics with perceptions of TV violence perpetrated by law-enforcers and criminals in Britain and America

	Violent	Realistic	Frightening	Likely to disturb people in general	Suitable for children	Humorous
Demographics						
Sex	-.01	-.02	.20	.15	-.24	-.34
Age	.20	-.43	.14	.21	.04	-.21
Class	.19	-.14	-.04	-.06	.28	-.04
Education	.13	-.08	-.01	-.12	.39	.23
Social beliefs						
Fear	-.07	1.01	.36	.13	.74	.36
Anomia	.35	.21	.59	.47	.38	.05
Just world	-.10	-.45	.28	-.45	-.73	.10
Locus of control	.34	.36	-.45	.03	.93	.31
Character-type						
Law-enforcer violence						
British crime	.44	.07	-.32	.04	-1.28	-.37
American crime	.02	1.25	.41	-.11	.65	-.36
Criminal violence						
British crime	-.35	.36	-.28	1.01	-1.32	-.07
American crime	.87	.54	.66	.07	.37	-.31
Multiple correlation coefficient r_c	.85	.66	.67	.70	.65	.75
Significance level $P <$	.001	.01	.01	.001	.01	.001

looked at the sex of attackers and attacked. Comparisons were made of viewers' ratings of episodes featuring either males attacking females or females attacking males. The results, which are discussed in Chapter Four, indicated that whether male-perpetrated violence was rated as more violent and more emotionally upsetting than female-perpetrated violence or vice versa, depended on the geographical location of the action. In British settings, male attackers were judged in more serious terms than were female attackers, but in American settings, the latter were, less expectedly, perceived as more violent and more disturbing. However, perceptions of these incidents may also vary according to viewers' own beliefs about the world they live in. In order to find out if this was so, respondents' social beliefs were related to their ratings of male- and female-perpetrated TV violence.

Separate canonical correlations were computed for each rating scale, with ratings of programme excerpts entered as the dependent variables and scores on the four dimensions of social belief (fear of victimisation, anomia, belief in a just world, and internal–external locus of control) entered with demographic and TV viewing inform- ation as independent variables. The results of these analyses are summarised in Table 13.4 which shows that significant canonical variates emerged on four scales.

Results indicated that respondents scoring higher on external locus of control and anomia, who had weak just world beliefs, tended to perceive male-perpetrated violence as more violent, more frightening, more personally disturbing, and as more likely to disturb people in general, and female-perpetrated violence as less serious in these terms.

Programme excerpts in this study were taken from British and American crime–drama series, and differences emerged between these two fictional settings in the relative perceived seriousness of male and female violence. In order to see whether respondents' social beliefs related in different ways to these portrayals according to their geographical location, further canonical correlations were computed in which male and female coercive portrayals were further divided into those set in Britain and those located in America.

Table 13.5 shows that significant canonical variates emerged for four scales again. However, these scales were not exactly the same as for the previous analysis. On this occasion the canonical correlation was significant for ratings of how humorous respondents perceived programme excerpts to be, but was non-significant for ratings on the personally disturbing scale.

External controllers with weak just world beliefs rated male- perpetrated violence in British settings as more violent, more fright- ening, more likely to disturb other people and less humorous, while in general such respondents were less concerned about male violence in

Table 13.4

Canonical correlations of social beliefs and demographics with perceptions of TV violence perpetrated by males and females

	Violent	Frightening	Personally disturbing	Likely to disturb people in general
Demographics				
Sex	-.27	.11	.11	.22
Age	.93	-.02	.34	-.08
Class	-.43	-.45	.41	-.65
Education	-.44	-.92	.96	-.91
Social beliefs				
Fear	-.12	.05	-.07	.20
Anomia	.37	-.26	-.55	.26
Just world	-.36	.60	.75	-.22
Locus of control	.32	-.12	-.56	.08
Character-type				
Male perpetrator	1.68	-2.28	-1.76	.82
Female perpetrator	-2.08	2.05	1.23	-1.59
Multiple correlation coefficient r_c	.58	.64	.53	.56
Significance level $P <$	.001	.001	.01	.001

Table 13.5

Canonical correlations of social beliefs and demographics with perceptions of TV violence perpetrated by males and females in Britain and America

	Violent	Frightening	Likely to disturb people in general	Humorous
Demographics				
Sex	-.04	.14	-.03	-.34
Age	.15	.11	.40	.17
Class	.16	.16	-.31	.03
Education	.18	.05	-.16	.32
Social beliefs				
Fear	.04	.26	.46	-.09
Anomia	.09	.62	.04	.03
Just world	-.21	-.43	-.74	-.19
Locus of control	.67	.01	.36	.68
Character-type				
Male perpetrator				
British crime	.99	1.22	.65	-.74
American crime	-.13	-.35	-.33	.24
Female perpetrator				
British crime	.08	-.20	-.20	.35
American crime	.01	-.29	-.97	.07
Multiple correlation coefficient r_c	.82	.73	.68	.78
Significance level $P <$	.001	.001	.001	.001

American settings or female violence generally.

Different physical forms of televised violence

The physical nature of violence can vary considerably and has an important bearing on the judgements observers make about particular incidents. Experiment Seven indicated that respondents rated some physical forms of violence as more violent and disturbing than others. These perceived differences corresponded with variations in the content of violent episodes and were averaged across respondents. To what extent, however, do individuals differ in their perceptions of different kinds of physical violence, and are these judgements related to more general beliefs they hold about the world?

Respondents' ratings of the four categories of physical violence examined in Experiment Seven were related, separately for each rating scale to their positions on four dimensions of social belief. As Table 13.6 shows, canonical correlations yielded significant canonical variates on four scales. Results indicated that respondents who believed that their lives are determined by fate, who were slightly more fearful and more alienated and held relatively weak just world beliefs tended to perceive shootings as less violent and upsetting, and all other forms of violence, especially stabbings, as more serious in these terms.

Further canonical correlations were computed to relate social beliefs to perceptions of each category of physical violence within programme genres. The results of these analyses are shown in Table 13.7. Significant canonical variates emerged for perceptions of British crime—drama materials but not for perceptions of Western materials. Within the former genre, social beliefs were related in particular to how violent, realistic, personally disturbing, likely to disturb people in general, exciting and humorous violent portrayals were perceived to be.

Stronger fearful and fateful beliefs were related to perceptions of shootings and stabbings in British crime—drama settings as being more violent, more realistic, more frightening, more likely to disturb others, more exciting, and less humorous. Again, individuals who perceived the world around them in a fearful or fateful manner exhibited greater concern about those portrayals classified by panel members in general as the most serious kinds of violence. Certain kinds of social beliefs appear to mediate exaggerated reactions to forms of violence on TV which observers in general tend to regard as most disturbing.

Table 13.6

Canonical correlations of social beliefs and demographics with perceptions of different physical forms of TV violence

	Violent	Frightening	Personally disturbing	Likely to disturb people in general
Demographics				
Sex	-.08	.17	-.48	-.09
Age	-.12	.48	-.33	-.26
Class	-.21	-.09	.09	.02
Education	.09	-.10	-.16	.38
Social beliefs				
Fear	-.08	.15	-.24	-.14
Anomia	.12	.40	-.16	-.15
Just world	-.03	-.77	.64	.33
Locus of control	.73	.22	-.27	-.77
Physical form				
Shootings	-.91	-.62	.32	.44
Fights	.42	.09	.64	-.35
Explosions	.47	.35	-.01	.42
Stabbings	.94	1.73	1.74	1.44
Multiple correlation				
coefficient r_c	.61	.68	.59	.66
Significance level $P <$	.01	.02	.02	.05

Table 13.7

Canonical correlations of social beliefs and demographics with perceptions of different physical forms of TV violence in British crime drama

	Violent		Realistic	Frightening	Personally disturbing		Likely to disturb people in general	Exciting	Humorous	
Demographics										
Age	.07	.63	.24	.39	.48	.18	-.21	-.07	.37	.63
Sex	.05	-1.02	-.26	.38	.41	-.78	-.42	-.43	.03	-1.54
Class	.07	.11	.24	.17	.10	.13	-.14	.37	.19	-.36
Education	.22	.26	.04	.35	.22	-.08	.02	-.05	.31	-.89
Social beliefs										
Fear	.02	-.34	-.80	.14	.34	-.00	-.24	.12	.33	.36
Anomia	-.06	-.62	-.31	.17	.27	-.47	.53	.35	-.00	.91
Just world	.16	.29	.36	-.30	-.26	.47	.12	-.56	.00	-1.15
Locus of control	.67	-.03	-.23	.40	.30	-1.41	-.85	.78	.52	.66
Scene type										
Shootings	.14	-2.90	-.75	.75	.59	-1.76	-.31	-.96	.28	-1.63
Fights	.59	-.33	1.33	.83	-.79	2.58	-.88	.12	-.03	-.38
Explosions	-.08	.27	-.36	-.34	-.94	.93	.97	.12	.25	-.09
Stabbings	.64	-2.86	-1.16	1.17	1.99	-1.35	-.73	-.22	.58	-1.05
Multiple correlation coefficient r$_c$	.83	.54	.67	.76	.70	.52	.72	.76	.77	.44
Significance level P<	.001	.05	.001	.001	.001	.05	.001	.001	.001	.05

203

Harmful and harmless TV violence

Some portrayals of violence on TV result in observable harm to those who are attacked, whilst others do not. The *degree* of harm caused by a violent attack can vary, and with it, as Experiment Nine indicated, so too, do viewers' judgements of its seriousness. Sensitivity to the harm caused by violence may vary across viewers who exhibit different beliefs about their social environment. In an analysis of this respondents' social beliefs were related in a series of canonical correlations, to their ratings of the programme excerpts presented to them in Experiment Nine. Table 13.8 summarises the results of these computations.

Significant canonical variates emerged for only two scales. Results indicated that strong beliefs in fate (or external locus of control) and weak belief in a just world were associated with perceptions of harmful (fatal and non-fatal) violence as more violent and more likely to disturb people in general. Harmless violence, on the other hand, was rated by such respondents as relatively less violent and less generally likely to disturb.

Relationships between social beliefs and perceptions of harmful and harmless violence were examined further for portrayals from different categories of programming. Canonical correlations yielded significant canonical variates on all scales. The results shown in Table 13.9 indicate that more fearful and fateful beliefs were associated with perceptions of most types of portrayal as more violent, more realistic, more disturbing and less suitable for children. An exception was for harmless portrayals from science fiction which panel members with fearful and fateful beliefs about the world thought were more suitable for children.

TV violence in different physical settings

Experiments Eleven and Twelve examined viewers' perceptions of violent incidents which occurred in different physical settings. Experiment Eleven compared day-time with night-time portrayals, and Experiment Twelve looked at incidents depicted indoors or outdoors. Significant differences in respondents' perceptions of portrayals emerged which corresponded with the physical setting. Of particular salience to audience judgements about violence was whether incidents occurred in indoor or outdoor locations, with violence in the former rated as more violent. To what extent though did respondents with different beliefs about their social environment vary in their reactions to televised violence depicted in different physical settings? Further

Table 13.8

Canonical correlations of social beliefs and demographics with perceptions of harmful and harmless TV violence

	Violent	Likely to disturb people in general
Demographics		
Sex	.04	-.04
Age	-.44	.26
Class	.07	-.33
Education	.25	-.27
Social beliefs		
Fear	.21	.15
Anomia	-.45	.16
Just world	.22	-.68
Locus of control	-.83	.56
Degree of harm		
Fatal	-.24	.26
Non-fatal	-1.45	1.67
No harm	.84	-1.10
Multiple correlation coefficient r_c	.69	.64
Significance level $P <$	.01	.01

Table 13.9
Canonical correlations of social beliefs and demographics with perceptions
of harmful and harmless TV violence as a function of fictional setting

	Violent	Realistic	Fright-ening	Personally disturbing	Likely to disturb people in general	Suitable for children	Exciting	Humorous
Demographics								
Sex	-.06	.04	-.33	-.37	.11	-.28	-.08	-.33
Age	.39	-.17	-.19	.13	.41	.01	.16	-.09
Class	.04	.24	.18	.05	-.01	.26	-.36	-.00
Education	.13	.11	.10	-.60	.08	.36	-.07	.24
Social beliefs								
Fear	-.05	-1.12	-.57	-.45	.38	-.30	.17	.33
Anomia	.12	-.01	-.02	-.61	.32	-.38	.19	.26
Just world	.00	.38	-.02	-.00	-.20	.53	-.52	-.35
Locus of control	.62	-.36	-.45	-.77	.68	-.83	.71	.64
Scene type								
Fatal								
American crime	.43	-.39	.09	-.10	.56	.42	-.18	.75
Science-fiction	.08	-.90	-.96	-1.19	.40	1.01	.61	-.42
Non-fatal injury								
American crime	.83	-.45	-.84	-.53	.31	.47	-.93	.31
Science-fiction	.22	-1.62	-2.46	-2.27	.74	.42	-.28	.32
Harmless								
American crime	.31	-.13	-.08	-.38	.00	.13	.14	-.01
Science-fiction	.22	-.28	1.68	1.66	-1.17	-.80	-.16	-.01
Multiple correlation coefficient r_c	.81	.71	.68	.75	.65	.71	.71	.81
Significance level $P <$	.001	.01	.05	.05	.05	.01	.05	.001

series of canonical correlations were computed in which social beliefs were related to perceptions of day-time and night-time portrayals, and then to indoor and outdoor portrayals of violence. No significant canonical variates emerged from eight separate canonical analyses on data from Experiment Eleven. However, significant canonical variates emerged for seven scales in Experiment Twelve. The latter results are presented in Table 13.10. These indicate that higher scores on external locus of control, anomia and fearfulness, and low scores on belief in a just world were related to perceptions of indoor portrayals as more violent, more realistic, more frightening, more personally disturbing, less suitable for children and less humorous, and of outdoor portrayals as less realistic and less frightening, and to some extent as less violent and likely to disturb others (but nevertheless still as not especially suitable for children).

Additional analyses were computed between social beliefs and perceptions of indoor and outdoor portrayals within different fictional settings. None of these, however, revealed any significant or meaning-ful relationships between panel members' perceptions of the world and their ratings of TV portrayals.

Table 13.10

Canonical correlations of social beliefs and demographics with perceptions of TV violence in indoor and outdoor locations

	Violent	Realistic	Frightening	Personally disturbing	Likely to disturb people in general	Suitable for children	Humorous
Demographics							
Sex	-.01	-.41	.09	.31	.17	-.29	-.54
Age	.13	.05	.05	-.17	.10	-.23	-.23
Class	-.06	.00	.16	.05	-.16	.15	-.15
Education	.09	-.01	-.00	.13	-.31	.32	.34
Social beliefs							
Fear	-.05	.58	-.03	.17	.30	.25	.25
Anomia	.24	.22	.80	.65	.23	.22	.19
Just world	.02	.03	-.75	-.66	-.30	-.89	-.24
Locus of control	.45	.44	-.09	-.08	.31	.37	.33
Location							
Indoors	1.26	2.21	2.38	2.16	.70	-.63	-.88
Outdoors	-.27	-1.33	-1.49	-1.28	-.30	-.38	.13
Multiple correlation coefficient r_c	.77	.54	.71	.58	.66	.53	.62
Significance level $P <$	.001	.01	.001	.01	.002	.05	.002

14 Personal aggressiveness and perceptions of television violence

Viewers' reactions to violence performed by others, whether in real life or on the TV screen, may depend on the extent to which they are predisposed to violence themselves. Relationships have been demonstrated by a number of researchers between preferences for violent programmes and the extent to which viewers say they would be willing to use violence under frustrating circumstances (Dominick and Greenberg, 1972; Greenberg and Atkin, 1977). Substantial increases in behavioural aggression following a heavy diet of violent TV are most likely to occur amongst viewers who already exhibit strong aggressive tendencies (Parke *et al*, 1977). Proneness to displays of physical aggressiveness has been found by one longitudinal study to be a good indicator of future violence-viewing preferences (Atkin *et al*, 1979).

Research has indicated that personal aggressiveness may indicate preferences for action—adventure programmes which frequently contain violence, and that behavioural reactions to such programming may also be determined by aggressive predispositions of viewers. In all this work, however, violence has been treated as some sort of homogenous, undifferentiated entity, which more aggressive personalities prefer and react to. But violence can occur in a variety of forms, both on TV and in the way it is displayed by individuals in reality. To what extent, and in what ways do aggressively predisposed individuals differ from less aggressive persons in their perceptions of various types of violence — is it in terms of fictional or physical setting, the types of actors involved, the kinds of weapons used, or the degree of harm suffered by victims? Furthermore, do individuals who are themselves characterised as predominantly aggressive in a physical sense, or in a verbal sense, differ in the types of violence they perceive as most serious or unacceptable? In this chapter, data are reported from seven experiments in which respondents' perceptions of programme excerpts featuring different kinds of violent portrayal were related to their scores on four sub-scales of a personal hostility inventory. Each sub-scale measured different kinds of personal aggressiveness; use of physical violence against others (*assault*); malicious gossip and proneness to throw anger tantrums (*indirect hostility*); readiness to show anger and to be rude to other people (*irritability*); and tendencies towards arguing, shouting, swearing and using verbal threats (*verbal aggression*). These sub-scales were treated as separate indicators of personal aggressiveness and related as such to perceptions of violent excerpts.

Violence in different programme genres

To assess relationships between viewers' personal predispositions towards aggressiveness and their perceptions of TV violence from different programme genres, eight canonical correlations were computed in which sex, age, socio-economic class and education details for each respondent were entered along with scores from each sub-scale of the Buss—Durkee Hostility Inventory as independent variables, and ratings of violence in each genre were entered as dependent variables. The results of these analyses are summarised in Table 14.1.

One significant canonical variate emerged for each scale. Following Levine (1977) each canonical variate was interpreted in terms of the items loading most strongly on it. Results showed that viewers with stronger propensities towards indirect hostility or verbal aggression rated violence in British crime—drama settings as less violent, and violence depicted in American crime—drama settings as less realistic, less frightening, less personally disturbing and as less likely to disturb others, and not suitable for children. Viewers with stronger propensities towards all four types of personal hostility, however, perceived violence in British crime programmes as more humorous and more exciting.

Violence perpetrated by law-enforcers and criminals

Individuals who profess to be disposed towards aggressiveness themselves may be more tolerant of violent conduct in others. But are they more tolerant of aggression in certain types of actors than in others?

Table 14.1

Personal aggressiveness and viewers' perceptions of violent portrayals from five genres of TV programming

	Violent	Realistic	Fright-ening	Personally disturbing	Likely to disturb people in general	Suitable for children	Exciting	Humorous
Demographics								
Sex	.20	.15	.27	-.37	-.44	-.41	-.21	-.36
Age	-.46	-.20	.07	.09	-.30	.08	.02	.29
Class	.05	-.15	-.32	-.30	.01	-.01	.26	.17
Education	.28	-.55	-.99	-.95	-.16	.19	.08	.51
Aggressiveness								
Assault	.19	-.68	.22	-.09	.33	.08	.27	.64
Indirect hostility	-.44	.37	.71	.31	-.11	.16	.48	-.92
Irritability	.03	-.37	-.11	-.40	-.11	-.36	.22	-.50
Verbal aggression	-.48	-.24	-.45	-.49	-.67	-1.05	.39	-.48
Genres								
British crime	-1.05	-.73	.37	-.28	-.26	.33	.85	.56
American crime	.08	-.26	-1.30	-.81	-.82	1.21	.11	.46
Westerns	.08	.20	-.94	-.37	.19	.29	-.29	-.06
Cartoons	.02	.02	-.42	-.42	-.04	-.56	.18	-.07
Science-fiction	.14	.53	.28	-.57	.19	-.01	-.06	-.09
Multiple correlation coefficient r_c	.88	.72	.73	.69	.71	.66	.79	.79
Significance level $P <$	.001	.001	.001	.001	.01	.01	.05	.001

In particular, do physically or verbally aggressive people differ from each other, or from non-aggressive sorts in their perceptions of violence perpetrated by law-enforcers and by criminals? And do self-endorsed aggressive types afford greater legitimacy to violence performed by the forces of justice or to that perpetrated by wrongdoers?

In an effort to answer at least some of these questions, respondents' personal aggressiveness scores were related to their perceptions of programme excerpts featuring violence perpetrated by law-enforcers and by criminals. From a series of eight canonical correlations, significant canonical variates emerged for every scale. These results are shown in Table 14.2.

The general picture to emerge from these analyses was that the greater the degree of self-endorsed personal aggressiveness or hostility, the less seriously violent, less likely to disturb people generally, less frightening and less personally disturbing were both law-enforcer and criminal violence perceived to be. More personally aggressive respondents were more likely to perceive both types of violence as suitable for children and as non-humorous. More aggressive or hostile types, particularly on the physical assault sub-scale, differentiated between law-enforcer and criminal violence on two scales however. These respondents rated law-enforcer violence as both more realistic and more exciting, and criminal violence as less realistic and exciting.

Personal aggressiveness scores were related also to their perceptions of law-enforcer and criminal violence in British crime—drama and American crime—drama settings independently. Further canonical correlations yielded significant variates on seven scales. Results shown in Table 14.3 indicate that lower assault scores together with higher verbal aggression were associated with perceptions of law-enforcer violence as less realistic, less disturbing and less exciting, and of criminal violence as more realistic and disturbing. These characteristics of aggressiveness among panel members were associated also with perceptions of law-enforcer violence and of criminal violence in British crime—drama settings only as more violent. Hence, there was some indication that individuals whose personal aggressive tendencies were more verbal than physical thought that violent portrayals set in geographically proximal locations were especially violent.

Violence perpetrated by males and females

Further distinction was made between character-involvement in violence in TV fiction on the basis of sex.

Experiment Five indicated that respondents' ratings of violent excerpts differed according to the sex of the attacker and victim. An

Table 14.2

Canonical correlations of personal aggressiveness and demographics with perceptions of TV violence perpetrated by law-enforcers and criminals

	Violent	Realistic	Frightening	Personally disturbing	Likely to disturb people in general	Suitable for children	Exciting	Humorous
Demographics								
Sex	-.15	-.13	.34	.46	.10	-.41	-.29	-.42
Age	.45	.34	.52	-.02	.40	.21	-.24	.26
Class	-.03	.08	.12	.04	-.18	-.22	.46	.31
Education	.28	.22	.31	.25	-.17	.42	-.02	.48
Aggressiveness								
Assault	.33	.56	-.15	-.03	.22	.41	.49	.70
Indirect hostility	.36	.13	.03	.42	.02	.37	.47	1.08
Irritability	.01	-.28	.25	.40	.42	.63	.04	-.39
Verbal aggression	.62	.31	.03	-.34	.65	.45	-.01	.82
Character-type								
Law-enforcer	-.34	1.26	-.08	-.73	-.00	.65	1.90	.68
Criminal	-.67	-.28	-1.07	-.29	-1.00	.37	-.98	.37
Multiple correlation coefficient r_c	.85	.54	.57	.45	.64	.56	.79	.82
Significance level $P <$	.001	.05	.001	.05	.001	.001	.001	.001

Table 14.3

Canonical correlations of personal aggressiveness and demographics with perceptions of TV violence perpetrated by law-enforcers and criminals in British and American settings

	Violent	Realistic	Frightening	Likely to disturb people in general	Suitable for children	Exciting	Humorous
Demographics							
Sex	-.12	.05	.37	.19	.43	.32	.45
Age	.45	-.28	.66	.40	-.15	.28	-.25
Class	.03	.08	.11	-.18	-.05	-.45	-.33
Education	.26	-.07	.42	-.10	-.18	.02	-.52
Personal aggressiveness							
Assault	-.31	-.40	-.31	-.37	-.26	-.46	-.74
Indirect hostility	.37	.26	-.20	-.18	-.05	-.72	-1.13
Irritability	.05	.26	-.01	.50	.23	.07	.31
Verbal aggression	.52	.93	.39	.79	.84	.11	1.02
Scene types							
Law-enforcer violence							
British crime series	.41	-.30	-.54	-.21	-.09	-.86	-.02
American crime series	.02	-1.04	-.30	-.19	-.96	-1.04	-.60
Criminal violence							
British crime series	.55	.50	.28	.30	.08	.07	-.23
American crime series	.04	.12	.96	.78	-.05	.92	-.26
Multiple correlation coefficient r_c	.86	.59	.60	.67	.59	.83	.82
Significance level $P <$	.001	.05	.05	.001	.01	.001	.001

important question then was whether the extent and nature of this distinction varied across respondents who were characterised by different degrees of self-professed personal aggressiveness.

Table 14.4 shows that from a series of canonical correlations in which personal aggressiveness scores were related to perceptions of male-perpetrated and female-perpetrated violence, significant canonical variates emerged for just four scales. These variates indicated that particular kinds of personal aggressiveness rather than personal aggressiveness in general were associated with differential perceptions of male and female violence. Respondents who claimed to be relatively verbally aggressive but essentially not physically aggressive judged male-perpetrated violence as more violent, more likely to disturb people in general, more frightening and more personally disturbing, and female-perpetrated violence as relatively less seriously on each of these scales.

Table 14.5 shows the results of further canonical correlations computed to find out whether personal aggressiveness was related to differential perceptions of male and female violence in different fictional settings. Results indicated that individuals with weaker aggressive dispositions tended to perceive male violence and female violence in more serious terms, especially male-perpetrated violence in British crime—drama settings. Those panel members who endorsed themselves to be to some extent or in certain ways aggressive persons were inclined to give less serious ratings to those portrayals which the average panel member judged most seriously.

Different physical forms of televised violence

The physical form of violence was found in Experiment Seven to be an indicator of panel members' perceptions of TV portrayals, with those portrayals depicting shootings and stabbings perceived as more violent and disturbing than those depicting fights or explosions. Do physically violent people judge these various forms of physical violence differently than non-physically violent or non-violent individuals?

A series of canonical correlations was carried out which examined relationships between measures of personal aggressiveness and viewers' ratings of different forms of physical violence on each scale. As Table 14.6 shows, significant canonical variates emerged for just five scales. These analyses indicated that stronger propensities towards the use of physical aggression (i.e. assault) amongst viewers were associated with perceptions of stabbings and fist-fights as less violent, less frightening and personally disturbing, and odd shootings and explosions as more serious on each of these scales. Stronger perceptions towards other less

Table 14.4

Canonical correlations of personal aggressiveness and demographics with perceptions of TV violence perpetrated by males and females

	Violent	Likely to disturb people in general	Frightening	Personally disturbing
Demographics				
Sex	.21	.20	.13	.26
Age	.95	.44	.24	-.01
Class	-.62	-.16	-.65	.24
Education	-.41	-.18	-1.00	.50
Aggressiveness				
Assault	-.61	-.76	-.20	-.60
Indirect hostility	.01	.44	.58	.48
Irritability	.17	.60	.06	.51
Verbal aggression	.87	.64	1.17	.20
Character-type				
Male perpetrator	1.78	1.16	2.24	1.57
Female perpetrator	-2.10	-.19	-2.19	-.82
Multiple correlation coefficient r_c	.55	.52	.64	.51
Significance level $P <$	.001	.001	.001	.01

Table 14.5

Canonical correlations of personal aggressiveness and demographics with perceptions of TV violence perpetrated by males and females in British and American settings

	Violent	Frightening	Personally disturbing	Likely to disturb people in general	Suitable for children	Exciting	Humorous
Demographics							
Sex	-.18	.01	.31	.20	-.08	-.12	-.31
Age	.37	-.08	-.07	-.28	-.64	.08	.47
Class	-.03	-.52	.26	.01	.31	.23	.24
Education	.21	-.61	.41	-.00	.78	-.02	.49
Personal aggressiveness							
Assault	-.31	-.16	-.39	.28	-1.28	.25	.47
Indirect hostility	.30	-.49	.46	-.32	.85	.68	.76
Irritability	.17	-.47	-.51	-.45	-1.61	-.24	-.15
Verbal aggression	.62	-.97	-.29	-.49	-.81	.28	-.63
Scene types							
Male aggression							
British crime series	.86	1.16	.81	-.96	-1.19	.14	.62
American crime series	-.15	.46	.42	-.05	-.04	-.06	-.29
Female aggression							
British crime series	.20	.11	.39	-.11	-.10	1.01	.55
American crime series	.06	.81	.79	.16	-.28	-.23	-.11
Multiple correlation coefficient r_c	.88	.69	.68	.71	.56	.73	.77
Significance level $P <$	.001	.001	.05	.001	.01	.001	.001

Table 14.6

Canonical correlations of personal aggressiveness and demographics with perceptions of different physical forms of TV violence

	Violent	Frightening	Personally disturbing	Likely to disturb people in general	Exciting
Demographics					
Sex	-.22	-.21	.65	-.07	.48
Age	.45	-.61	.42	-.49	.65
Class	-.32	.22	-.10	.02	-.48
Education	.16	-.00	.14	.33	.15
Aggressiveness					
Assault	-.57	1.25	.47	.33	-.50
Indirect hostility	.58	-.68	-.70	-.61	-1.22
Irritability	.21	-.14	-.44	.08	.00
Verbal aggression	.64	-.67	.25	-.61	.84
Instrumental form					
Shootings	-.86	1.08	.18	.79	-2.32
Fist-fights	1.15	-1.38	-.44	-.53	.82
Explosions	.30	.97	.17	.28	.35
Stabbings	.33	-1.38	-1.65	-1.43	.58
Multiple correlation coefficient r_c	.63	.74	.55	.66	.43
Significance level $P <$	.01	.001	.01	.01	.05

physical forms of personal hostility, however, were related to perceptions of stabbings and fist-fights as more violent and disturbing.

Ratings of different physical categories of violence from British
crime—drama and from Western settings were related independently to
personal aggressiveness measures. Significant canonical variates
emerged only for British crime—drama materials and are shown in
Table 14.7. Stronger self-endorsed tendencies towards physical assault-
iveness amongst panel members were associated with perceptions of
fights and stabbings as being less frightening, less personally disturbing,
and less likely to disturb others. Non-physically aggressive tendencies
were associated on the other hand with perceptions of these portrayals
in more serious terms. Generally the findings indicate that those
individuals who say that they are themselves aggressive in certain
physical ways (e.g. fighting) judge portrayals featuring fist-fights and
other close up combat (e.g. stabbings) in less serious terms than do
non-physically aggressive persons.

Harmful and harmless TV violence

Experiment Nine showed that violent portrayals resulting in observable
harm to victims were rated as more violent and disturbing than were
portrayals resulting in no observable harm to victims by panel members
generally. However, individuals with self-endorsed propensities to be
aggressive may react differently than less aggressive individuals to harmful and harmless violence on TV.

Canonical correlations were computed to relate respondents'
personal aggressiveness scores to their rating of harmful and harmless
violent portrayals on all scales. Significant canonical variates emerged
for three scales, and those results are displayed in Table 14.8. Across
these three scales, indirect hostility was related most consistently and
most powerfully to viewers' perceptions of any of the sub-scales of
personal aggressiveness. Stronger tendencies towards indirect hostility
and verbal aggression were related to perceptions of fatal and non-fatal
harmful violence as more violent and more likely to disturb others, and
of harmful *and* harmless violence as more frightening. Age also emerged
as an indicator of perceptions of TV violence here. Older respondents
rated harmful violence as more violent and likely to disturb people in
general, and rated harmful and harmless violent scenes as more frightening than did younger respondents.

Further canonical correlations were computed to assess relationships between personal aggressiveness and perceptions of harmful and
harmless violence from different types of programme. Unfortunately,
no meaningful relationships as such emerged to indicate more refined

Table 14.7

Canonical correlations of personal aggressiveness and demographics with perceptions of different physical forms of TV violence in British crime drama

	Violent		Realistic		Frightening	Personally disturbing	Likely to disturb people in general	Suitable for children	Exciting	Humorous
Demographics										
Sex	.01	.69	.38	.51	-.40	.46	-.15	-.42	.20	.33
Age	.18	1.13	-.77	-.21	-.30	.35	-.39	.44	.07	-.27
Class	.06	.17	.32	.66	-.05	.07	.13	.32	-.25	-.25
Education	.22	-.03	-.01	.63	-.41	.13	.17	.67	.13	-.55
Personal aggressiveness										
Assault	-.18	.41	-.20	.54	.76	-.25	.35	1.27	-.11	-.40
Indirect hostility	.29	-.26	-.34	.06	-.07	.44	-.11	.98	-.53	-.69
Irritability	.08	-.05	.38	.59	-.55	.10	-.18	1.34	.21	.48
Verbal aggression	.61	.03	-.62	-1.57	-.23	-.01	-.89	-.80	-.65	.10
Scene types										
British crime drama										
Shootings	-.10	2.52	-.39	1.09	1.12	-.54	.18	1.09	-.87	-.36
Fights	.39	-.63	1.61	1.23	-.94	.48	-.51	.41	.99	-.15
Explosions	-.34	-.21	-.67	-1.86	.43	-.80	.89	-1.77	.80	-.39
Stabbings	1.03	3.17	-1.41	-.07	-1.44	1.67	-1.15	1.32	.15	-.21
Multiple correlation coefficient r_c	.90	.51	.62	.49	.80	.69	.78	.56	.78	.45
Significance level $P <$	.001	.05	.001	.05	.05	.001	.001	.05	.001	.001

Table 14.8

Canonical correlations of personal aggressiveness and demographics with perceptions of harmful and harmless TV violence

	Violent	Likely to disturb people in general	Frightening
Demographics			
Sex	.14	-.13	-.36
Age	.62	-.50	.51
Class	.17	.33	.16
Education	.03	.16	.31
Aggressiveness			
Assault	.26	.49	-.18
Indirect hostility	.52	-.56	.68
Irritability	-.22	.17	-.75
Verbal aggression	.29	-.92	.18
Consequences of violence			
Fatal injury	.53	-1.23	.67
Non-fatal injury	1.24	-.59	2.32
No observable harm	-.94	.96	.88
Multiple correlation coefficient r_c	.58	.57	.49
Significance level $P <$	.05	.05	.05

perceptual discrimination between portrayals on the basis of their fictional setting and the physically or verbally aggressive predispositions of individuals.

Violence in different physical settings

Two experiments were carried out which examined the mediating affects on viewers' judgements of televised violence of the physical setting and location of portrayals. Canonical correlations were computed to relate personal aggressiveness scores to perceptions of violence depicted in different physical environments. Table 14.9 shows that differential perceptions of violent portrayals occurring during day-time or night-time were related to personal aggressiveness at a significant level on only one scale.

Higher scores on all hostility sub-scales were related to perceptions of day-time violence as more violent and night-time violence as less violent.

Table 14.10 presents the results of canonical correlations which related personal aggressiveness to televised violence occurring indoors and outdoors. Significant canonical variates emerged for seven out of eight rating scales. Respondents who had higher scores on the assault, (e.g. fighting, vandalism) and indirect hostility (e.g. malicious gossip, practical jokes, temper tantrums) rated indoor violence as less violent, less realistic, less likely to disturb other people, less frightening, less personally disturbing, more exciting, and more humorous and rated outdoor violence as more serious and less entertaining and amusing. More verbally aggressive individuals, with higher scores on the irritability and verbal aggression sub-scales judged outdoor violence generally in less serious terms than they did indoor violence. Further canonical analyses between personal aggressiveness and perceptions of indoor and outdoor portrayals from different fictional settings yielded no additional significant or meaningful relationships.

Table 14.9

Canonical correlations of personal aggressiveness and demographics with perceptions of TV violence in day-time and night-time settings

	Violent
Demographics	
Sex	-.25
Age	.90
Class	-.28
Education	.05
Aggressiveness	
Assault	.82
Indirect hostility	1.01
Irritability	.50
Verbal aggression	.32
Physical setting	
Day-time violence	1.92
Night-time violence	-1.03
Multiple correlation coefficient r_c	.54
Significance level $P <$	.05

Table 14.10

Canonical correlations of personal aggressiveness and demographics with perceptions of TV violence in indoor and outdoor locations

	Violent	Realistic	Frightening	Personally disturbing	Likely to disturb people in general	Exciting	Humorous
Demographics							
Sex	-.07	-.41	.39	.20	.51	-.23	-.51
Age	.49	.69	.45	.50	.10	.01	.21
Class	-.14	.25	.22	-.16	.12	.23	.36
Education	.26	.39	.20	-.13	.30	.01	.72
Aggressiveness							
Assault	-.41	-.19	.22	.39	.45	.61	.67
Indirect hostility	-.45	-.67	.22	.62	.48	.17	1.09
Irritability	.09	.86	.03	-.09	.24	-.23	-.56
Verbal aggression	.70	.39	.13	.54	.05	.44	-.88
Location							
Indoor violence	.87	2.53	-1.25	-1.23	-1.41	1.86	.46
Outdoor violence	-.13	-1.70	.26	.24	.43	-.96	.57
Multiple correlation coefficient r_c	.79	.49	.52	.53	.65	.64	.59
Significance level $P <$	.001	.05	.05	.05	.01	.01	.05

15 Personality and perceptions of television violence

Studies of individual differences between viewers and their responses to TV violence have typically been extremely limited in the measures of personality employed. There can be little doubt, either on a common-sense level or on the evidence of early isolated studies, that people do exhibit variations in the way they interpret and react to different kinds of TV content. There is a need, however, for more systematic and comprehensive examination of TV content within well-developed theoretical frameworks which incorporate standardised, tried and tested measures of personality. One such frame is Eysenck's three-dimensional model of personality (Eysenck and Eysenck, 1967, 1975). Extensive empirical testing led Eysenck to define the variance in human personality largely in terms of three factors: extraversion (E), neuroticism (N), and psychoticism (P).

The E factor represents the sociability or outgoingness of an individual, and ranges from highly outgoing (or extraverted) to quiet and retiring (or introverted). The N factor represents the emotionality of an individual and varies from highly stable and emotionally calm to highly anxious and emotionally sensitive. The P factor indicates how tough-minded and callous versus how tender-minded and gentle an individual is.

Eysenck (1967) reported that neuroticism and extraversion interact to determine personal propensities towards aggressiveness, and that unstable or neurotic extraverts often show stronger anti-social and unruly tendencies than other personality types. This fact opens up the possibility that such individuals also perceive the violence of others, including that depicted on TV, in a fashion that is distinct from the perceptions of individuals with a different blend of these characteristics.

In his theory of crime and personality Eysenck (1964) further suggested that criminals and delinquents tend to score highly on all three scales (E, N and P), and so it may be hypothesised that people with high scores are not only more likely to engage in anti-social acts, but may be less likely to perceive violent TV portrayals as violent, disturbing or anti-social than people with lower scores on all three variables.

To investigate the significance of the E, N and P factors as mediators of audience perceptions of TV violence members of Panel One were given the Eysenck Personality Questionnaire (Eysenck and Eysenck, 1969) to fill out, and their scores on the three dimensions were related to their perceptions of violent excerpts.

Five programme genres

In Experiment One, respondents on Panel One were invited to make judgements about violent excerpts from five different categories of fictional programming: British crime—drama, American crime—drama, Westerns, science-fiction and cartoons. Results showed that the panel as a whole considered incidents from contemporary crime—drama series as significantly more serious than those from more fantastic fictional settings, along a number of evaluative scales. However, individuals may differ in their reactions to televised violence and such variations in judgement could be associated with differences in personality.

In order to examine the independent effects of the neuroticism, extraversion and psychoticism dimensions on perceptions of violent episodes, with the contribution to these judgements of other factors such as demographics statistically controlled, eight canonical correlations were run (one per rating scale) in which neuroticism, extraversion and psychoticism scores were entered along with demographic data as independent variables. As Table 15.1 shows, these analyses yielded at least one significant canonical variate per scale. Following Levine (1977) each canonical variate was interpreted in terms of the strength of loadings of items on them. Results indicated that for these TV stimuli and ratings scales, neuroticism and psychoticism dimensions were more consistently and powerfully related to viewers' perceptions of violent TV scenes than was extraversion.

High neuroticism scorers with a tendency also to score more highly

Table 15.1

Canonical correlations of personality factors and demographics with perceptions of TV violence from five programme genres

	Violent		Realistic		Frightening			Personally disturbing		Likely to disturb people in general		Suitable for children	Exciting	Humorous
Demographics														
Sex	-.19	-.33	.12	-.28	.36	.44	-.15	-.30	-.21	.27	.13	-.08	.12	.02
Age	-.11	.73	.31	.36	-.10	.35	.41	.10	-.04	.02	.51	.18	.08	.33
Class	-.27	.04	.20	-.26	.31	.10	.07	-.09	-.04	.23	.23	.32	.39	.11
Education	-.68	.24	.77	.48	.65	.57	.41	-.57	-.55	.71	.02	.53	.46	.80
Personality														
Neuroticism	.37	.57	-.35	.39	-.49	-.13	.45	.59	.42	.36	.50	-.26	-.49	-.29
Extraversion	.13	-.08	.21	.51	.06	-.35	.33	-.23	-.28	.30	.07	-.46	-.20	-.10
Psychoticism	.13	.44	-.42	.12	-.11	.49	.33	.51	-.21	.50	.24	-.09	-.14	-.15
Programme genres														
British crime	-.00	1.07	-.76	.23	.13	.11	.16	.16	.34	-.01	.07	-.48	.45	.42
American crime	.71	.36	.03	.82	-1.05	.04	.50	.49	.61	.84	.61	.11	.07	.43
Westerns	.59	.66	-.09	.52	-.79	.70	-.04	.48	.19	.75	.43	.16	-.37	-.31
Science-fiction	.31	.06	-.57	.12	-.15	.51	.12	.28	.45	.45	-.06	.59	-.21	-.15
Cartoons	-.20	.20	-.37	1.07	-.08	.91	-.82	.30	-1.01	.23	.28	.38	-.28	-.09
Multiple correlations coefficient r_c	.77	.74	.72	.52	.83	.57	.44	.77	.59	.74	.57	.67	.74	.62
Significance level $P <$	.001	.001	.001	.01	.001	.001	.05	.001	.001	.001	.01	.01	.001	.01

227

on the psychoticism dimension rated portrayals from British crime—drama series and Westerns as more violent. This judgement was also more likely among older panel members. Lower neuroticism scorers with better education perceived scenes from American crime—drama series and from Westerns as less frightening, whilst higher neuroticism scorers tended to judge contemporary American crime—drama portrayals and also cartoon portrayals as more frightening. Higher psychoticism scorers tended to rate non-contemporary and cartoon materials as more frightening, whilst higher scorers on neuroticism and psychoticism tended to be more personally disturbed by violence in most fictional settings. Higher neuroticism scorers who did not score highly on either extraversion or psychoticism dimensions claimed to be less personally disturbed by cartoons.

Individuals who exhibited higher scores on neuroticism, extraversion and psychoticism dimensions judged violence in most fictional settings (except British crime—drama) as more likely to disturb people in general, whilst higher neuroticism scorers believed this only of violence in American crime—drama and Western settings. Panel members with introverted tendencies judged violent portrayals from British crime—drama settings as less suitable for children, and violence in science-fiction and cartoon settings as more suitable.

On the perceived realism of TV violence, lower neuroticism scorers judged portrayals from British crime—drama, science-fiction, and cartoon shows as less true to life. However, higher neuroticism and extraversion scorers rated violent incidents from all genres as more realistic. Finally on personality differences, there was a tendency for lower neuroticism scorers to perceive violent portrayals in British crime—drama settings as more exciting and more humorous.

Violence perpetrated by law-enforcers and criminals

Experiment Three examined respondents' ratings of programme excerpts in which violence was perpetrated either by law-enforcers or by criminals. Judgements about these two types of portrayal varied according to the geographical location of their setting. In American locations, law-enforcer violence was perceived as less violent and disturbing than criminal violence, whilst in British settings the reverse finding emerged.

The previous three chapters indicated certain variations across respondents in their perceptions of these portrayals which were associated with self-perceptions, social beliefs and self-endorsed propensities towards aggressiveness. Was there any evidence of relationships between deep-seated personality characteristics of respondents and judgements about violence perpetrated for legal or criminal ends?

Table 15.2 shows the results of canonical correlations in which neuroticism, extraversion and psychoticism were related to ratings of law-enforcer violence and criminal violence (the latter averaged across programme types). No indication emerged from these analyses of any strong or consistent relationships between any of the three personality variables and judgements made about these portrayals. There were weak tendencies for higher neuroticism to rate law-enforcer violence as more exciting, more suitable for children and less personally disturbing and to perceive criminal violence as more realistic, more personally disturbing and less exciting.

Stronger relationships emerged between age and education, and perceptions of violence. Older and better educated respondents rated both kinds of portrayals as more violent (but law-enforcer violence more so). These respondents also rated criminal violence as more realistic, more frightening, more personally disturbing, more likely to disturb people in general, less suitable for children, less humorous and less exciting than law-enforcer violence.

Violence perpetrated by males and females

Experiment Five compared respondents' perceptions of violent excerpts which featured either male attacks on females, or female attacks on males. Over the panel as a whole, the former was perceived as more violent and disturbing in British fictional settings, while the latter was rated as more serious in American settings. To what extent, however, did respondents vary in their ratings of male- and female-perpetrated violence on opposite sex victims, and were such variations associated with particular personality characteristics?

Canonical correlations were computed which were designed to indicate the strength of relationships of neuroticism, extraversion and psychoticism to ratings of the TV scenes featuring male- or female-perpetrated violence, in the presence of statistical controls for demographic factors. Table 15.3 shows that significant canonical variates were found for seven scales, and that personality variables loaded noticeably on four of these. Higher neuroticism scorers rated male-perpetrated violence as much more violent and less humorous than female-perpetrated violence. Extraversion coupled with neuroticism were associated with ratings of both kinds of violent portrayal as being more suitable for children; and extraversion and psychoticism together loaded with greater perceived realism of these excerpts.

Further canonical correlations were computed with male- and female-perpetrated violence broken down in terms of geographical

Table 15.2

Canonical correlations of personality factors and demographics with perceptions of TV violence perpetrated by law-enforcers and criminals

	Violent	Realistic	Frightening	Personally disturbing	Likely to disturb people in general	Suitable for children	Exciting	Humorous
Demographics								
Sex	.03	.04	.37	.53	.27	-.38	-.14	-.28
Age	.55	.43	.52	.68	.66	.22	-.27	.37
Class	.23	.22	.18	.15	.15	.44	.72	.32
Education	.71	.68	.37	.56	.35	.84	.53	.91
Personality								
Neuroticism	-.04	.34	.11	.35	-.01	.22	.44	.04
Extraversion	-.06	-.15	.06	-.01	-.02	-.12	-.04	.07
Psychoticism	.17	.23	.16	.19	.05	.11	.36	-.07
Character-type								
Law-enforcer	.71	.27	.08	-.36	-.14	1.24	2.67	.41
Criminal	.30	.74	.92	1.33	1.13	-.26	-1.92	-.64
Multiple correlation coefficient r_c	.72	.54	.58	.47	.52	.47	.63	.63
Significance level $P < .001$	.01	.01	.01	.01	.01	.01	.001	.001

Table 15.3

Canonical correlations of personality factors and demographics with perceptions of TV violence perpetrated by males and females

	Violent	Realistic	Frightening	Personally disturbing	Likely to disturb people in general	Suitable for children	Humorous
Demographics							
Sex	-.25	.06	.18	.35	.37	-.24	-.28
Age	.80	.43	.50	-.05	.62	.26	-.03
Class	-.44	.20	-.36	.45	-.26	-.41	.39
Education	-.35	.29	-.65	.63	-.34	.41	.61
Personality							
Neuroticism	-.32	-.04	-.06	.10	.12	.45	.51
Extraversion	.28	.28	.02	-.10	.12	.54	.33
Psychoticism	.19	.58	.39	-.04	.30	-.09	.06
Character-type							
Male perpetrator	-1.90	.61	-1.83	1.73	-.68	2.81	-.55
Female perpetrator	2.10	.41	2.24	-1.16	1.51	2.15	1.34
Multiple correlation coefficient r_c	.61	.42	.58	.41	.46	.64	.42
Significance level $P <$	.001	.05	.001	.01	.002	.05	.02

location of the action (i.e. the United Kingdom or America). Table 15.4 shows that these analyses yielded significant canonical variates on seven scales out of eight, but personality factors featured noticeably on only two. Higher neuroticism was linked with the perceptions that male-perpetrated violence in British settings was more violent, while high neuroticism and extraversion together were associated with ratings of all forms of violence as more suitable for children.

Further canonical correlations were computed to relate personality with perceptions of law-enforcer violence and criminal violence perpetrated in British and American crime—drama settings. These analyses, however, yielded no significant relationships, and indicated no tendencies of individuals with different personality characteristics to exhibit varying degrees of perceptual discrimination between these portrayals from different fictional settings.

Different physical forms of televised violence

Experiment Seven made a study of viewers' perceptions of different types of physical violence — violence involving guns, explosives or knives, or simply unarmed combat. Differences emerged in the relative perceived seriousness of these varieties of violence, and scenes that depicted shootings and stabbings were generally judged by respondents to be the most violent and disturbing. It was of interest to know in addition, however, whether individuals of differing personality characteristics also exhibited variations in their judgements of different physically violent forms.

Relationships between neuroticism, extraversion and psychoticism and perceptions of four categories of physical violence were assessed in a series of canonical correlations. The results of these analyses are summarised in Table 15.5 and whilst significant canonical variates emerged on seven scales, there was no evidence on these of any marked association between personality and perceptual differentiation of the categories of physical violence.

On assessing relationships between personality factors and perceptions of different physical forms of televised violence within British crime—drama and Western settings independently, no significant findings emerged.

Harmful and harmless TV violence

Experiment Nine examined the effect on viewers' judgements of TV violence of the degree of observable harm caused to victims in each

Table 15.4

Canonical correlations of personality factors and demographics with perceptions of TV violence perpetrated by males and females in different programme genres

		Violent	Realistic	Frightening	Personally disturbing	Likely to disturb people in general	Suitable for children	Humorous
Demographics								
Sex	-.02	-.27	.11	-.22	.52	.15	.02	.13
Age	.46	.94	-.44	-.21	-.07	-.07	-.28	-.59
Class	.32	-.38	-.29	-.45	.39	-.49	-.37	-.23
Education	.70	-.17	-.79	.58	.52	-.72	-.43	-.70
Personality								
Neuroticism	.06	-.51	.10	.09	-.13	.09	.37	-.05
Extraversion	-.18	.21	-.17	.11	.01	.30	.37	.21
Psychoticism	.16	.02	-.21	.12	-.25	.07	.02	.02
Scene types								
Male violence British crime series	1.09	-1.06	-1.37	-1.14	.90	-.91	.22	-.75
Male violence American crime series	-.16	-.65	-.27	.00	.22	-.08	.70	.45
Female violence British crime series	.01	.67	.07	-.17	.54	-.32	1.53	-.44
Female violence American crime series	-.01	1.35	.79	.59	-1.02	.95	.41	.24
Multiple correlation coefficient r_c	.71	.58	.54	.62	.60	.57	.54	.69
Significance level $P <$	.001	.01	.01	.001	.01	.01	.01	.001

Table 15.5

Canonical correlations of personality factors and demographics with perceptions of different physical forms of violence

	Violent	Realistic	Frightening	Personally disturbing	Likely to disturb people in general	Exciting	Humorous
Demographics							
Sex	.09	.07	.51	.54	-.34	-.01	.27
Age	.40	-.69	-.34	.50	-.60	-.23	.38
Class	.26	-.09	-.22	.13	-.23	-.43	.33
Education	.74	.56	-.39	.22	-.29	-.75	.90
Personality							
Neuroticism	-.03	-.12	-.05	-.01	.01	.04	.01
Extraversion	-.00	-.22	-.09	.05	-.00	-.14	.06
Psychoticism	.12	-.25	.06	-.08	-.01	.35	.04
Physical forms of violence							
Shootings	.26	-.46	.87	.74	-.35	.47	.13
Fist-fights	.02	.74	.74	-.95	-.51	-.93	.03
Explosions	-.10	.30	.36	-.96	1.09	-.58	.59
Stabbings	.83	-1.49	-1.37	2.01	-1.16	.06	.33
Multiple correlation coefficient r_c	.72	.64	.71	.65	.61	.57	.68
Significance level $P <$	.001	.001	.01	.01	.01	.01	.001

portrayal. In general, respondents on Panel One rated harmful violence in more serious terms than violence which resulted in no apparent or observable pain and suffering to the target of an attack.

In order to assess the strength of association between personality and perceptions of portrayals depicting harmful and non-observable harmful violence, canonical correlations were computed over the eight rating scales. Table 15.6 shows that significant canonical variates emerged for four scales.

Interpreting these variates in terms of the highest loading items on them, results indicated that harmful violence (fatal and non-fatal) was perceived as less violent by younger people and higher psychoticism scorers. Harmful violence was rated as more frightening and more likely to disturb people in general by older viewers and lower psychoticism scorers, whilst harmless violence was rated as less likely to disturb others by these viewers. Finally younger people with somewhat higher neuroticism, extraversion and psychoticism scores were more likely than the average respondent to perceive some humour in scenes depicting harmful violence.

Further canonical correlations were computed to assess relationships between personality factors and perceptions of harmful and harmless violence in different fictional settings. Table 15.7 shows that significant canonical variates emerged on all scales, but that loadings of personality factors on these variates were generally quite small. Higher psychoticism scorers perceived harmful and harmless violence in American crime—drama and science-fiction settings as less violent and less realistic, and less likely to disturb other people. Introverts perceived most types of violence, harmful and harmless across fictional settings, as less suitable for children, compared with extraverts.

Violence in different physical settings

Viewers' perceptions of violent incidents in different physical settings were investigated in Experiments Eleven and Twelve. In Experiment Eleven, comparisons were made of ratings of violence in day-time and night-time settings. Was violence depicted after darkness perceived in more serious terms than similar forms of violence portrayed in daylight? Results reported in Chapter Seven indicated that night-time portrayals were perceived to be more frightening and personally disturbing (though not as significantly more violent) than day-time portrayals. Emotionally toned reactions to portrayals in the dark may vary across viewers, however, as some people are more frightened of the dark than are others. These reactions may be related in particular to an individual's character, and more nervous, less outgoing types may

Table 15.6

Canonical correlations of personality factors and demographics with perceptions of harmful and harmless TV violence

	Violent	Humorous	Likely to disturb people in general	Frightening
Demographics				
Sex	.05	-.19	.27	.33
Age	-.76	-.58	.67	.66
Class	-.05	.45	.03	-.04
Education	-.44	.44	.15	-.04
Personality				
Neuroticism	-.11	.23	.11	.12
Extraversion	-.18	.25	.03	.17
Psychoticism	.31	.31	-.26	-.37
Consequences of violence				
Fatal	-.81	.61	.95	.40
Non-fatal injury	-.41	1.66	.50	1.40
No observable harm	.24	-.43	-.49	-.49
Multiple correlation coefficient r_c	.55	.55	.46	.56
Significance level $P <$	.01	.01	.05	.05

Table 15.7

Canonical correlations of personality factors and demographics with perceptions of harmful and harmless TV violence as a function of fictional setting

	Violent	Realistic	Fright-ening	Personally disturbing	Likely to disturb people in general	Suitable for children	Exciting	Humorous
Demographics								
Sex	-.00	.13	-.39	-.33	-.09	-.21	-.04	-.36
Age	-.58	-.47	-.63	-.10	-.58	.23	-.11	.13
Class	-.05	-.08	-.01	-.03	-.19	.34	-.48	.36
Education	-.71	-.72	-.36	-.79	.03	.62	-.52	.67
Personality								
Neuroticism	.15	.19	.17	.16	-.35	-.11	.25	.09
Extraversion	.08	.85	-.31	-.32	.35	-.49	.41	.42
Psychoticism	-.27	.61	.08	.44	.65	-.08	-.09	.36
Scene types								
Fatal								
American crime	1.22 .81	1.61 -.58	-.04	-.12	-.15	.14	-.64	.11
Science-fiction	.53 .14	-4.50 -2.77	.88	1.48	-1.20	-1.15	.60	.43
Non-fatal injury								
American crime	2.55 .01	.17 -.32	-.76	-.28	-.08	-.82	-.49	.22
Science-fiction	1.81 .32	1.49 -2.75	-2.25	-1.52	-.36	-.11	.52	1.98
Harmless								
American crime	1.27 .18	-2.16 .03	.07	-.58	-.66	-.25	.34	.12
Science-fiction	.99 .20	3.14 .64	1.54	.83	1.32	-.56	-.62	-1.10
Multiple correlation coefficient r_c	.74 .53	.64 .52	.62	.73	.63	.72	.66	.61
Significance level $P <$	.001 .01	.001 .01	.01	.01	.01	.01	.01	.01

exhibit stronger reactions to threatening night-time scenes than more tough-minded, stable and sociable personalities. In order to investigate these possible differences in viewers' perceptions of day-time and night-time episodes, respondents' neuroticism, extraversion and psychoticism scores were related to their ratings of the TV stimuli used in Experiment Eleven.

A series of canonical correlations were computed which were designed to show the strength of association between each personality variable and perceptions of violent programme excerpts in the presence of controls for demographic differences between respondents. The results summarised in Table 15.8 show that significant canonical variates emerged for four scales. These results indicated that the neuroticism and psychoticism dimensions of personality were related to differential perceptions of the day-time and night-time episodes. Higher neuroticism and lower psychoticism scores were associated with perceptions of day-time and night-time violence (particularly the former) as more violent and more likely to disturb people in general (and day-time violence as somewhat less likely to do so) and as more frightening. Clearly then, more anxious and gentle people are more upset by televised violence occurring in darkness.

Interestingly though, these respondents tended to rate day-time incidents, in which the overt physical characteristics of the violence were more apparent, as more violent than similar incidents depicted at night-time. This indicates that for certain types of people perceptions of how violent televised incidents seem to be (meaning perhaps how overtly physically violent) do not always correspond with how upsetting they are.

In Experiment Twelve comparisons were made between ratings of violent scenes along another feature of physical setting — whether violence occurred indoors or outdoors. On the basis of an analysis of content effects alone, results indicated that indoor portrayals were judged to be more violent, more realistic, less exciting and less suitable for children than were outdoor portrayals. Personality differences and associated variations in perceptions of these two kinds of portrayal were also assessed the same way as for Experiment Eleven. Once again, the question was tackled as to whether those portrayals judged by respondents in general as more violent were perceived as even more so by particularly anxious, gentle or introverted individuals.

Table 15.9 shows the results of canonical correlations which yielded significant canonical variates for seven out of eight rating scales. Results indicated fewer and weaker relationships between the three personality dimensions and differential perceptions of violence in different settings than did the previous experiment. Demographic factors were more powerful indicators of viewers' perceptions than was

Table 15.8

Canonical correlations of personality factors and demographics with perceptions of TV violence in day-time and night-time settings

	Violent	Realistic	Likely to disturb people in general	Frightening
Demographics				
Sex	-.29	.21	.22	.17
Age	.75	.46	.50	.72
Class	.11	.02	.11	-.02
Education	.24	.10	.22	-.09
Personality				
Neuroticism	.43	.03	.61	.19
Extraversion	.02	.30	-.13	.11
Psychoticism	-.48	-.53	-.39	-.39
Physical setting				
Day-time violence	.74	1.39	-.32	.06
Night-time violence	.28	.43	1.29	.94
Multiple correlation coefficient r_c	.69	.45	.62	.50
Significance level $P <$	.001	.05	.001	.01

Table 15.9

Canonical correlations of personality factors and demographics with perceptions of TV violence in indoor and outdoor locations

	Violent	Realistic	Frightening	Personally disturbing	Likely to disturb people in general	Exciting	Humorous
Demographics							
Sex	.02	-.33	.38	.61	.35	-.12	-.46
Age	.57	.64	.45	.09	.63	.21	.24
Class	.16	.36	.29	.22	.15	.53	.35
Education	.65	.61	.27	.38	.22	.77	.89
Personality							
Neuroticism	.07	.08	.02	-.04	.09	.06	.24
Extraversion	-.00	.21	.07	-.03	.08	.05	.20
Psychoticism	-.28	-.31	-.27	-.33	-.12	-.10	-.09
Location							
Indoor violence	1.21	2.11	1.06	1.12	.79	1.22	.31
Outdoor violence	-.21	-1.22	-.07	-.13	.21	-.23	.72
Multiple correlation coefficient r_c	.70	.50	.57	.50	.53	.45	.56
Significance level $P <$	.001	.001	.001	.01	.01	.05	.001

personality. Neuroticism and extraversion were essentially unrelated to respondents' perceptions of indoor and outdoor portrayals, whilst there was a weak association between psychoticism and how violent, realistic, frightening and personally disturbing these excerpts were perceived to be. Lower psychoticism scorers to some extent rated indoor violence as more violent, more realistic, more frightening and more personally disturbing. More powerfully related to these programme excerpts were age and education. Older respondents and respondents with a better education perceived indoor violence as more violent, realistic, generally and personally disturbing, relative to outdoor portrayals.

Further canonical analyses computed to examine possible relationships between personality factors and perceptions of indoor and outdoor portrayals from different fictional settings failed to yield any significant findings.

16 Implications of a perceptual analysis of television violence for monitoring of programme content

This research began with the premise that violence is not a unitary concept or entity, or even one that can be reduced simply to one or two principal defining features. The perception of an act as violent depends not only upon the physical form it takes, but also upon the setting in which the act occurs. Not all acts which satisfy the necessary criteria to be called 'violent' are perceived as equally violent or upsetting. Subjective judgements about violent acts can be influenced by the presence of a variety of features within a particular scenario. A further point of importance is that individuals vary considerably in their perceptions of violence. Not all people judge the same violent incident in the same way. Some may perceive certain acts as violent, while others will not. Consequently, when attempting to derive a system of content classification based on viewers' perceptions of content, it is essential that the nature of the judges themselves is taken fully into account, as well as the nature of the content that is being judged.

In this final chapter, consideration will be given to the implications which the major findings of this research hold for the classification and assessment of violent content in fictional TV programming. The discussion will be presented in two parts. First, it will discuss implications for the control of TV violence arising out of evidence showing which facets of programme content determine most powerfully how violent portrayals are differentially perceived, and more importantly which portrayals are perceived in general as the most serious forms of violence, and which are perceived as relatively less serious. Second, further implications for content control will be examined that can be drawn with reference to differences between individuals in their perceptions of the relative seriousness of various forms of fictional TV violence. It is apparent from the current research data that whilst there may often be considerable agreement amongst individuals concerning the perceived seriousness of violence on a number of evaluative scales, certain individuals may find violence in general or particular forms of violence more serious in certain terms than do other individuals. Indeed, whilst some portrayals of violence may be rated as not especially violent by individuals generally, there may still be a few people who regard them seriously.

Features of violence and content control

The research reported in this book has taken a step towards classifying violent portrayals from fictional TV programmes in a way that is related directly to viewers' responses to programme content. Whilst there were certain genres of programming and certain objectively identifiable forms of violence not covered by this research, nevertheless it did reveal a number of attributes of portrayals along which individuals discriminated quite strongly between different kinds of violence.

Five broad objective categories of content attributes were examined for their possible mediating effects on individuals' perceptions of TV portrayals. To recap, these were:

1   the fictional setting of a portrayal or the type of programme from which it was taken;
2   the types of characters who were involved as perpetrators of violence;
3   the physical forms of the violence or the weapons or techniques used;
4   the degree of harm caused by violence to victims;
5   the physical setting of the violence.

In each experimental study, one or two of these characteristics were manipulated across a set of programme excerpts whilst other features were held constant. Whilst the complexity of this sort of procedure curtailed the range of features it was possible to investigate during the term of the project, the observed differences in judgements of the stimulus materials employed were sufficient in number and significance to indicate the complexity and multidimensionality of individuals' perceptions of fictional TV violence.

In traditional content analysis all the portrayals examined in this research would have been given equal weights (e.g. Gerbner, 1972). The current perceptual analysis has indicated, however, that these violent materials were not judged to be equally violent by two panels of individuals recruited from the public who were untutored in any specific content coding scheme. In summarising the main findings relating to differentiation of violent TV content then, what kinds of portrayals did these panels endorse as ones about which special vigilance perhaps ought to be employed?

The impact of fictional setting

The genre or fictional type of programme from which a violent portrayal originated had a powerful influence on the way it was perceived by the panels, even though other features such as the form of violence, degree of harm caused, etc. were held constant over all materials. The main finding was that as the fictional setting of violent episodes approached closer to everyday reality (temporally and/or geographically), the terms in which portrayals were rated became more serious. Violence depicted in clearly fantastic settings such as cartoons or science-fiction were perceived as essentially non-violent, non-frightening and non-disturbing. Furthermore, most panel members were prepared to endorse portrayals from the latter two types of programme as suitable for children. There was some discrimination between violent scenes from science-fiction and cartoon settings however. Animated cartoon portrayals, for example, were perceived as very humorous, whilst similar kinds of portrayals from science-fiction programmes were given low humour ratings that approximated the perceived humourless levels of violent portrayals occurring in the contemporary fictional settings. Nevertheless, futuristic settings of science-fiction shows were evidently perceived to be so divorced from everyday life that any violence occurring in them was dismissed as relatively harmless (if not necessarily humorous) fantasy.

With respect to individuals' evaluations of violent portrayals in crime—drama programmes and in Westerns, however, the story changes. In these fictional settings, violence generally was rated as considerably more violent and disturbing. Interestingly, though, the scenes perceived to be the most true to life were not also rated as the most violent or disturbing. Violent acts depicted in contemporary American crime—drama were rated as more realistic and less violent than those in contemporary British crime—drama settings. These British panels evidently perceived violence in American crime shows as typical of the kinds of incidents that actually occur in American society and violent portrayals of a similar nature in British series as not so accurately reflective of events in their own society.

The general picture that emerges from the studies reported in Chapter Six was that televised violence in contemporary settings is normally rated as more seriously violent than is that depicted in non-contemporary settings. There was one exception to this pattern. Gunfights or shootings were judged to be as violent in Westerns, and just as unsuitable for children, as were similar forms of violence in crime—drama settings. Thus the panels were concerned most about violence portrayed in contemporary and geographically proximal settings, and also in the case of Panel One about shootings in Western feature films, especially when children are likely to be watching. It is in these settings of realism and familiarity to viewers then that violent content needs to be monitored most carefully.

The impact of the types of characters involved

Four studies were carried out which investigated panel members' perceptions of violence perpetrated by different types of characters. Two of these compared perceptions of violence perpetrated either by law-enforcers or by criminals. In each scenario, the depicted conflict was between a character operating on the side of the law and one operating against it. The 'good guy' was usually a well known fictional character or if relatively unfamiliar was clearly identifiable as a law-enforcer by the uniform he was wearing. Two further studies examined perceptions of violence between males and females. In these excerpts, either a male was depicted attacking a female victim, or a female was shown attacking a male. Across each category of violence, portrayals were matched as far as possible along other attributes such as fictional setting, types of weapons used, and degree of observable harm caused by violence.

Scenes which portrayed violence perpetrated by law-enforcers were judged differently than those which depicted criminal violence, but the relative perceived seriousness of each, in terms of how violent or upsetting they were rated to be, varied significantly according to the geographical location of the action.

In American crime—drama settings, violence was rated as more violent and disturbing if it was performed by a criminal. However, in British crime—drama settings, violence was judged to be more serious on these scales if it was performed by a law-enforcer. Whilst the brief durations of these excerpts provided little storyline information about the moral or legal context in which a portrayal occurred, it was generally fairly clear to panel members on which side of the law each character was. Yet, these individuals were nevertheless more concerned about violence depicted as occurring in a British location when it was perpetrated by a law-enforcer, even though in the line of duty.

Panel members' perceptions of male-perpetrated and female-perpetrated violence against opposite-sex victims were investigated for stimulus materials from three programme genres: British crime—drama American crime—drama and science-fiction. As with judgements about violence performed by law-enforcers or criminals, the relative perceived seriousness of male- and female-perpetrated violence varied across categories of programming.

For portrayals from British crime—drama settings, male-perpetrated violence on a female victim was perceived as more violent and more disturbing than was female violence on a male victim. In American crime—drama or science-fiction settings, however, the violent female was judged to be the more violent, although in the latter genre differences between perceptions of male and female violence were only small. How can we explain such differences in the direction of individuals' judgements about these two kinds of portrayals when they occur in different fictional settings?

One answer may lie in the societal norms regarding the use of violence. Traditionally, society approves of some forms of violence under certain circumstances, and disapproves of others. Certain forms of legitimised violence are approved of. For example, violence used by police officers to uphold the law; that used by the armed forces to protect the nation against an enemy, and that used by private individuals in self-defence against an attacker. Under all these circumstances, however, the employment of a violent response must not far outweigh the magnitude of the behaviour of the intimidator or attacker. Where the force used to repel an attacker is much greater than that justified by initial provocation, it will not be found so acceptable.

Amongst the kinds of violence of which society disapproves most is that performed by men, the physically dominant and stronger sex, against women, who are generally regarded as physically weaker. Violent TV portrayals set in contemporary British locations are closer to home for British viewers than those set in contemporary America or in the future. Thus, perceptions of violence in familiar British settings involving British characters may be strongly influenced by norms of conduct that prevail in the society in which British viewers live. Therefore the violent attack of a male character on a female character in a British setting will be judged according to the appropriate norms of conduct and rated as something which is normally acceptable.

Similar types of portrayals in American crime—drama or science-fiction settings, however, are sufficiently distanced from the everyday reality of the panel members for the same rules of judgement not to apply. Instead, such factors as the frequency and familiarity of particular types of portrayal within these programmes, but not in relation to everyday life, may be more important mediators of judgements made about them. More unusual or less familiar portrayals may have a stronger impact than more frequently occurring portrayals, for example, and may therefore be perceived in different ways. One reason for this could be that individuals become differentially habituated to portrayals depending on how often they occur in programmes. In particular, individuals may become desensitised to regularly occurring portrayals. Quantitative assessments of programme content have indicated that violence in fictional TV drama is perpetrated much more often by men than by women (Gerbner *et al*, 1977, 1978, 1979) and therefore it is possible that viewers grow more accustomed to seeing male aggressors than female aggressors. As a result of differential degrees of desensitisation to these two kinds of portrayal (with habituation presumably stronger for male violence), viewers rate male-perpetrated violence as less violent and disturbing than that perpetrated by female characters in programme settings remote from their everyday reality.

To sum up, the findings here indicate that the types of characters involved in portrayals are not simply objectively specifiable features of violence, whose frequency of involvement in TV violence can be quantified through counting of appearances, but they also represent a qualitative feature which can affect the subjective perceptions of viewers about violent portrayals. Character-involvement, however, does not function in isolation to mediate viewers' judgements about violent portrayals, but interacts with fictional setting. Sharp reversals in patterns or directions of perceptual ratings were observed in four separate experimental studies of violence perpetrated by certain character-types in different fictional settings. Thus, with regard to violence portrayed in British crime—drama programmes, panel members were most concerned about that performed by law-enforcers and by male characters on females. For American programming of the same genre, however, greatest concern was displayed about criminal violence and that of women on men. Overall, the British portrayals received the most serious ratings and from a programme-monitoring perspective represent the types of violent content over which greatest vigilance is to be recommended on the basis of the current findings.

The impact of different physical forms of violence

Violent portrayals in TV fiction take on a variety of forms. Some portrayals feature the use of weapons, while others depict unarmed combat or fighting between actors. When weapons are used, these too come in a variety of forms. Some forms of armed violence such as shootings can take place with the perpetrator at a distance from the intended victim, whilst other forms such as stabbings, require attacker and victim to be at close quarters.

Two experimental studies were carried out to examine panel members' perceptions of different physical forms of violence. In the first of these studies panel members gave perceptual ratings of programme excerpts which depicted four types of violence: shootings, fist-fights, explosions and stabbings. These clips were taken from British-produced crime—drama programmes and from Westerns. In the second study, six excerpts, all taken from the same Western film, were rated in pairs. These scenes depicted violence in which victims were hurt by clubbing, by a knife, by cannon fire, by a sword, by shooting, and during a fist-fight.

From the first study, averaging over ratings of portrayals from British crime—drama and Western settings, shootings and stabbings emerged as the most violent and disturbing portrayals, and as the least suitable for children. There were some differences in perceptions of these portrayals as a function of the fictional setting in which they occurred. Whereas shootings were judged to be the most violent portrayals in Westerns, stabbings were rated as most violent in British crime—drama settings. Another important variation in perceptions of portrayals within different programme categories was the fact that physical forms of violence were more markedly differentiated between in British crime—drama settings than in Westerns. It appears that within programmes whose settings more closely approximate everyday reality as it is known by judges, the more discriminating do the latters' judgements about different kinds of portrayals become.

Among the six physical categories of violence assessed in the second study, portrayals which featured cutting or stabbing instruments were perceived as the most violent and disturbing, followed by cannon fire and shootings. Unarmed fighting was perceived to be the least violent and disturbing of all portrayals. Thus in making direct paired comparisons of portrayals, panel members rated violence with stabbing instruments as more violent than shootings, a reversal of their rank order in the previous study when clips were rated singly. This difference may be a function of the different methods employed in these studies, or perhaps in part of the different groups of individuals who participated in these two studies.

On examining the mean scores for each category per scale, it is apparent that whilst all of these forms of physical violence were perceived as moderately to very violent, they were generally not perceived to be frightening or disturbing. The latter feature was particularly true of ratings of Western scenes. So even though significant differences emerged between ratings of certain categories of physical violence, as a general rule none was judged to be especially upsetting on an absolute level. Perhaps the only real exception here was that of stabbings in British crime—drama settings. These portrayals emerged as the ones over which particular vigilance perhaps needs to be employed.

Impact of observable harm

The perpetration of violence is more often than not intended to cause harm, and frequently in violent scenarios on TV someone does get hurt or even killed. The degree of harm caused to a victim has been shown to mediate observers' behavioural reactions to a violent media portrayal (Hartmann, 1969), but what role does this feature play in viewers' perceptions of TV violence? Two studies were run to investigate panel members' perceptual reactions to televised violence which resulted either in fatal consequences for the victim, non-fatal though still injurious consequences, or no observable harm. In both studies, excerpts depicting examples of each of these types of portrayal were obtained from two programme types — American crime—drama and science-fiction — and were presented to the panels for perceptual analysis.

In general, whether judgements were obtained for excerpts singly or via paired-comparisons of portrayals, any kind of observably harmful violence was perceived as more violent and more disturbing than was violence with no observable harmful consequences for intended victims. Although the difference between them was typically small, there was some tendency for non-fatally harmful scenes to be rated as more serious than the fatally harmful ones. This difference might have been a function of greater depicted pain and suffering among victims following non-fatally violent incidents. In contrast, killings often resulted in what appeared to be relatively painless deaths. These perceived differences suggest that the amount of suffering endured by victims of violence, as well as the ultimate outcome is a crucial factor influencing judgements about violent TV portrayals. Reinforcing further earlier observations made about the varying strength of effects of different violent forms across different fictional contexts, it was found that the consequences of violence had a much stronger influence on viewers' perceptions of portrayals in contemporary settings than in futuristic settings. In science-fiction contexts, discrimination between violent episodes on the basis of degree of depicted harm was much weaker and occurred on fewer evaluative scales than did this discrimination among American crime—drama episodes.

What emerges once again from this research is the fact that on a perceptual level and using their own frame of judgemental reference, panel members were able to make more refined discriminations between portrayals in realistic fictional settings than in less realistic ones. Within realistic fictional settings such as those occurring in contemporary crime—drama shows (and perhaps also other kinds of programmes in which a story unfolds in a contemporary fictional setting), portrayals of violence that result in injury, pain, suffering and death need to be weighted more heavily than portrayals in which no observable harm to victims occurs. Within fictional settings divorced from everyday reality (e.g. science-fiction, cartoons, and possibly Westerns) such differential weighting can still be applied to portrayals on the basis of these characteristics, but is less important here because ratings of violent portrayals tend to be much lower in terms of perceived seriousness anyway, and discrimination between portrayals is less refined. For monitoring purposes, results reported in this research indicate that special attention needs to be paid to any portrayal in a contemporary fictional setting in which violence causes observable pain and suffering to victims. The more closely a fictional setting approaches or resembles everyday life, and the more graphic the portrayals of pain and suffering, the greater should be the care taken over the decision of whether such a portrayal should be shown, and when the programme that contains it should be transmitted.

The impact of physical setting

Two final studies were carried out which examined the effects of two aspects of physical setting on panel members' perceptions of violent portrayals. Controlling the content of portrayals along other important dimensions such as fictional setting, character-involvement, physical form and degree of harm, these studies compared perceptions of portrayals depicted during the day and at night, and of portrayals depicted either indoors or outdoors. The excerpts used in the first of these experiments were taken from two genres of programming — American crime—drama series and Western films and TV series — whilst the second study used excerpts from the latter two genres and also from British crime—drama series. Day-time and night-time proved to be relatively weak discriminating features of violent portrayals. Night-time portrayals were rated as somewhat more violent and more likely to disturb other people than were day-time portrayals but no really substantial differences emerged on any of the other scales. Differences between perceptions of violence occurring indoors or outdoors were more pronounced, however, and indoor portrayals were typically perceived as more seriously violent and disturbing than were outdoor portrayals.

The perceived seriousness of violence within a particular physical setting also varied as a function of fictional setting, and as observed above, differences in the rated seriousness of portrayals were more refined in realistic fictional settings than in less realistic ones. There were also differences in the kind of effect physical setting had upon ratings of portrayals in different fictional settings. Thus, whilst night-time portrayals were perceived to be more violent than day-time portrayals in Western settings, the latter were rated as the more violent in American crime–drama settings. Amongst indoor and outdoor portrayals, there was consistency in the direction of rated seriousness of portrayals across American crime–drama and Western settings, with outdoor portrayals rated as more violent and potentially disturbing to others than indoor portrayals. Within British crime–drama contexts, however, indoor portrayals were rated in more serious terms than outdoor portrayals.

Although weaker in their influence on panel members' perceptions of violent TV materials than other objective features of content, physical setting did have some effect on subjective judgements of episodes within contemporary crime–drama programmes. Greatest concern emerged for indoor portrayals of violence in British crime–drama programmes, and whilst this feature may not be potent on its own, in association with other disturbing features such as degree of harm caused to victims, types of weapons employed and characters involved, it could add to the overall impact of a portrayal on viewers.

In pulling these findings together, attempts have been made to identify certain combinations of the features studied which, if put together in a single sequence, would constitute a portrayal likely to be found especially violent or disturbing. Figures 16.1, 16.2 and 16.3 depict attempts to specify recipes for portrayals which, on the evidence of this research, are those most likely to be perceived respectively as very violent, likely to disturb people in general, or personally disturbing. As can be seen, these recipes have many ingredients in common, but are not exactly alike. The nature of the judgement in question determines to some extent the precise ingredients to be added to the recipe. Thus, for example, law-enforcers perpetrating shootings are less likely to feature as essential ingredients of portrayals found to be personally disturbing than they are to feature in portrayals judged to be relatively violent or likely to disturb people in general.

The audience and content control

Panel members were not all alike in the way they judged the violent

252

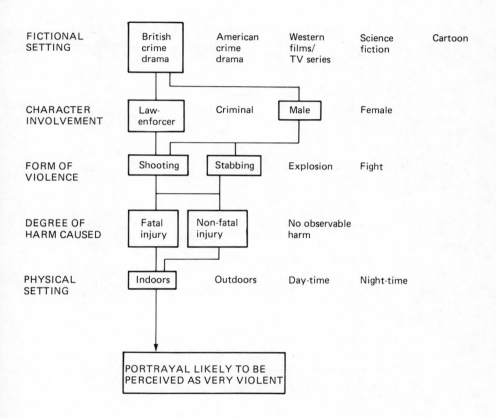

FICTIONAL SETTING: British crime drama · American crime drama · Western films/TV series · Science fiction · Cartoon

CHARACTER INVOLVEMENT: Law-enforcer · Criminal · Male · Female

FORM OF VIOLENCE: Shooting · Stabbing · Explosion · Fight

DEGREE OF HARM CAUSED: Fatal injury · Non-fatal injury · No observable harm

PHYSICAL SETTING: Indoors · Outdoors · Day-time · Night-time

PORTRAYAL LIKELY TO BE PERCEIVED AS VERY VIOLENT

Figure 16.1 Ingredients of a scene most likely to be perceived as very violent

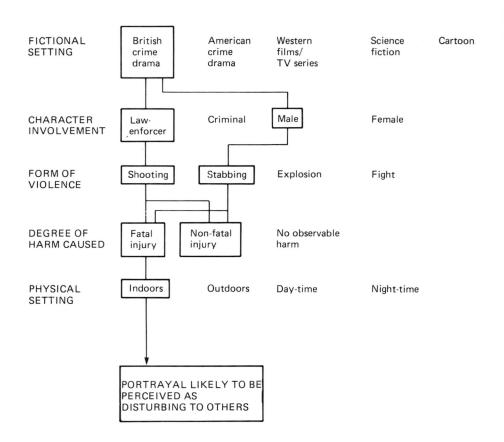

FICTIONAL
SETTING
British crime drama | American crime drama | Western films/ TV series | Science fiction | Cartoon

CHARACTER
INVOLVEMENT
Law-enforcer | Criminal | Male | Female

FORM OF
VIOLENCE
Shooting | Stabbing | Explosion | Fight

DEGREE OF
HARM CAUSED
Fatal injury | Non-fatal injury | No observable harm

PHYSICAL
SETTING
Indoors | Outdoors | Day-time | Night-time

PORTRAYAL LIKELY TO BE PERCEIVED AS DISTURBING TO OTHERS

Figure 16.2   Ingredients of a scene most likely to be perceived as disturbing to others

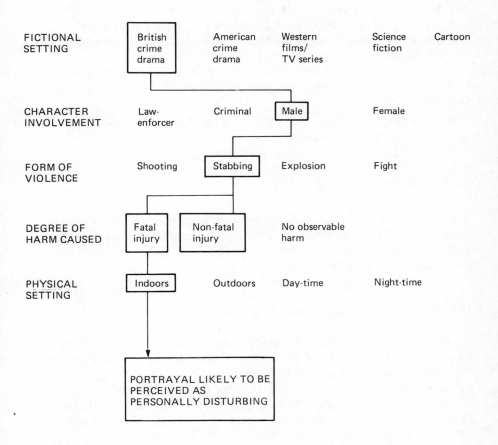

FICTIONAL
SETTING

| British crime drama | American crime drama | Western films/ TV series | Science fiction | Cartoon |

CHARACTER
INVOLVEMENT

Law-enforcer   Criminal   Male   Female

FORM OF
VIOLENCE

Shooting   Stabbing   Explosion   Fight

DEGREE OF
HARM CAUSED

Fatal injury   Non-fatal injury   No observable harm

PHYSICAL
SETTING

Indoors   Outdoors   Day-time   Night-time

PORTRAYAL LIKELY TO BE
PERCEIVED AS
PERSONALLY DISTURBING

Figure 16.3   Ingredients of a scene most likely to be perceived as personally disturbing

materials they saw. Whilst a number of general patterns of response emerged, some individuals perceived all or certain portrayals as more seriously violent than did others. The different patterns of ratings outlined in the previous sections of this chapter were based on the average opinions of the panels as a whole. However, the finding that certain portrayals were perceived by most or some panel members as essentially non-violent or non-disturbing does not preclude the possibility that some individuals were not so untroubled by the same materials. If a minority of the audience is disturbed by particular kinds of violence even though the majority are not bothered by them, this is enough to justify consideration.

Five categories of individual difference characteristics were examined in relation to respondents' perceptions of TV violence, for Panel One only:

1   demographic factors (sex, age, class, education) and amount of TV viewing;
2   self-perceptions relating to sexuality;
3   social beliefs;
4   attitudes towards aggression;
5   personality.

What do current findings indicate are the kinds of individuals who are most likely to be concerned by TV violence in general? Do they show also that certain types of person are particularly concerned by particular kinds of violent portrayal?

Demographics and amount of TV viewing

Beginning with differences in perceptions of violence from different fictional settings, weight of viewing was more powerfully and consistently related to panel members' judgements than any demographic variables. Heavier viewers tended to judge portrayals from British crime—drama series as particularly violent and realistic. Female and lighter viewers, however, tended to rate all kinds of violence except cartoon content as less suitable for children. Heavier viewers among the panel who had a higher terminal age of full-time education perceived British law-enforcer violence as more frightening and American law-enforcer and criminal violence as less frightening compared with other panel members. Sex, age and socio-economic class were less clearly related to perceptions of the latter portrayals. Heavier viewers also rated male violence on female victims in British crime—drama settings as more violent, more realistic, more frightening and more personally disturbing than did other individuals. Heavier viewers were also more upset by female violence in British fictional settings than were other panel members, though they also thought that such content was relatively less violent. It is interesting to note that the actual sex of panel members was neither consistently nor strongly related to differential perceptions of male- and female-perpetrated violence here.

Amount of TV viewing was differentially related to perceptions of different physical categories or forms of violence, along with the actual sex of respondents. Female and heavier viewers were more concerned about nearly all forms of violence, especially in British crime—drama settings. No such relationships emerged for Western materials. In particular these individuals were most frightened and disturbed by stabbings and shootings, the types of violence generally perceived by the panels as the most seriously violent materials. Heavier viewing was associated with perceptions of fatal and non-fatal harmful violence as more violent, more frightening and more likely to disturb people in general than were other characteristics of panel members. On physical setting, finally, heavier viewing and better-educated panel members perceived indoor violence as especially more violent, more frightening, more personally disturbing and as less humorous and suitable for children.

The consistent pattern to emerge throughout all correlations of viewing and demographic factors with perceptions of violent portrayals was:

1   that weight of TV viewing was more consistently and powerfully related to perceptions of violence than any demographic factor; and
2   that heavier viewers tended to perceive as especially more violent and disturbing those categories of TV violence which panel members in general rated as the most violent and most disturbing.

Self-perceptions

Actual gender of panel members emerged as a relatively weak correlate of perceptions of violent materials used in this research. However, at an experiential—judgemental level, the extent to which individuals perceive attributes associated with masculine or feminine tendencies as descriptive of their own character may be more important to their perceptions of TV scenarios than is their actual sex. In a series of separate analyses which related self-perceptions as such to perceptions of televised violence this assumption was supported. Actual gender was found to be less consistently and more weakly related to ratings of different categories of TV violence than was self-perceived masculinity—femininity.

Respondents who scored higher on masculinity judged violence from all fictional settings examined in this research as less violent than did other panel members. Higher self-perceived femininity and lower self-perceived masculinity were together associated with perceptions of law-enforcer violence in British crime—drama settings as particularly more realistic, more frightening, and less suitable for children. Higher femininity alone was associated with perceptions of criminal violence in British settings as especially more disturbing.

Panel members characterised by low masculinity and high femininity perceived male-perpetrated violence in British crime—drama settings as more realistic and more personally disturbing than did other respondents. Female violence in American crime—drama settings, on the other hand, was seen by those panel members in less serious terms. Higher femininity scorers also thought that male violence in British settings would be especially likely to disturb people in general.

On perceptions of TV violence of different physical forms or which cause different degrees of observable harm to victims, results indicated that lower masculinity and higher femininity were associated with particular concern about those portrayals which panel members in general rated as the most seriously violent and disturbing (e.g. stabbings and shootings in British crime—drama contexts and harmful violence in realistic fictional settings). This same pattern emerged for relationships between perceptions of indoor and outdoor portrayals of violence and self-perceived masculinity—femininity. Higher femininity and lower masculinity were associated with judgements of indoor violence as being more violent, more frightening, more personally disturbing and more likely to disturb people in general than when these portrayals were judged to be by panel members as a whole.

In summary, relatively higher levels of self-perceived femininity, coupled often with relatively low levels of self-perceived masculinity, were associated with even higher ratings of seriousness for those scenes which were regarded by the panels as a whole as the most seriously violent or disturbing.

Social beliefs

Four social belief factors were related to perceptions of televised violence: fear of victimisation, anomia, belief in a just world, and internal—external locus of control. Recent research has indicated that more apprehensive individuals may exhibit particular attraction to crime—drama programming (Wakshlag *et al*, 1983) or that individuals may selectively view such programmes for information about how to cope with crime (Mendelsohn, 1983) or which offer support to beliefs they hold about the world (Gunter and Wober, 1983). The current research has indicated that individuals who hold different kinds of social beliefs exhibit different perceptions or judgements about violent portrayals from crime—drama and other fictional settings, and about portrayals which differ from each other in terms of character involvement, physical form, degree of harmfulness, and physical setting.

Panel members whose beliefs were characterised by external locus of control, or who, in other words, believed that events in their lives are governed primarily by forces beyond their personal control, tended to rate violent portrayals from British and American crime—drama settings as more realistic, more violent and more upsetting than did the average respondent. On differentiation between violent portrayals according to the types of characters featured as perpetrators or victims of violence, higher external locus of control, stronger anomia, stronger fearfulness and weaker belief in a just world were associated with perceptions of law-enforcer violence in British crime—drama settings as being more violent and less humorous, and also as less suitable for children. External locus of control and weak just world beliefs were also associated with greater perceived seriousness of male-perpetrated violence on female victims in British settings.

More fearful and fateful beliefs were related to perceptions of shootings and stabbings in British crime—drama settings as being particularly serious in terms of degree of perceived violence, realism and emotional distress caused. Such beliefs were associated in addition with perceptual reactions of a serious nature to portrayals which depicted observable harm to victims, and which were located indoors.

In summary two major sets of findings emerged from correlations of social beliefs with perceptions of different kinds of TV violence:

1   Internal—external locus of control was related most robustly to perceptions of TV violence of all social belief factors examined in this research.
2   External controllers, who also exhibited stronger fearfulness and weaker just world beliefs, tended to perceive as even more serious terms those portrayals which panel members in general rated as most violent and most disturbing.

Personal aggressiveness

People differ in their attitudes towards aggression and in their dispositions to behave aggressively themselves. Several studies have indicated that aggressive predispositions may mediate preferences for violent TV programmes (Atkin *et al*, 1979; Fenigstein, 1979; Freedman and Newton, 1975). These findings suggest that need for a more complex transactional model to account for the relationships between watching TV violence and subsequent behavioural tendencies amongst viewers (see Gunter, 1983).

The current research investigated the significance of personal aggressiveness or attitudes towards the use of aggression as mediators of observers' perceptions of different kinds of televised violence. Panel members' scores on four sub-scales of a personal hostility inventory (Buss and Durkee, 1957) were related to their perceptual judgements of violent portrayals. The four sub-scales represented four types of personally aggressive dispositions. To recap these were:

1   *assault* — or the tendency to endorse the use of physical violence against others;
2   *indirect hostility* — malicious gossip and proneness to throw temper tantrums;
3   *irritability* — or the readiness to show anger and to be rude to people; and
4   *verbal aggression* — or tendencies towards arguing, shouting, swearing, and issuing verbal threats.

In relation to perceptions of violent portrayals from different fictional settings, it was found that individuals with stronger self-endorsed aggressive dispositions generally — over all sub-scales — tended to rate British crime—drama scenes as more humorous and more exciting than did other panel members. Stronger indirect hostility and verbal aggressiveness were related to perceptions of British crime—drama scenes in rather less serious terms than for the panel as a whole. Thus, personal aggressiveness was associated with differential perceptions of portrayals from different fictional settings, and in such a way that more aggressive panel members tended to perceive those scenes rated on average as the most violent in rather less violent terms.

Personal aggressiveness was related in different ways to perceptions of televised violence perpetrated by different character-types. Weaker self-endorsed physical aggressiveness coupled with stronger self-endorsed verbal aggressiveness were associated with ratings of law-enforcer violence as relatively less disturbing and criminal violence as relatively more disturbing compared with average ratings for panel members generally. This pattern was particularly clear among British crime—drama materials. On perceptions of male-perpetrated and female-perpetrated violence, individuals with weaker self-endorsed aggressive dispositions perceived both types of portrayal as relatively more violent and more disturbing than did panel members as a whole, and this was again especially pronounced for male violence in British crime—drama contexts.

There was an interesting interaction between personal aggressiveness and perceptions of different categories of physical violence. Panel members with weak physically aggressive dispositions (low assault scorers) rated stabbings and fist-fights as relatively less violent, less frightening and less personally disturbing than did the panel generally, and shootings and explosions as relatively more serious in these terms. Individuals who endorsed statements such as 'People who continually pester me are likely to get a punch on the nose', or 'There have often been times when people pushed me so far that we came to blows', or who rejected statements such as 'I can think of no good reason for ever hitting anyone', or 'I seldom strike back, even if someone hits me first' were less likely to perceive fights between TV characters to be as violent as did individuals who gave the opposite responses to these statements. Individuals who condoned the use of physical violence and who claimed to be inclined to use it themselves were less concerned than were other individuals about fighting between TV characters. However, for other categories of violence such as shootings and explosions, which they would be probably less likely to use themselves, personally aggressive respondents gave much more serious judgemental ratings.

Initial comparisons of harmful and harmless violent incidents for panels as a whole yielded higher ratings of violence for the former. In addition, harmful violence was found to be rated as especially more violent and more likely to disturb other people than was harmless violence by individuals with relatively strong self-endorsed dispositions towards non-physical forms of aggression such as indirect hostility and verbal aggressiveness. Individuals with both physical and non-physical aggressive dispositions tended to endorse indoor portrayals as relatively less violent, less realistic, less likely to disturb others and as less personally disturbing than did other panel members.

Personality

Personality was operationalised here via Eysenck's Personality Questionnaire (Eysenck and Eysenck, 1975). Three separate personality factors: extraversion, neuroticism and psychoticism, were related to panel members' perceptions of televised violence. Although regarded by Eysenck as core structures of human personality and behavioural dispositions across situations, these factors exhibited largely inconsistent or weak relationships with perceptions of televised violence amongst the materials and individuals tested in this research. There were a number of relationships worth mentioning, however, which indicated a tendency for individuals with stronger neuroticism to be especially concerned about those categories of portrayal rated by panel members generally as most seriously violent or disturbing.

Higher neuroticism scorers rated British crime–drama, American crime–drama and Western materials as more violent and more frightening than did other panel members. On perceptions of violence perpetrated by males on females or by females on males, it was found that higher neuroticism scores were associated with judgements that male violence in British crime–drama settings was particularly violent. Higher psychoticism scorers were less frightened by violent portrayals that depicted harm to victims, whilst individuals who scored relatively highly on extraversion, neuroticism *and* psychoticism perceived more humour in harmful portrayals than did other panel members.

References

Argyle, M., Furnham, A., and Graham, J.A. (1981) *Social Situations*. Cambridge: Cambridge University Press.

Atkin, C., Greenberg, B., Korszenny, F., and McDermott, S. (1979). 'Selective exposure to televised violence', *Journal of Broadcasting*, Vol. 23, pp.5–13.

Bandura, A. (1965). 'Vicarious processes: A case of no-trial learning'. In L. Berkowitz (ed.), *Advances in Experimental Social Psychology*. New York: Academic Press, Vol. 2, pp.1–55.

Bandura, A., Ross, D., and Ross, S.A. (1963). 'Imitation of film-mediated aggressive models', *Journal of Personality and Social Psychology*, Vol. 66, pp.3–11.

Bandura, A., and Walters, R.H. (1963). *Social Learning and Personality Development*. New York: Holt, Rinehart and Winston.

Barclay, R.A., Ullman, D.G., Otto, L., and Brecht, J.M. (1977). 'The effects of sex-typing and sex appropriateness of modelled behaviour on children's imitation', *Child Development*, Vol. 48, pp.721–725.

Barker, R., Dembo, T. and Levin (1941). *Frustration and regression: An experiment with young children*. University of Iowa, Studies in Child Welfare, no. 18.

Baron, R.A. (1971a). 'Magnitude of victim's pain cues and level of prior anger arousal as determinants of adult aggressive behaviour', *Journal of Personality and Social Psychology*, Vol. 17, pp.236–243.

Baron, R.A. (1971b). 'Aggression as a function of magnitude of victim's pain cues, level of prior anger arousal and aggressor—victim similarity', *Journal of Personality and Social Psychology*, Vol. 18, pp.48—54.

Baron, R.A. (1977). *Human Aggression*. New York: Plenum Press.

Baron, R.A., and Kepner, C.R. (1970). 'Model's behaviour and attraction toward the model as determinants of adult aggressive behaviour', *Journal of Personality and Social Psychology*, Vol. 14, pp.335—344.

Belson, W.A. (1978). *Television Violence and the Adolescent Boy*. Farnborough: Saxon House.

Bem, S.L. (1974). 'The measurement of psychological androgyny', *Journal of Consulting and Clinic Psychology*, Vol. 52, pp.155—162.

Bem, S.L., and Lenney, E. (1976). 'Sex typing and the avoidance of cross-sex behaviour', *Journal of Personality and Social Psychology*, Vol. 33, pp.48—54.

Berkowitz, L. (1965). 'Some aspects of observed aggression', *Journal of Personality and Social Psychology*, Vol. 2, pp.359—369.

Berkowtiz, L. (1971). 'The "weapons effect", demand characteristics and the myth of the compliant subject', *Journal of Personality and Social Psychology*, Vol. 20, pp.332—338.

Berkowitz, L., and Alioto, J.T. (1973). 'The meaning of an observed event as a determinant of its aggressive consequences', *Journal of Personality and Social Psychology*, Vol. 28, pp.206—217.

Berkowitz, L., and Le Page, A. (1967). 'Weapons as aggression-eliciting stimuli, *Journal of Personality and Social Psychology*, Vol. 7, pp.202—207.

Blank, D.M. (1977a). 'The Gerbner violence profile', *Journal of Broadcasting*, Vol. 21, pp.273—279.

Blank, D.M. (1977b). Final comments on the violence profile. *Journal of Broadcasting*, Vol. 21, pp.287—296.

Blumenthal, R., Kahn, R., Andrews, F., and Head, K. (1972). *Justifying Violence: Attitudes of American Men*. Ann Arbor, Mich: Survey Research Centre, Institute for Social Research, University of Michigan.

Boyanowsky, E.O. (1977). 'Film preferences under condition of threat: Whetting the appetite for violence, information or excitement?' *Communication Research*, Vol. 4, pp.133—144.

Boyanowsky, E.O., Newtson, D., and Walster, E. (1974). 'Film preferences following a murder', *Communication Research*, Vol. 1, pp.32—43.

British Broadcasting Corporation (1972). *Violence on Television: Programme Content and Viewer Perceptions*. London: British Broadcasting Corporation.

British Broadcasting Corporation (1979). *The Portrayal of Violence in*

Television Programmes: Suggestion for a Revised Note of BBC Guidance. London: British Broadcasting Corporation.

Brown, R.C., Jr., and Tedeschi, J.T. (1976). 'Determinants of perceived aggression', *Journal of Social Psychology*, Vol. 100, pp.77–87.

Buckhart, K. (1973). *Women in prison*. New York: Doubleday.

Buss, A.A. (1961). *The Psychology of Aggression*. New York: John Wiley and Sons Inc.

Buss, A.A., and Durkee, A. (1957). 'An inventory for assessing different kinds of hostility', *Journal of Consulting Psychology*, Vol. 21, pp.343–349.

Butler, M., and Paisley, W. (1980). *Women and the Mass Media*. New York: Human Sciences Press.

Cattell, R.B., and Scheier, I. (1958). 'The nature of anxiety: A review of thirteen multivariate analyses comparing 814 variables', *Psychological Reports*, Vol. 4, pp.351–388.

Christie, R., and Geis, F.L. (1970). *Studies in Machiavellianism*. New York: Academic Press.

Coffin, T.E., and Tuchman, S. (1973). 'Rating television programmes for violence: a comparison of five surveys', *Journal of Broadcasting*, Vol. 17, pp.3–22.

Couch, C.J. (1968). 'Collective behaviour: An examination of some stereotypes', *Social Problems*, Vol. 15, pp.310–322.

Diener, E., and De Four, D. (1978). 'Does television violence enhance programme popularity?', *Journal of Personality and Social Psychology*, Vol. 36, pp.333–341.

Diener, E., and Woody, L.W. (1981). 'TV violence and viewer liking', *Communication Research*, Vol. 8, pp.281–306.

Dominick, J.R., and Greenberg, B.S. (1972). 'Attitudes toward violence: The interaction of television, exposure, family attitudes and social class'. In G.A. Comstock and E.A. Rubinstein (eds.), *Television and Social Behaviour*, Vol. 3. *Television and Adolescent Aggressiveness*. Washington, D.C. U.S. Government Printing Office, pp.314–335.

Doob, A.N., and Macdonald, C.E. (1979). 'Television viewing and fear of victimization: Is the relationship causal?', *Journal of Personality and Social Psychology*, Vol. 37, pp.170–179.

Ekman, P., Liebert, R.M., Friesen, W.V., Harrison, R., Zlatchin, C., Malmstrom, E.J., and Baron, R.A. (1972). 'Facial expressions of emotion while watching televised violence as predictors of subsequent aggression'. In G.A. Comstock, E.A. Rubinstein, and

J.P. Murray (eds.), *Television and Social Behaviour*, Vol. 5, *Television's Effects: Further Explanations*. Washington, D.C. U.S. Government Printing Office, pp.22–58.

Eysenck, H.J. (1964). *Crime and Personality*. London: Routledge and Kegan Paul.

Eysenck, H.G. (1967). *The Biological Basis of Personality*. Springfield: Thomas.

Eysenck, H.J., and Eysenck, S.B.G. (1969). *Personality Structure and Measurement*. London: Routledge and Kegan Paul.

Eysenck, H.J., and Eysenck, S.B.G. (1975). *Manual for the Eysenck Personality Questionnaire*. London: Hodder and Stoughton.

Eysenck, H.J., and Nias, D.K.B. (1978). *Sex, Violence and the Media*. London: Maurice Temple Smith.

Fenigstein, A. (1979). 'Does aggression cause a preference for viewing media violence?', *Journal of Personality and Social Psychology*, Vol. 37, pp.2307–2317.

Feshbach, S. (1970). 'Aggression'. In P.H. Mussen (ed.), *Carmichael's Manual of Child Psychology*. New York: John Wiley, pp.159–259.

Feshbach, S. (1972). 'Reality and fantasy in filmed violence'. In J.P. Murray, E.A. Rubinstein, and G.A. Comstock (eds.), *Television and Social Behaviour*, Vol. 2, *Television and Social Learning*. Washington, D.C. U.S. Government Printing Office, pp.318–345.

Feshbach, S., and Singer, R.D. (1971). *Television and Aggression: An Experimental Field Study*. San Francisco: Jossey-Bass.

Feshbach, S., Stiles, W.B., and Bitter, E. (1967). 'Reinforcing effect of witnessing aggression'. *Journal of Research in Personality*, Vol. 2, pp.133–139.

Forgas, J.P. (1979). *Social Episodes: The Study of Interaction Routines*. New York and London: Academic Press.

Forgas, J.P., Brown, L.B., and Menyhart, J. (1980). 'Dimensions of aggression: The perception of aggressive episodes'. *British Journal of Psychology*, Vol. 19, pp.215–227.

Fraczek, A. (1979). 'Functions of emotional and cognitive mechanisms in the regulation of aggressive behaviour'. In S. Feshbach and A. Fraczek (eds.), *Aggression and Behaviour Change*. New York: Praeger, pp.139–157.

Freedman, J., and Newtson, R. (1975). *The effect of anger on preference for filmed violence*. Paper presented at the annual conference of American Psychological Association, Chicago, September 1975.

Furnham, A.F. (1982). 'Personality and activity preference'. *British Journal of Social Psychology*, Vol. 20, pp.57–68.

Gamson, W.A., and McEvoy, J. (1972). 'Police violence and its public support', in J.F. Short and M.E. Wolfgang (eds.), *Collective Violence*. Chicago: Aldine.

Gans, H.J. (1980). 'The audience for television and in television research', in S.B. Withey and R.P. Abeles (eds.), *Television and Social Behaviour: Beyond Violence and Children*. Hillsdale, New Jersey: Lawrence Erlbaum Associates, Inc.

Geen, R.G. (1970). 'Perceived suffering of the victim as an inhibitor of attack-induced aggression', *Journal of Social Psychology*, Vol. 81, pp.209–215.

Geen, R.G., (1976). *Personality: The Skein of Behaviour*. Henry Kingston Publishers.

Geen, R.G., and Rakosky, J.J. (1973). 'Interpretations of observed aggression and their effect on GSR', *Journal of Experimental Research in Personality*, Vol. 6, pp.289–292.

Gerbner, G. (1972). 'Violence in television drama: Trends and symbolic functions', in G.A. Comstock and E.A. Rubinstein (eds.), *Television and Social Behaviour*, Vol. 1, *Media Content and Control*. Washington, D.C. U.S. Government Printing Office, pp.28–187.

Gerbner, G., and Gross, L. (1976). 'Living with television: The violence profile', *Journal of Communications*, Vol. 26, pp.173–199.

Gerbner, G., Gross, L., Eleey, M.E., Jackson-Beeck, M., Jeffries-Fox, S., and Signorielli, N. (1977). 'Television violence profile No. 8: The highlights', *Journal of Communication*, Vol. 27, pp.171–180.

Gerbner, G., Gross, L., Jackson-Beeck, M., Jeffries-Fox, S., and Signorielli, N. (1978). 'Cultural indicators: Violence profile No. 9', *Journal of Communication*, Vol. 28, pp.176–207.

Gerbner, G., Gross, L., Signorielli, N., Morgan, M., and Jackson-Beeck, M., (1979). 'The demonstration of power: Violence profile No. 10', *Journal of Communication*, Vol. 29, pp.177–196.

Goldstein, J.H. (1972). *Preference for aggressive movie content. The effects of cognitive salience*. Unpublished manuscript, Temple University, Philadelphia.

Goranson, R.E. (1969). 'A review of recent literature on psychological effects of media portrayals of violence', in R.K. Baker and S.J. Ball (eds.), *Violence and the media. A Staff Report to the National Commission on the Causes and Prevention of Violence*. Washington, D.C. U.S. Government Printing Office, pp.395–413.

Greenberg, B.S. (1974). 'Gratifications of television viewing and their correlates for British Children', in J. Blumler and E. Katz (eds.), *The Uses of Mass Communications. Current Perspectives on Gratifications Research. Sage Annual Reviews of Communications*

Research, Vol. 3. Beverley Hills, Ca. Sage, pp.71—92.

Greenberg, B., and Dominick, J.R. (1970). 'Racial and social class differences in teenagers' use of television', *Journal of Broadcasting*, Vol. 13, pp.331—344.

Greenberg, B.S., and Gordon, T.F. (1972a). 'Perceptions of violence in television programmes: Critics and the public', in G.A. Comstock and E.A. Rubinstein (eds.), *Television and Social Behaviour, Vol. Content and Control*. Washington, D.C. U.S. Government Printing Office, pp.244—258.

Greenberg, B.S., and Gordon, T.F., (1972b). 'Social class and racial differences in children's perception of televised violence', in G.A. Comstock and E.A. Rubinstein (eds.), *Television and Social Behaviour, Vol. 5. Television's Effects. Further Explorations*. Washington, D.C. U.S. Government Printing Office, pp.

Greenberg, B.S., and Reeves, B. (1974). 'Children and the perceived reality of television'. *Journal of Social Issues*, Vol. 4, pp.86—97.

Gross, L., and Jeffries-Fox, S. (1978). 'What do you want to be when you grow up little girl?', in G. Tuchman, A.K. Daniels and J. Benet (eds.), *Health and Home: Images of Women in the Mass Media*. New York: Oxford University Press, pp.240—265.

Gunter, B. (1981). 'Measuring television violence: A review and suggestions for a new analytical perspective'. *Current Psychological Reviews*, Vol. 1, pp.91—112.

Gunter, B. (1983). 'Do aggressive people prefer violent television?' *Bulletin of the British Psychological Society*, Vol. 36, pp.166—168.

Gunter, B., and Wober, M. (1983). 'Television viewing and public trust'. *British Journal of Social Psychology*, Vol. 22, pp.174—176.

Halloran, J.D., and Croll, P. (1972). 'Television programmes in Great Britain', in G.A. Comstock and E.A. Rubinstein (eds.), *Television and Social Behaviour, Vol. 1. Content and Control*. Washington, D.C. U.S. Government Printing Office, pp.415—492.

Harre, R., and Secord, P. (1972). *The Explanation of Social Behaviour*. Oxford: Blackwell.

Hartmann, D.P. (1969). 'Influence of symbolically modelled instrumental aggression and pain cues on aggressive behaviour'. *Journal of Personality and Social Psychology*, Vol. 11, pp.280—288.

Hawkins, R.P. (1977). The dimensional structure of children's perceptions of television reality', *Communication Research*, Vol. 4, pp.299—320.

Head, S.W., (1954). 'Content analysis of television drama programmes', *Quarterly of Film, Radio and Television*, no. 9, pp.175—194.

Himmelweit, A.T., Oppenheim, A.N., and Vince, P. (1958). *Television and the Child. An empirical Study of the Effect of Television on the Young.* London: Oxford University Press.

Himmelweit, H.T., Swift, B., and Biberian, M.J., (1978). 'The audience as a critic: An approach to the study of entertainment', in P. Tannenbaum (ed.), *Entertainment Functions of Television.* New York: Lawrence Erlbaum Associates.

Hoffman-Bustamente, D. (1973). 'The nature of female criminality', *Issues in Criminology*, Vol. 8, pp.117–136.

Howitt, D., and Cumberbatch, G. (1974). 'Audience perceptions of violent television content', *Communication Research*, Vol. 1, pp.204–223.

Howitt, D., and Cumberbatch, G. (1975). *Mass Media Violence and Society.* New York: Halstead.

Johnson, R.L., Friedman, H.L., and Gross, H.S. (1972). 'Four masculine styles in television programming: A study of the viewing preferences of adolescent males', in G.A. Comstock and E.A. Rubinstein (eds.), *Television and Social Behaviour, Vol. 3. Television and Adolescent Aggressiveness.* Washington, D.C. U.S. Government Printing Office, pp.361–371.

Kahn, R.L. (1972). 'The justification of violence: Social problems and social issues'. *Journal of Social Issues,* Vol. 28, pp.155–172.

Kane, T., Joseph, J.M., and Tedeschi, J.T. (1976). 'Personal perception and the Berkowitz paradigm for the study of aggression', *Journal of Personality and Social Psychology*, Vol. 33, pp.663–673.

Kaplan, R.M., and Singer, R.D. (1976). 'Television violence and viewer aggression: A re-examination of the evidence', *Journal of Social Issues*, Vol. 32, pp.35–70.

Lagerspetz, K.M.J., Wahlroos, C., and Wendelin, C. (1978). 'Facial expression of pre-school children while watching televised violence', *Scandinavian Journal of Psychology*, Vol. 19, pp.213–222.

Lansky, L.M., Crandall, V.J., Kagan, J., and Baker, C.T. (1961). 'Sex differences in aggression and its correlates in middle-class adolescents', *Child Development*, Vol. 32, pp.45–48.

Larsen, O.N., Gray, L.N., and Fortis, J.G. (1963). 'Goals and goal achievement in television content: Models for anomie?', *Sociological Inquiry*, Vol. 33, pp.180–196.

Latane, B., and Darley, J.M. (1970). 'Social determinants of bystander intervention in emergencies', in J. Macawley and L. Berkowitz (eds.), *Altruism and Helping Behaviour.* New York:

Academic Press, pp.13—27.

Lefkowitz, M.M., Eron, L.D., Walder, L.O., and Huesmann, L.R., (1972). 'Television violence and child aggression: A follow-up study', in G.A. Comstock and E.A. Rubinstein (eds.), *Television and Social Behaviour, Vol. 3. Television and Adolescent Aggressiveness*. Washington, D.C. U.S. Government Printing Office.

Lefkowitz, M.M., Eron, L.D., Walder, L.O., and Huesmann, L.R., (1977). *Growing Up to be Violent: A Longitudinal Study of the Development of Aggression*. New York: Pergavon.

Lerner, M.J. (1970). 'The desire for justice and reactions to victims', in I.J. Macawley and L. Berkowitz (eds.), *Altruism and Helping Behaviour*. New York: Academic Press Inc., pp.205—229.

Levin, H., and Sears, R.R. (1956). 'Identification with parents as a determinant of dull play aggression', *Child Development*, Vol. 27, pp.135—153.

Levine, M.S. (1977). *Canonical analysis and factor comparison*. Sage University Paper, Beverley Hills: Sage.

Leyens, J.P., and Parke, R.D. (1975). 'Aggressive slides can induce a weapons effect', *European Journal of Social Psychology*, Vol. 5, pp.229—236.

Liebert, R.M., and Baron, R.A. (1972). 'Some immediate effects of televised violence on children's behaviour', *Development Psychology*, Vol. 6, pp.469—475.

Lincoln, A., and Levinger, G. (1972). 'Observers' evaluations of the victim and the attacker in an aggressive incident', *Journal of Personality and Social Psychology*, Vol. 22, pp.202—210.

Lloyd, B.B., and Archer, J. (1981). 'Problems and issues in research on gender differences', *Current Psychological Reviews*, Vol. 1, pp.287—304.

Maccoby, E., and Jacklin, C. (1974). *The Psychology of Sex Differences*. Palo Alto, Calif. Stanford University Press.

Maccoby, E.E., and Wilson, W.C., (1957). 'Identification and observational learning from films', *Journal of Abnormal and Social Psychology*, Vol. 55, pp.76--87.

Maccoby, E.E., Wilson, W.C., and Burton, R.V. (1958). 'Differential movie-viewing behaviour of male and female viewers', *Journal of Personality*, Vol. 26, pp.259—267.

McGlynn, R.P., Megas, J.C., and Benson, D.H. (1976). 'Sex and race as factors affecting the attribution of insanity in a murder trial', *Journal of Psychology*, Vol. 93, pp.93—99.

McLeod, J., Atkin, C., and Chaffee, S. (1972). 'Adolescents, parents and television use: Adolescent self-report measures from Maryland

and Wisconsin samples', in G.A. Comstock and E.A. Rubinstein (eds.), *Television and Social Behaviours, Vol. 3. Television and Adolescent Aggressiveness*. Washington, D.C. U.S. Government Printing Office.

McLeod, J.M., and Reeves, B. (1980). 'On the nature of mass media effects', in S.B. Withey and R.P. Abeles (eds.), *Television and Social Behaviour: Beyond Violence and Children*. Hillsdale, New Jersey: Lawrence Erlbaum Associates, Inc.

Mendelsohn, H. (1983). *Using the mass media for crime prevention*. Paper presented at the Annual Conference, American Association for Public Opinion Research, Buck Hill Falls, Pennsylvania, May 21.

Milgram, S., and Shotland, R.L. (1973). *Television and Antisocial Behaviour: Field Experiments*. New York: Academic Press.

National Coalition on Television Violence (1981). 'TV violence on the average'. *NCTV News*, no. 2, p.1.

Noble, G. (1970). 'Film-mediated aggressive and creative play', *British Journal of Social and Clinical Psychology*, Vol. 9, pp.1–7.

Noble, G. (1975). *Children in Front on the Small Screen*. London: Constable.

Osborn, D.K., and Endsley, R.C. (1971). 'Emotional reactions of young children to TV violence', *Child Development*, Vol. 42, pp.321–331.

Parke, R.D., Berkowitz, L., Leyens, J.P., West, S.G., and Sebastian, R.J. (1977). 'Some effects of violent and non-violent movies on the behaviour of juvenile delinquents', in L. Berkowitz (ed.), *Advance in Experimental Social Psychology*, Vol. 10. New York: Academic Press.

Perry, D.G., and Perry, L.C., (1975). 'Observational learning in children: Effects of sex of model and subject's sex-role behaviour', *Journal of Personality and Social Psychology*, Vol. 31, pp.1083–1088.

Rappaport, H., and Katkin, E. (1972). 'Relationships among manifest anxiety, response to stress, and the perception of autonomic activity', *Journal of Consulting and Clinical Psychology*, Vol. 38, pp.219–224.

Rarick, O.L., Townsend, J.E., and Boyd, D.A. (1973). 'Adolescent perceptions of police: actual and as depicted in TV drama'. *Journalism Quarterly*, Vol. 50, pp.438–446.

Reeder, L.G., Donohue, G.A., and Biblarz, A. (1960). 'Conceptions of self and others', *American Journal of Sociology*, Vol. 66, pp.153—159.

Reeves, B. (1978). 'Perceived TV reality as a predictor of children's social behaviour', *Journalism Quarterly*, Vol. 55, pp.682—689 and p.695.

Reeves, B., and Greenberg, B. (1977). 'Children's perceptions of television characters', *Human Communication Research*, Vol. 3, pp.113—127.

Reeves, B., and Lometti, G. (1979). 'The dimensional structure of children's perceptions of television characters. A replication', *Human Communications Research*, Vol. 5, pp.247—256.

Rotter, J.B., (1965). 'Generalized expectancies for internal versus external control of reinforcement', *Psychological Monographs*, Vol. 80, Whole no. 609.

Rubin, Z., and Peplau, A. (1973). 'Belief in a just world and reactions to another's lot: A study of participants in the national draft lottery', *Journal of Social Issues*, Vol. 29, pp.73—93.

Rubin, Z., and Peplau, L.A. (1975). 'Who believes in a just world?', *Journal of Social Issues*, Vol. 31, pp.65—89.

Schramm, W., Lyle, J., and Parker, E.B. (1961). *Television in the lives of our children*. Stanford: Stanford University Press.

Searle, A. (1976). 'The perception of filmed violence by aggressive individuals with high or low self-concept of aggression', *European Journal of Social Psychology*, Vol. 6, pp.175—190.

Smythe, D.W. (1954). *Three years of New York television: 1951—1953*. Urbana I11: National Association of Education Broadcasters.

Snow, R.P. (1974). 'How children interpret TV violence in play context', *Journalism Quarterly*, Vol. 51, pp.13—21.

Spence, J.T., and Helmreich, R.L. (1978). *Masculinity and femininity: Their psychological dimensions, correlates and antecedents*. Austin: University of Texas Press.

Spielberger, C. (1966). 'Theory and research on anxiety', in C. Spielberger (ed.), *Anxiety and Behaviour*. New York and London: Academic Press.

Spielberger, C., and Smith, L. (1966). 'Anxiety (drive), stress and serial position effects in serial-verbal learning', *Journal of Experimental Psychology*, Vol. 72, pp.589—595.

Srole, L. (1957). 'Social interpretation and certain corrollaries', *American Sociological Review*, Vol. 21, pp.709—716.

Stein, A.H., and Friedrich, L.K. (1972). In J.P. Murray, E.A. Rubinstein and G.A. Comstock (eds.), *Television and Social Behaviour: Vol. 2, Television and Social Learning*. Washington,

D.C. U.S. Government Printing Office, pp.202—317.

Steuer, F.B., Applefeld, J.M., and Smith, R. (1971). 'Televised
   aggression and the interpersonal aggression of pre-school children',
   Journal of Experimental Child Psychology, Vol. 11, pp.442—447.

Strauss, A. (1964). *George Herbet Mead of Social Psychology*.
   Chicago: University of Chicago Press.

Surgeon General's Scientific Advisory Committee on Television and
   Social Behaviour. (1972). Washington, D.C. U.S. Government
   Printing Office.

Sutherland, E.H., and Cressey, D.R. (1974). *Principles of criminology*.
   Philadelphia/New York: Lippincott.

Tannenbaum, P. (1971). 'Emotional arousal as a mediator of erotic
   communication effects', in *Technical Report of the Commission on
   Obscenity and Pornography*, Vol. 8. Washington, D.C. U.S.
   Government Printing Office.

Thomas, M.H., and Tell, P.M. (1974). 'Effects of viewing real versus
   fantasy violence upon interpersonal aggression', *Journal of
   Research in Personality*, Vol. 8, pp.153—160.

Tichenor, P.J., Nnaemeka, A.I., Oliens, C.N., and Donohue, G.A.
   (1976). 'Community pluralism and perceptions of television
   content', *Journalism Quarterly*, Vol. 53, pp.254—261.

Tuchman, G. (1978). 'Introduction: The symbolic annihilation of
   women by the mass media', in G. Tuchman, A.K. Daniels and J.
   Benet (eds.), *Health and Home: Images of Women in the Mass
   Media*. New York: Oxford University Press, pp.4—38.

Wakshlag, J.J., Bart, L., Dudley, J., Groth, G., McCutcheon, J., and
   Rolla, C. (1983). *Fear of crime and the appreciation of crime
   drama*. Paper presented to the Mass Communication Division,
   Internation Communication Association, Dallas, Texas, May 31.

Walters, R.H., and Thomas, E.L. (1963). 'Enhancement of
   punitiveness by visual and audiovisual displays', *Canadian Journal
   of Psychology*, Vol. 17, pp.244—255.

Walters, R.H., Thomas, E.L., and Acker, C.W. (1962). 'Enhancement
   of punitive behaviour by audiovisual displays', *Science*, Vol. 136,
   pp.872—873.

Wober, M. (1978). 'Televised violence and paranoid perception: The
   view from Great Britain', *Public Opinion Quarterly*, Vol. 42,
   pp.315—321.

Wober, M., and Gunter, B. (1982). 'Television and personal threat:
   Fact or Antifact: A British survey', *British Journal of Social
   Psychology*, Vol. 21, pp.43—51.

Wolf, T.M. (1973). 'Effects of televised modelled verbalisations on children's delay of gratification', *Journal of Experimental Child Psychology*, Vol. 18, pp.333—339.

Index

Control, 17
Thomas, M.H. and Tell, P.M.
(1974), 39, 61, 273
Tichenor, P.J. *et al.* (1976),
62, 273
Tuchman, G. (1978), 45, 106,
119, 273

Unintentional violence, 3 4
United Kingdom, 24, 74, 93,
95, 118, 232
United States of America, 13,
14, 27, 36, 45, 68, 232
University of Pennsylvania, 5,
105, 109
University of Toronto, 48
The Untouchables, 48, 49

Victimisation, 6, 22, 24, 30
see also
Violence, harmful and
harmless
Violence, perceptions of
Violence,
character involvement, 18,
21, 22—24, 38, 42—43,
50—51, 75, chpt. 7,
246—248
characters seen as violent
by nature, 106—108
characters' use of violence
criminals and law
enforcers, 43—44,
108—118, 156—158,
159, 160, 176, 177,
193, 195, 196, 197,
210, 212, 213, 214,
228—229, 230, 232,
246—248, 253—255
female, 45—46, 58,
59—61, 107—108,
119—128, 158—162,
163, 175, 178—181,
195, 198—201, 212,

215, 216, 217, 229, 231,
233, 246—248, 253—255
male, 45—46, 58, 59—61,
107, 108, 119—128,
158—162, 163, 175,
178—181, 195, 198—201,
212, 215, 216, 217, 229,
231, 233, 246—248,
253—255
definitions, 2—4, 5
demographic factors and, chpt.
11, 256—258
see also
Androgyny
characters' use of violence,
female, male
harmful and harmless, 38,
50—54, 75, chpt. 9, 164,
167, 168, 183, 186, 187,
204—206, 219, 221, 232,
235, 236—237, 250,
253—255
perceptions of,
anomia, 63, 82, 83, 191,
192, 194, 196—198, 199,
200, 202, 203, 205—208,
258—259
belief in a just world,
64—65, 82, 83, 84, 191,
192, 194, 196—198, 199,
200, 202, 203, 205—208,
258—259
locus of control, 63—64, 82,
83, 191, 192, 193, 194,
195—203, 205—208,
258—259
social beliefs, 61—62, chpt.
13, 258—259
victimisation, fear of,
62—63, 82, 83, 191, 192,
194—203, 205—208,
258—259
perceptual analysis, 10—11,
chpt. 5, chpt. 16